JESUS—JESHUA

JESUS—JESHUA

STUDIES IN THE GOSPELS

by

GUSTAF DALMAN, D.D.

Authorised Translation

by the Rev.

PAUL P. LEVERTOFF

KTAV PUBLISHING HOUSE, Inc.

NEW YORK

1971

FIRST PUBLISHED 1929
REPRINTED BY PERMISSION OF S.P.C.K.
HOLY TRINITY CHURCH, MARYLEBONE ROAD, LONDON N.W. 1.

SBN 87068-154-0

LIBRARY OF CONGRESS CATALOG CARD NUMBER: 77-149608
MANUFACTURED IN THE UNITED STATES OF AMERICA

CONTENTS

PART FOUR

THE PASSOVER MEAL

PART FIVE

AT THE CROSS

APPENDIX

NOTE BY THE TRANSLATOR

Any literary production of the veteran scholar, Prof. Gustaf Dalman, deserves to be made accessible to English readers. His fame as a reliable authority on Early Rabbinic Theology and Aramaic has long been established. Many, even scholarly, works on the Gospels often show that their authors lack a first-hand knowledge of contemporary Palestinian life and thought. In Dalman, however, we find one who from his earliest years was imbued with an ardent desire to be satisfied with nothing less than this. A perusal of his autobiography, which appears in Volume IV of Dr Erich Stange's series of autobiographies of contemporary theologians,[1] reveals a character in which thoroughness and closeness of application were attributes even from earliest childhood, and a passionate desire to learn and understand everything connected with Biblical and post-Biblical Jewish Literature, one might almost say, was absorbed with his mother's milk. The deeply religious atmosphere in which he was reared, eventually awoke in him an ardent missionary zeal. In fact, what the late Prof. Franz Delitzsch said of himself[2] might with equal truth have been said by Dalman: 'the purely scientific interest in the literature of the Jews and the spiritual interest in their conversion, have long struggled for the mastery in my soul'. But, whereas in Delitzsch this was probably a 'call of the blood', in Dalman it was the result of his Moravian upbringing.

The present volume is not only a translation but also a new edition, since it contains additional notes by the author and a few other improvements.

[1] *Die Religionswissenschaft der Gegenwart* (Felix Meiner, Leipzig, 1928).
[2] Cf. Prof. Kaufmann, *J.Q.R.* II. 386.

The translation was undertaken as a labour of love and as an expression of gratitude to the 'scribe...who bringeth forth out of his treasure things new and old'.*

מִיָּדְךָ נָתַנּוּ לָךְ, 1 Chronicles xxix. 14.

PAUL P. LEVERTOFF

HOLY TRINITY CHURCH
OLD NICHOL STREET
SHOREDITCH
In Lent 1929

* The following are the latest works of Dr Dalman:

Orte und Wege Jesu, 3rd ed. with 52 illus. 1924.

Hundert deutsche Fliegerbilder aus Palästina, with explanations. 1925.

Arbeit und Sitte in Palästina. (2 vols.) I. Jahreslauf und Tageslauf, with 76 illus. 1928.

Jerusalem und seine Umgebung, with illus. and map. 1929.

Publisher: C. Bertelsmann, Gütersloh.

FOREWORD

It has possibly been expected in some quarters that I should follow up *The Words of Jesus* by an Aramaic translation of the discourses of our Lord. But this was never my aim. A better understanding of the Dominical words would be promoted as little by a new Targum of the Gospels as by the already existent Aramaic and Hebrew translations. These latter were chiefly intended for practical purposes: either to make the Gospels intelligible to those who are entirely ignorant of, or not sufficiently familiar with, the original; or with the view of rendering the Greek into a language which, to the Jew at least, is the holy language. The mere fascination of linguistic activity in connexion with a dialect which has long been dead, and the supposed 'genuine' colouring in expression and sound of the words of Jesus gained in the process, would not alone have justified my work of the last thirty years upon the structure of the language of our Lord. It is the examination, as such, of how the thoughts of Jesus, the formulation of which has been transmitted to us in Greek, were expressed in the original idiom, that I consider of importance. But this cannot be separated from the consideration of the conceptions and thoughts which the Jewish sources offer for a comparison as regards subject-matter and the relation of the thoughts and words of our Lord to them. Examples of such weighings of language and subject-matter in connexion with momentous words of our Lord are now presented in this book. At the same time I have attempted to illumine the background, and depict the environment in which our Lord's words were uttered, and have, therefore, thought it necessary to discuss the Jewish synagogal service, the Passover meal, and the Cross.

I hope that my introducing anew the linguistic problem in all its fulness will not be considered superfluous. Here, in the land of Jesus, in a house dedicated to the continuation of our Lord's own work among the sick of Palestine, apart from the interest in the places of His activity,[1] the soul burns with the ardent desire to draw nearer to His Person, and to visualise Him as He was among Jews, Samaritans, and pagans, from all of whom He differed. For this reason, I finally decided to designate these studies 'Jesus—Jeshua', instead of the originally chosen title: 'Jesus and Judaism'. The real problem is, how our Lord, whose portrait is preserved to us in a Greek form, looked among the 'Hebrews'. The fact that, although *of* Israel, He was yet not merely a Jew, admits no question. But to define with detailed exactitude both aspects of this fact is the great problem, to the solution of which this book purports to offer some contribution.

GUSTAF DALMAN

JERUSALEM, in the Moravian
Leper Home 'Jesushilfe'

First Sunday in Advent 1921

[1] See my *O.W.* where I have inserted a number of the Words of Jesus in their primitive form.

ABBREVIATIONS EMPLOYED

I. GENERAL

Gram. = Dalman, *Grammatik des jüdisch-palästinischen Aramäisch*, 2nd ed. Leipzig, 195.

Jubil. = The Book of Jubilees.

M.G.W.J. = *Monatsschrift für Geschichte und Wissenschaft des Judentums*, Breslau.

Midr. on Ten Commandments, Beth ha-Midr. = A. Jellinek, *Beth ha-Midrasch.*

O.W. = Dalman, *Orte und Wege Jesu*, 3rd ed. Gütersloh, 1924.

Pal. Evang. = The Palestinian Aramaic Evangeliarium.

P.E.F.Q. = *Palestine Exploration Fund Quarterly.*

Pesh. = Peshito.

P.J.B. = *Palästinajahrbuch.*

W.J. = Dalman, *The Words of Jesus*, authorised version by D. M. Kay, Edinburgh, 1902.

Z.D.P.V. = *Zeitschrift des Deutschen Palästina-Vereins.*

II. TALMUDIC, MIDRASHIC, AND TARGUMIC LITERATURE

Tos. = Tosæfta. b., p. = the G^{e}mārā of the Babylonian and Palestinian Talmud respectively. Names of the tractates without the addition of b. or p. refer to the Mišna. The abbreviations of the names of the tractates are those commonly used. Thus: Ber. = B^{e}rāk̄ōþ, Sab. = Šabbāþ, Pes. = P^{e}sāḥim.

Mech. = M^{e}k̄ilþā; Gen. R., Exod. R., Lev. R., Num. R., Deut. R. = B^{e}rešiþ; Rabbā, etc., Pes. R. = P^{e}siqþā Rabbāþi; Tanch. = Tanḥumā; Yalk. Shim. = Yalquṭ Šim'oni.

Tg. Onk. = Targum Onkelos. Tg. Yer. I = Targum Jerushalmi I (the complete Jerusalem Targum). Tg. Yer. II = Targum Jerushalmi II (the fragmentary Jerusalem Targum).

SOURCES OF RABBINICAL LITERATURE

Babylonian and Palestinian Talmud; Mišnā, Tōsephtā (edit. Zuckermandel) and Gemārā.

The Targums.

Miđrāšim:

- Meḵilþā, ed. Constantinople, 1515; Friedmann, Wien, 1870.
- Siphre, ed. Venice, 1545; Friedmann, Wien, 1867.
- Siphrā, ed. Venice, 1545.
- Pesiqþā de Raƀ Kāhanā, ed. Buber, Lyck, 1868.
- Pesiqþā Rabbāþi, ed. Friedmann, Wien, 1880.
- Midrash Rabbā, ed. Constantinople, 1512, ed. 8vo. Wilna, 1897.
- Tanḥūmā, ed. Venice, 1545, ed. Buber, Wilna, 1885.
- Miđraš Tehillim, ed. Constantinople, 1512, ed. Buber, Wilna, 1891.
- Miđraš Tannā'im to Deuteronomy, ed. D. Hoffmann, Berlin, 1908, 1909.
- Yalquṭ Šim'oni, 2 vols. ed. Salonica, 1526, Frankfort-on-the-Maine, 1687.

PART ONE

THE THREE LANGUAGES OF PALESTINE IN THE TIME OF JESUS CHRIST

I. JESUS AND THE GREEK LANGUAGE

IT is indeed a great event to set foot upon the native soil of Jesus: in Bethlehem, to descend into the Grotto of the Nativity with its manger niche; to survey, from *nebi sa'īn* above Nazareth, the district in which He grew up; to tarry at the places where He taught, round the Sea of Galilee, between basaltic rocks and the synagogue ruins; to visualise, meditatively, His Cross and Sepulchre at the Golgotha cleft in Jerusalem; to meditate, under the olive trees of the Mount of Olives, on the Risen Lord who returned to take leave of His loved ones—these are incomparable experiences to the student, as well as to him whose only wish is to be a simple follower of the Master who here gathered His disciples about Him. My book *Orte und Wege Jesu* (3rd edition, 1924) is meant to supply these experiences, in some measure, even to those who are unable themselves to visit the Holy Land.

But to hear Him *speak* there (words fitting into the scene of their delivery), who spoke as one who has power (Aramaic *keshallīṭā*)[1] and not as the *sāpherīn* (the 'scribes', who did not proclaim, but merely interpreted God's Word), is more important. This necessitates an understanding of the language which Jesus spoke. What was it? What was His mother-tongue? What were the linguistic forms into which His thoughts shaped themselves?

To the world at large the Words of our Lord were transmitted in Greek. Even the lost Gospel to the Hebrews was scarcely an original work, independent of the Greek tradition. On the eastern shores of the Mediterranean Greek was, at the time, the common language. It had obtained a firm footing also in

[1] Pal. Evang. Mt. vii. 29, AC *hēk shallīṭ*, Pesh. *aik meshalleṭā*. For *shallīṭā* see Lev. R. 9 (23 b).

Palestine. The representatives of the Roman government, Pilate, Felix, and Festus, must have used it, for the Palestinian inscriptions referring to the Roman Emperors, when not of a military nature, were written mostly in Greek; and they designate Caesar not as *Divus* but as θεός.[1] Only in the army did the Roman language rule supreme, as Josephus[2] testifies, and as also, among other things, the inscriptions of the milestones on the Palestinian military roads prove.[3] Yet even these show that among the people another language was commoner; for on the roads which radiate from Jerusalem, the finger-posts, which also mentioned the distances, were almost all done in Greek.[4] Our Lord did not see any of these emblems of Roman rule, for they were not set up before the time of Vespasian. Their testimony, however, is supplemented by the coins which the Hasmoneans, since Alexander Janneus (103–76 B.C.), and also Herod, Archelaus, and Antipas, as well as the Roman Procurators, commanded to be minted.[5] On the denarion, which Jesus desired His adversaries to show Him (Mt. xxii. 19 f., Mk. xii. 15 f., Lk. xx. 24 f.), the words Καίσαρος Σεβάστου, not *Caesaris Augusti*,[6] must have been stamped. The last kings of the Jews designated themselves βασιλεύς on the coins. To the towns and strongholds which they founded they gave Greek names. Even the Hasmonean princes had, since 135 B.C., together with Jewish, also Greek names, after the precedent of the High Priests, Jason and Menelaos, 175 B.C. It can also be seen from the inscriptions on the sarcophagi in the neighbourhood of Jerusalem to what extent the use of Greek names among the Jews spread. Names like Papias, Tryphon, Thodos, and Bernike, must have been fully assimilated for them to have been

[1] See Hadrian's inscriptions at Gerasa, Dalman, *Z.D.P.V.* 1913, 260 f.

[2] *Bell. Jud.* III. 5. 4.

[3] Thomsen, *Z.D.P.V.* 1917, 11, but see also e.g. 'The Trajan Inscription on the Zion gate in Jerusalem', *Z.D.P.V.* 1921, 1.

[4] Thomsen, *ibid.* Nos. 260 f., 266 f., 288, 297 a, 300, 305. On the other hand, in Latin, Nos. 282, 286, Greek and Latin No. 305.

[5] A catalogue of these coins is given by Thomsen, *Kompendium der pal. Altertumskunde*, 95 f.

[6] See Wroth, *Catalogue of the Greek coins of Galatia, Cappadocia, Syria*, 166 f.—the coins of Antioch from the time of Augustus and Tiberius. The stamping of the imperial silver coins of Phoenicia seems to have begun later.

transcribed in Hebrew characters.[1] They were not merely alternative names, to facilitate intercourse with the outer world, as, for example, Paul was used for the Hebrew *Sha'ul* (Acts ix. 4). Antigonos of Sokho was a renowned scribe.[2]

Greek-speaking Jews had their own synagogues in Jerusalem, and, accordingly, formed (see Acts vi. 1, 9) their own special communities. A Rabbinical source makes mention of a synagogue of the Alexandrians.[3] From the Greek inscription found by Weill at the southern end of old Jerusalem[4] it is evident that the synagogue must have been built for Roman Jews, to judge from the name of the builder, Theodotos, son of Vettenos. In Jaffa,[5] and probably also in Sepphoris,[6] there was a congregation of the Cappadocians (cf. Acts ii. 9). Thus, Jews who assimilated the Greek language outside Palestine transplanted this foreign language into the Holy Land. The tablets of warning in the Temple in Jerusalem,[7] written in Greek and Latin (a Greek one was found in the year 1871[8]), were meant for all non-Jews, even those of Palestine. But the Greek synagogue-inscriptions in Ashdod and Gaza,[9] as well as the Greek inscription on the lintel of the door of the synagogue of Zippori, which mentions thrice a chief of the synagogue,[10] were intended for Palestinian Jews, as were also the numerous inscriptions, written wholly or partly in Greek, on the ossuaria of Jews in Jerusalem and of Jaffa,[11] with names like Jesus, Joses, Juda, Nathanaelos, Salome, Elisabe, Mariame. The *titulus crucis* was not without strong reasons written in Greek, Latin and Hebrew (Lk. xxiii. 38, A, D).

In Jerusalem, because of its relation to the outside world, the contact with the Greek language was particularly close. It could not have been otherwise in Nazareth, which was so near to one of the chief towns of Herod Antipas, and in close touch with the

[1] Klein, *Jüdisch-Palästinisches Corpus Inscriptionum* [*J.P.C.I.*], I. 13; 18. 19. 114; 36; 9. 89; 24.
[2] Ab. i. 3.
[3] Tos. Meg. iii. 6; p. Meg. 73 d.
[4] Clermont-Ganneau, *Syria*, I. 1920, 190 f.
[5] Klein, *J.P.C.I.* I. 132.
[6] p. Schebi, 39 a.
[7] Jos. *Ant.* XV. 11. 5; *Bell. Jud.* V. 5. 2; VI. 2. 4.
[8] Clermont-Ganneau, *Rev. Arch.* 1872, 214 f., 290 f.; Klein, *J.P.C.I.* II. 16.
[9] Klein, *ibid.* II. 2. 15.
[10] Ewing, *P.E.F.Q.* 1895, 354; Lammens, *Le Musée Belge*, 1902, 55, No. 112.
[11] Klein, *ibid.*: 42 examples from Jerusalem, 48 from Jaffa.

great traffic of the chief roads.[1] The Mother of our Lord was related to a priestly family in Judaea (Lk. i. 36), in which higher culture and wider social intercourse can be assumed.[2] Joseph considered himself to belong to Judaean Bethlehem (Lk. ii. 4 f.), if, as it would seem from Mt. ii. 1, it was not actually his home. In later times Nazareth was considered to have been a priestly town.[3] All this indicates that our Lord, having been brought up there, could not have lived in isolation from the influence of Greek.

At the Galilaean Sea the language of Trans-Jordania made its influence felt. Since the third century B.C. a number of Hellenistic cities had arisen there, of which Philadelphia was perhaps the oldest.[4] Greek-speaking colonies, Greek religion and constitution, also Greek popular places of amusement, helped in the diffusion of the Greek language. The inscriptions (of which, it is true, but a few go back to the time of our Lord) on public and private buildings, on gifts to the temples, and on tombstones, are for the most part entirely in Greek. Jesus Himself passed occasionally through the district of Hippos, probably also through that of Gadara, Pella, and Skythopolis.[5] Although it is not probable that He actually visited the capital cities of those districts, He found Himself, nevertheless, in the domain of their population and their language. It is also probable that the hippodrome of Magdala-Taricheae,[6] the Augustan temple of Sebaste,[7] the amphitheatre and the hippodrome of Jericho,[8] as well as the theatre in Jerusalem,[9] did not escape His notice. At the same time we realise that His was a different world, and that the vocabulary of sport, of race-running and prize-fighting,[10] favoured by St Paul, was foreign to Him,[11] and that He never

[1] Dalman, *O.W.* 68 f. [2] *Ibid.* 56 f. [3] *Ibid.* 65 f.

[4] Schürer, *G.J.V.* 4th ed. II. 155; Guthe, *Die griechisch-römischen Städte des Ostjordanlandes*, 12.

[5] Dalman, *O.W.* 180 f. [6] *Bell. Jud.* II. 21. 3.

[7] *Ant.* XV. 8. 5; *Bell. Jud.* I. 21. 2.

[8] *O.W.* 259. [9] *Ibid.* 293.

[10] It is true that Lk. xiii. 24 has: '*Struggle* that ye may enter the narrow door', but Mt. xi. 12 has: '*Enter*'. The 'struggling' puts the Semitic translator into a difficulty. Delitzsch, with his Hebrew *hit'ammeṣū*, 'endeavour', has given up the simile, and the *etkatteshū* of the Syrian sounds more like the fighting of quarrelling persons.

[11] In none of the Gospels, nor in the Epistles of St John and St Peter, is there any reference to this.

found it necessary to discuss paganism. It is, however, impossible to believe that the linguistic sphere connected with these things, which had taken a firm hold also in Jewry, should have left Him entirely unaffected.

In John xii. 20 it is taken for granted that our Lord did not belong to the Greek-speaking Jews. Greeks who desired to speak to Him in the Temple in Jerusalem, approached His disciple, Philip, who came from 'the Galilaean Bethsaida', who, again, took Andrew, also from Bethsaida (John i. 44), to help him, and both went to Jesus. The genuinely Greek names of just these two among our Lord's disciples (names which occur, in the form of Andray and Philippay, also as those of Galilaean Rabbis[1]), prove relationship to the Greek cultural circle. It is very probable that the brother of Andrew, Simon, was not called in the family circle by the Hebrew form Shim'ōn (cf. Συμεών Lk. ii. 25), but by the hellenised form Simon (= Σίμων), a form which, together with Shim'ōn, is also found in Jewish literature.[2] Even his second name Petros, in its Greek form, is not rare there.[3] Among the disciples of our Lord Θαδδαῖος (Mt. x. 3), which through Θευδᾶς (Acts v. 36) goes back to Θεόδοτος or a similar Greek name,[4] points also to Greek origin.

The Gospel of St John rightly takes for granted that the knowledge of Greek was common in Galilee. Then it cannot exclude our Lord, who was a Galilaean, from this common knowledge, who, also according to this Gospel, speaks to the Roman Procurator (John xviii. 34 f.; xix. 11). And St Mark not only suggests this, but relates the conversation of Jesus with the Canaanite woman, who, in respect of language, was a Greek (Mk. vii. 26). He who knows the East is aware that familiarity with several languages is not necessarily proof of higher education, but is rather a state of things arising out of the conditions of intercourse between the different populations. He will not, therefore, have a different conception of the Palestine of the first century which was permeated with Hellenistic culture. That the people, and especially Jesus, Who came into contact with

[1] p. Ber. 2 c; Meg. 75 a; Gen. R. 71 (155 a).
[2] p. Shek. 49 c; Ber. 2 c; Mo. k. 82 a; Gen. R. 71 (155 a); *Gram.* 179.
[3] p. Ab. z. 42 c; *Gram.* 185; Kraus, *Lehnwörter*, II. 443.
[4] *Gram.* 179.

such a variety of types, should not have understood Greek, and should have used foreign words only unconsciously, as Schulthess thinks,[1] is not credible, and, taking into consideration the great difference between the Semitic and the Greek, one must even say impossible. The well-known treatment of the gutturals in Galilaean and Samaritan[2] would not have been possible without a very strong influence of a non-Semitic language, in this case Greek, which must have been felt not only in the intercourse with foreign officials, as Klein[3] assumes, but in everyday life. We have a perfect right to assume that Pilate, in putting the question to our Lord: 'Art thou the King of the Jews?', did not need to use an interpreter, and that our Lord answered him in the same language: 'Thou sayest' (Mk. xv. 2 f.; Mt. xxvii. 11; Lk. xxiii. 3), even though the form of the answer emanates less from the Greek than from the Semitic idiom (cf. Mt. xxvi. 64).[4]

A singular echo of the Greek Palestine of the time of our Lord is found in the fact that His name *Jesus*, Ἰησοῦς, as the hellenised form of the Hebrew *Jēshūaʿ*, has become not only the name by which He conquered the world, but also that which was used by the Aramaic-speaking Church of Palestine. Its *Evangeliarium* calls the Saviour of the world *Jēsūs Meshīḥā* (cf. Mt. i. 1), whilst the East-Syrian Church said *Jēshūʿ Meshīḥā*, and the Palestinian Jews, in order not to pronounce the real name,[5] changed *Jēshūaʿ* into *Jēshū*.[6] It is not credible that this was only done because the concluding guttural was no longer pronounced in Galilee (see above); for the name *Jeshu* is used in Jewish literature only of persons who were despised for one reason or another, and we have *Jēshūaʿ* together with Ἰησοῦς and Ἰεσοῦς on Jewish ossuaries.

That our Lord and those about Him were conversant with other languages, is a fact of no small historic import; not less so is the fact that this state of things continued in the early Church (Acts vi. 1). For it means that the first Christian

[1] *Das Problem der Sprache Jesu*, pp. 19, 47.
[2] *Gram.* 57 f., 96 f.
[3] *M.G.W.J.* 1925, 185.
[4] See also *W.J.* 253 f.
[5] See Siphre on Deut. xii. 3; Mech. to Ex. xxiii. 13; Gen. R. 49 (102 a) on Prov. x. 7; Tos. Ab. z. vi. 4; p. Ab. z. 43 a; Sabb. 11 d; b. Ab. z. 46 a.
[6] p. Sab. 14 d; Ab. z. 40 d; b. Ab. z. 27 b; Eccl. R. x. 8. Yet we also find *Jeshua*, Tos. Ḥall. ii. 22.

formulation of the words of our Lord on which our Gospels are based, belongs to a circle which, in its knowledge of the universal tongue of the time, was in close contact with our Lord and His disciples. Thus we gain the confident certainty that the Gospels present an essentially faithful reproduction of the genuine thoughts of Jesus. There is no necessity for conjecture concerning their original form, possessing, as we do, in the Greek text a sound bridge over the gap between us and it. But this does not exempt us from trying this bridge for ourselves; a bridge which, although it actually does span the gap, lies, nevertheless, between two so widely separated worlds—the world of Plato and Phidias on the one hand, and that of Moses and the Jewish scribes on the other.

II. ARAMAIC—THE MOTHER-TONGUE OF JESUS

That the Law was originally given not in one but in four languages (Hebrew, Latin, Arabic, and Aramaic), the Midrash deduces from Deut. xxxiii. 2.[1] This naïve idea was at the outset a mere theory, but from it we gather which languages were of chief importance to a Jew. The inscription on the Cross appeared in three languages. According to Lk. xxiii. 38, John xix. 20, apart from Latin (the language of the Roman army), and Greek (the language of the Government and of which everyone had to have some knowledge), Hebrew (mentioned *first* in John) was one of the three.[2] Evidently, this latter was considered to be the language of the Jews. Parallels to this are the bilingual inscriptions (those not dealing with military matters) on many ossuaries of the Jews from the time of Christ.[3] The Hebrew or Aramaic name is put first there and below it the Greek equivalent; more rarely is the reverse order to be found.[4] Hebrew and Aramaic seem to interchange here without any fixed principle, and the question is, therefore, which was at that time the vernacular of those Jews who, in contrast to the Hellenists, are designated 'Hebrews' in Acts vi. 1.

[1] Siphre Deut. 343 (142 b).

[2] Similarly English, Arabic, and Hebrew, are now the official languages in Palestine which are used in public announcements and on the postage stamps.

[3] Even Jeshua bar Jehoseph Ιεσ(ους) occurs on an ossuary.

[4] Klein, *J.P.C.I.* 1. i. 7, 11 f., the reverse 1. 9, 13, 24.

In the time of Hezekiah, the Assyrian war-lord spoke 'Judaean', *jehūdīt*, to the representatives of the Judaean king, at the wall of Jerusalem, and not 'Aramaic', *arāmīt*, since he wished to be understood by the common people (2 Kings xviii. 26). According to Schulthess,[1] 'Judaean' could only mean Aramaic, which language alone could be expected to have been known by the Assyrian; and 'Aramaic' means Assyrian. However, the narrative probably takes it for granted that there was an interpreter, as in Gen. xlii., where one gathers merely from a casual remark (verse 23) that Joseph used an interpreter, whilst from verse 7 on, the conversation with his brethren seems to have been carried on directly. In Eastern polyglot-countries even to-day it would not always be stated whether an interpreter was present during a personal negotiation between officials. Even 270 years after Hezekiah the 'Judaean' language must have been Hebrew, as Nehemiah, who fought for 'Judaean' and against the intrusion of the languages of Ashdod, Moab, and Ammon (Neh. xiii. 24), could not have referred to the widely-spread Aramaic as the language of the Judaeans, but only to the language in which he himself wrote his book, namely Hebrew. However, Nehemiah's struggle was, as far as Hebrew was concerned, in vain. Yet it was Aramaic that won the day, overwhelming all the other languages mentioned by him in connexion with certain marriages. Nehemiah might have mentioned Aramaic in connexion with the marriage of a High Priest's son with the daughter of the Persian governor Sanballat,[2] but he did not seem to see any danger there, as the Judaeans who returned from the exile had probably already brought two languages with them: Hebrew as the language of intercourse among themselves, and Aramaic as the medium of speech with the Babylonian natives. Nehemiah, who certainly must have known both languages, would not have had any scruples concerning this bilingual practice. What he deplored and wished to frustrate was the decay of Hebrew in Jewish families.

The spread of Aramaic in the originally Hebrew Palestine must already have begun in the year 721 B.C., when Samaria

[1] *Das Problem der Sprache Jesu*, 19, 47.
[2] Neh. xiii. 18; Jos. *Ant.* XI. 7. 2.

was peopled by Mesopotamian colonists. Through the influence of the Babylonian and, later, the Persian Governments it continued to spread: finally reaching Southern Palestine, when the leading classes were deported from there and supplanted by the alien element. The Judaean exiles on their return made a last attempt to preserve their native language.

From the documents relating to Jeb (Elephantine)[1] in Upper Egypt, the extent of the early intrusion of Aramaic is to be seen. These documents, discovered in 1906, were written in the second half of the fifth century B.C., i.e. in the time of Nehemiah. The members of this colony called themselves, and were called by others, corporately, *ḥēlā jehūdāyā*, 'the Judaic army', individually, *jehudai*, 'Judaean'; but sometimes the same person would also be called *arāmay*, 'Aramaean'.[2]

Originally they were Judaeans, that is, South Palestinians, and it may be taken for granted that it was not in Egypt that they acquired Aramaic. The same invasion of alien tongues took place in Eastern Palestine, where the languages of the Moabites and Ammonites finally disappeared without leaving any traces, the Nabataic dialect of Aramaic usurping them, wherever Greek and Arabic had not become predominant.

In the time of Nehemiah the Law could still be understood in the original Hebrew in Jerusalem. Nevertheless, it required interpretation when read at public services, probably not merely as to the contents (Neh. viii. 7 f.). Later a full translation into Aramaic was considered to be absolutely necessary, so that 'the clear and understandable' reading (Neh. viii. 8) was interpreted as meaning the addition of a full translation.[3] The oral Aramaic translation of the Hebrew text of the Old Testament in public reading was, in A.D. 200,[4] considered to be such a fixed institution in the divine service of the Synagogue, that discussions took place concerning the question which passages in the Law and

[1] See Ungnad, *Aram. Papyrus aus Elephantine*, Pap. 6, 2, 11; 11, 12; 18, 1.

[2] Staerk, *Alte und Neue Aram. Papyri*, 34. 36; cf. 41, 47, 49, 51.

[3] p. Meg. 74 d; b. Meg. 3 a; Ned. 37 a; Gen. R. 36; p. Meg. 71 b; b. Sanh. 21 b; Tos. Sanh. iv. 7 refer to an Aramaic translation and to the introduction of the square script of the Hebrew text, and not, as Hänel, *Der Schriftbegriff Jesu*, p. 143, erroneously concludes from this, that the Aramaic Bible, of which the Jewish texts say nothing, was then predominant.

[4] Meg. iii. 4, 6, 9, 10; cf. Tos. Meg. iv. 20, 21, 28, 31–38, 41.

the Prophets should be excluded from translation, and how the reading and the translating were to be executed. The Mishna does not in this point legislate anew, but merely records the tradition. Thus, a practical necessity in earlier times must have caused this usage of translating into Aramaic. This must have been the case at least at the time of our Lord. In the third century A.D. it had become a rule that even one who understood Hebrew must always, when reading the Law privately, supplement it with the traditional Aramaic translation; so essential for the understanding of the contents was the Aramaic translation[1] considered to be.

A similar necessity led the Church of Palestine, whose official language was Greek, into the same practice. When Etheria visited Jerusalem in 380, she observed that at the Holy Sepulchre the Greek homily of the Bishop and all the lessons were rendered into Syriac (as the Palestinian Aramaic was called there[2]) by a special minister. This, she explained, was made necessary, since one part of the population 'of this province' understood only Syriac, another part Syriac and Greek, and a third Greek alone.[3] The first Palestinian martyr in the third century was the Syrian interpreter of the community of Skythopolis.[4] The Palestinian-Syriac Bible, which we possess only in an incomplete condition, is probably connected with this custom. In Damascus, where fragments of this Bible were found, leaves of a Greek Bible also came to light, in which the word *ἑρμηνεία* is inserted between the verses.[5] This probably was meant to be a sign for the Syriac translator. A Greek and Syriac dedicatory inscription on the mosaic of a small village church, west of Jerusalem, is a documentary proof of the bilinguality of the Christian populace.[6]

This Syriac language, which Eusebius knew from the usage of the Palestinian Church, was considered by him to have been the language in which the Apostles grew up;[7] that is to say, he

[1] b. Ber. 8 a.
[2] For the corresponding Jewish term see *Gram.* p. 2.
[3] Geyer, *Itinera*, 99.
[4] Violet, *Die paläst. Märtyrer des Eusebius von Caesarea*, 4, 7, 110.
[5] Thus according to Prof. von der Goltz, who was shown these leaves by Prof. von Soden.
[6] *P.J.B.* 1914, 28.
[7] *Dem. Ev.* III. 7, 10.

considered the Palestinian Aramaic of his day as the continuation of the idiom of those who were our Lord's companions. The mother-tongue of Jesus, which, according to John xii. 20 f., was not Greek,[1] cannot be separated from this Palestinian Aramaic.

This conclusion is confirmed by His words preserved to us in the Gospel of St Mark in their Semitic form. Even if they should have had their origin in an Aramaic proto-Gospel, they would show what the Greek editor of Mark considered the language of Jesus to have been; and such an Aramaic proto-Gospel would, in itself, show to which linguistic circle Christianity originally belonged. At the eastern shore of the Lake of Tiberias Jesus called to the deaf and dumb (Mk. vii. 34): ἐφφαθά, i.e. in Aramaic, *itpattaḥ*, 'open thyself'.[2] This is not, as I previously used to think, really a plural referring to the ears—*itpattaḥā*; for, of a blind person it could be said: *itpattaḥ*, 'he was made to see', i.e. opened; of a she-ass: *itpatteḥat*, 'she was made to see'; as also 'he who sees' is called *petīaḥ* or *mephattaḥ*.[3] In Hebrew it is said of a once-deaf person *nitpaḳḳaḥ*,[4] 'he was opened', i.e. made to hear, and only of a once-blind person *nitpattaḥ*,[5] 'he was opened', i.e. made to see; but *nitpaḳḳaḥ*[6] can also be used of the latter, which, however, in Targum Isa. xlii. 7, 20 (cf. the Hebrew text) is avoided. Thus everything points to the conclusion that ἐφφαθά on the lips of our Lord was not Hebrew but Aramaic, though it is possible that *itpattaḥ* had been already changed into *ippattaḥ* in Aramaic.[7] ταλιθὰ κοῦμι is undoubtedly Aramaic—*ṭalyetā* (or *ṭelītā*) *ḳūmi*, Mk. v. 41. The reading κουμ presupposes in Syriac the usual falling off of the unaccentuated vowel of a feminine ending. According to Schulthess, it could be shown that this shortening of words had already taken place in the first century. But the Galilaean imperative form with the feminine ending *-īn*[8] is a proof against this theory. *Ṭalyetā* is a genuine Aramaic designation of a girl, which in Hebrew

[1] Cf. above, p. 5.
[2] Cf. *Gram.* 278; *O.W.* 214.
[3] Cf. Lev. R. 22 (58 a); Eccl. R. v. 8 (95 a); Midr. on Psalms, xxii. 7 (96 b).
[4] Gen. R. 53 (113 a); p. Keth. 25 b; b. Jeb. 113 a.
[5] Gen. R. 53 (113 a).
[6] Num. R. 18 (146 b); Midr. on Ten Commandments, Beth ha-Midr. I. 71, where *nitpattaḥ* is said of the deaf.
[7] Cf. *Gram.* 253.
[8] *Ibid.* 275 f., 321.

would be *yaldā*. It is foreign to the old Targumic idiom, but frequently used in the Galilaean and Jerusalem-Targumic dialects.[1]

The surnames given by our Lord to the disciples are yet another proof of the language which He used. Genuinely Aramaic is *kēphā*, 'rock', the surname of Simon (John i. 42; cf. Mt. xvi. 18; Mk. iii. 16). The Matthean passage calls to mind the Jewish narrative (suggested by Isa. li. 1 f.) concerning the Creator of the world who says of Abraham: 'I have found a rock (*peṭrā*) to build on it and to establish the world'.[2] The two brothers[3] He characterised as Βοανηργές (Mk. iii. 17), which word probably goes back to the Aramaic *benē regēsh*, 'sons of rage', and does not mean (as it is often understood) 'sons of thunder'. Among the names of the disciples are some of actual Aramaic origin. Θωμᾶς (Mk. iii. 18; John xi. 16) is the Aramaic *tōmā*, 'twin'; Καναναῖος, the name of the one Simon (Mk. iii. 19; cf. Lk. vi. 15), is derived from the Aramaic *ḳan'ānā* or *ḳannāyā*, 'the zealot'.[4] Akin to this is the interpretation which is given to Phinehas as a grandson of Aaron (Num. xxv. 11): it would suggest that he was 'a zealot, the son of the zealot', Hebrew *ḳannay ben ḳannay*.[5] *Bar* in Βαρθολομαῖος is the Aramaic for 'son' (Mk. iii. 18), which name has its double in Bar Telamyon in Jewish literature.[6] Βαριωνᾶς (Mt. xvi. 17; John i. 42), Βαρσαββᾶς (Acts i. 23) as well as Βαραββᾶς (Mt. xxvii. 16; Mk. xv. 7; Lk. xxiii. 18; John xviii. 40, which latter obviously does not mean 'son of the father' but 'the son of Abba'[7]) also contain this Aramaic *bar*. The names Ἀλφαῖος (Mk. ii. 14), Ζεβεδαῖος (Mt. x. 2), Μαθθαῖος (Mt. ix. 9), Θαδδαῖος

[1] Cf. also *Gram.* 150, 321.

[2] Jalk. Shim on Num. xxiii. 9, from Yelammedenu. Cf. Levertoff's note on this passage in the one-volume Commentary on the Bible ed. by Bishop Ch. Gore, S.P.C.K. 1928.

[3] *Gram.* 144. Schulthess, *Problem*, 52 f., suggests *benē reḥēm*, which would mean *fratres uterini*, but is as foreign to the Aramaic usage as to the tradition of the name and its meaning.

[4] *Gram.* 174.

[5] Siphre on Num. xxv. 11 (48 b) (Levertoff's ed. p. 141); Lev. R. 33; b. San. 82 b.

[6] Lev. R. 6 (17 a).

[7] *Gram.* 179. The name *Abba* is an abbreviation of *Abbiya*. Ḥiyya bar Abba was a well-known Tannaite; see Strack, *Einleitung in den Talmud*, 5th ed. p. 134.

(Mt. x. 3), Θολομαῖος (Mt. x. 3), presuppose the Aramaic ending *ay* in Chalphay, Zabday, Mattay, Thadday, Tholmay.[1]

Our Lord is addressed by Peter (Mk. ix. 5; xi. 21) and by the traitor (Mt. xxvi. 49; Mk. xiv. 45) as *rabbī*, 'my great one', the usual designation of a teacher, but also of a master craftsman[2] and of a chief of robbers.[3] This can be Hebrew as well as Aramaic;[4] but *rabbūnī* (= rabbōnī), with which the blind man in Jericho (Mk. x. 51) and Mary Magdalene (John xx. 16) addressed our Lord, is without doubt Aramaic. According to St John it would have to be translated with 'my teacher'. But it is in fact an intensified form of the usual *rabbī*, which can only be rendered adequately: 'my Lord and Master'. When Jesus was addressed (e.g. Mt. viii. 25) as κύριε,[5] we have to think of it as a form of politeness, while at the same time it could also express reverence. When used in a Semitic dialect it is always combined with the passive pronoun; and, in Aramaic, when addressed by one person it should be *mārī*,[6] 'my Lord'. The Aramaic origin of μαραναθά in 1 Cor. xvi. 22 (composed of *māran*, 'our Lord', and *etā*, 'come'), which has become a formula, is self-evident.[7] The sinking Peter could have addressed our Lord only with the words *mārī shēzēbni*, 'My Lord save me' (Mt. xiv. 30), and when a disciple addressed Jesus in the name of all (Lk. xi. 1), he said: *māran allephan*, 'Our Lord, teach us!'[8]

To the question of how Jesus was distinguished from other men of the same name in the primitive Hebrew Church, the answer would be: by the addition of Μεσσίας (John i. 41; iv. 25), which is the Semitic for Χριστός. Μεσσίας is not formed from the Hebrew *Mashīaḥ*, but from the Aramaic *Meshīḥā*, which is also used in the Syriac Bible of Palestine.

Thus, there is sufficient evidence that Aramaic was the language of Jesus. We add a few more examples. *Pharisee* is derived from the Aramaic *perīshā*, 'separated one'. The place

[1] *Gram.* 176, 178 f. The vowel ending is dissolved in Ζεβεδαῖος, Θολομαῖος.
[2] b. Ab. z. 17 b.
[3] b. Bab. m. 84 a.
[4] *W.J.* 272 f.
[5] *W.J.* 267, 269 f.
[6] *Gram.* 108.
[7] Differently in *Gram.* 152, 357.
[8] The Pal. Evang. has not preserved this passage, but it rendered rightly, e.g. Mt. xv. 11, *māran*; Mt. xiv. 30, *mārī*.

where our Lord was condemned, *Gabbatha*, is the Aramaic *gabbetā*, 'hunch', or *gabbaḥtā*, 'bald forehead',[1] but certainly not *gabbetā*, 'a bowl',[2] which has this meaning in *Christian* Palestinian Aramaic but not in Jewish Palestinian. The place where He was crucified, *Golgotha*, is in Aramaic *golgoltā*, 'skull'.[3] The field purchased with the price of His blood, is Akeldama, Aramaic *ḥaḳēl demā*, 'bloody ground'. The pool Siloam,[4] where He sent the man who was born blind (John ix. 7, 11), is the Aramaic *shilōḥā*; and the pool Bethesda, where He healed a lame person, is *beza'tā* in Aramaic (John v. 2).[5] The name of the festival Πάσχα, is the Aramaic *pasḥa*, 'Passah', and 'Ασάρθα[6] is the Aramaic *'aṣartā*, 'Pentecost'. Martha[7] (Lk. x. 38) is the Aramaic *māretā*, 'lady'; Sapphira[8] (Acts v. 1) is the Aramaic *shappīrā*, 'the beautiful one'; Tabitha (Acts ix. 36) is the Aramaic *ṭabyetā*, 'gazelle', and Shelamzion[9]—the Aramaic *shelām ṣiyōn*, 'the salvation of Zion'. The abusive word *raka*[10] (Mt. v. 22) is the Aramaic *rēḳā*, 'silly fool'. The treasury in the Temple was called *korbanas* (Mt. xxvii. 6) = the Aramaic *ḳorbānā*, 'sacrifice'.

On the Jewish ossuaries a part of the inscriptions was written in Aramaic, even when referring to a priestly family.[11] The solitary ossuary inscription found in Nazareth is in Aramaic.[12] The Aramaic memorial inscriptions of the synagogues in Zepporin, Kefr Kenna, Capernaum, Chorazin, Kefr Ber'im, and Gush Chalab in Galilee, in Chirbet Kanef, and Fik, east of the Sea of Tiberias, Naaran, near Jericho, and in Gaza,[13] are of later times. The fact is significant that, although when these inscriptions were made, Hebrew had become more and more prevalent in the synagogues, such memorial inscriptions of a

[1] *Gram.* 160.
[2] So Schulthess, *Problem*, 54.
[3] *Gram.* 166.
[4] So also is Σιλωα, Σιλωας, Jos. *Bell. Jud.* II. 16. 2; V. 4. 1, 6. 1, 12. 2 to be interpreted. Cf. *shilōḥā* Tg. 1 Kings i. 33; Isa. viii. 6.
[5] *O.W.* 325.
[6] This only in Jos. *Ant.* III. 10. 6.
[7] Shown by Klein, *J.P.C.I.* I. 54, 55, 173, also Tos. Yom. i. 14.
[8] In inscriptions, Klein, I. 14; see p. 90 there.
[9] Klein, *ibid.* 15, 64–66, 79; Jos. *Ant.* XVIII. 5. 4; Lev. R. 35 (97 b).
[10] *Gram.* 173 f.
[11] Klein, I. 1–5, 7.
[12] See *P.J.B.* 1913, 45; *O.W.* 54; Klein, I. 166.
[13] Klein, II. 2–5, 7, 9, 12, 13; Dalman, *Aram. Dialektproben*, 2nd ed. 38; *P.E.F.Q.* 1927, 101 f.

religious character were done in Aramaic. Concerning the Aramaic writing of documents of different kinds, see my *Gram.* p. 8 f. It would have been impossible for Gamaliel to have sent his three messages to the Jews of Southern Palestine, of Upper and Lower Galilee, and of Babylonia and Media, in Aramaic,[1] had not this language been the one which was understood by all the Jews of the East.

Aramaic became the language of the Jews to such an extent that the Gospel of St John as well as Josephus found it possible to designate such Aramaic words as *beza'ta*, *golgolta*, *gabbeta*, *asarta*, *rabbuni* (see above) as Hebrew.[2] This was partly due to the fact that of all the Semitic languages Aramaic is the nearest to Hebrew; and the affinity became even closer just at that time, for Aramaic influence had created a new Hebrew which, in vocabulary and syntax, essentially differs from ancient Hebrew and is more akin to Aramaic. The 'Hebrew' speech of St Paul to the Jews who were gathered in the Temple (Acts xxi. 40; xxii. 2); the addresses of Josephus to the besieged Jerusalemites in the 'language of the fathers' or in 'Hebrew';[3] and the shouts 'in the language of the fathers' of the watchmen in the towers of Jerusalem, giving warning of the Romans,[4] were doubtless in Aramaic. The emphasis is here not on the difference between various Semitic languages, but on the contrast between the dialects used by the Jews and the languages of the foreigners, namely, Greeks and Romans. The fact that Roman soldiers, natives of Syria, understood the table-talk of the Jews in Gamala,[5] is natural, as the Jewish Aramaic language was essentially the same as Syriac. Hence it is intelligible why St Paul emphasised the fact that he was a Hebrew (2 Cor. xi. 22), yea, a Hebrew of a Hebrew family (Phil. iii. 5). By this he meant that he was not just an Israelite (2 Cor. xi. 22), but that, unlike the Hellenists who adopted the language of the foreigners,

[1] p. San. 18 d; Maas. Sh. 56 c; Tos. San. ii. 6; b. San. 11 b; cf. Dalman, *Aram. Dialektproben*, 2nd ed. 3. That Midrash Tannaim on Deut. xxvi. 13 (176) gives two such messages in Hebrew is not astonishing, and shows that the linguistic form given by the other authorities is not accidental but historical.

[2] John v. 2; xix. 13, 17; xx. 16; *Ant.* III. 10. 6.

[3] *Bell. Jud.* v. 9. 2; VI. 2. 1.

[4] *Bell. Jud.* v. 6. 3.

[5] *Bell. Jud.* IV. 1. 5.

he used the language of the fathers, which language—Aramaic—he did not differentiate from the Hebrew. The Apostle was brought up in Jerusalem (Acts xxii. 3), but it is possible that his parents in Tarsus belonged to a 'Hebrew' community, since we know such communities to have existed in Rome, Corinth, and in a place in Asia Minor.[1] The family of the Apostle was supposed to have been Galilaean. Our Lord was, in an even fuller sense than St Paul, a 'Hebrew of the Hebrews'. The Jewish Aramaic was, and remained, His natural language for thought and speech. That Aramaic and not Hebrew was really the language of the people is proved by Aramaic proverbs and sentences which occur not only in the Midrashim, but also in the Mishna,[2] and first and foremost by rabbinical Hebrew itself, which is either an aramaicised Hebrew or an hebraicised Aramaic, and so presupposes Aramaic to have been the language of the country. Similarly, works of a scientific character written in modern Palestinian Hebrew cannot disguise the fact that the mother-tongue of the writers is one of the Western languages.

III. THE RELIGIOUS USE OF ARAMAIC

Because the conversational language of the majority of Palestinian Jews in the time of our Lord was Aramaic, it does not follow that the same language was used in the domain of religion and worship. The influence of the Scriptural language, which is primarily that of the Law, the Prophets, and the Psalms, must have been considerable (see below, VI). Indeed, the Jews used Hebrew during a long period of their history as the language of worship and as a medium for literary productions of a religious nature, even after having made other languages their own. Yet, in harmony with the old warning not to despise Aramaic,[3] this latter language was never entirely neglected, and in Cabbalistic literature even experienced a fresh revival. We have adequate proof that Aramaic was frequently used in the religious domain in more ancient times.

[1] Schürer, *G.J.V.* 4th ed. III. 83; Müller and Bees, *Die Inschriften der jüdischen Katakombe am Monteverde zu Rom*, 1919, 23 f., 58 f., 173.

[2] *Gram.* 9 f.

[3] p. Sot. 21 c; Meg. 71 b.

I. DIVINE ORACLES

Once at the royal court of Babylon a divine writing in Aramaic proclaimed that the Babylonian domination would come to an end (Dan. v. 25). It is expressly stated at a later date that 'Divine Oracles' were uttered in Aramaic, even when Hebrew would also have been understood.[1] Simon the Just, the acknowledged last representative of the time nearest to the last prophets,[2] is said to have heard the following oracle in Aramaic, uttered from the Holy of Holies in the Temple: 'Vain is the work which the enemy planned against the Temple'. The High Priest Joḥanan, most probably John Hyrcanus (135–104 B.C.), of whom Josephus says that he possessed prophetic gifts,[3] and whom later the Jews considered to have been the most bitter enemy of the Greeks,[4] is supposed to have heard a divine utterance in Aramaic, proceeding from the same place: 'The youths who went out to fight against Antioch have conquered'. In the time of the Hadrianic persecutions we have the prophetic oracle of the dying Samuel 'the small', referring to the coming travails of persecution: 'Simeon and Ishmael (two doctors of the Law)[5] are destined for the sword; his (Ishmael's?) associates—for execution; the rest of the people—for spoil; and many tribulations will follow'. The uttering of such Divine oracles and prophetic foretellings in Aramaic would have been senseless if it had not been thought natural for God to use this language, although, possibly, such oracles were looked upon as lower grades of prophecy.

Hence it is correct to assume that the utterances of the 'voice' heard from heaven in the Gospel story were in Aramaic. The words heard at our Lord's Baptism (Mk. i. 11) must have been: *att hū berī ḥabībā debākh itreʿīti*:[6] 'Thou art my son, the beloved, in thee I have pleasure'; the words to the three disciples at the

[1] Tos. Sot. xiii. 4–6; p. Sot. 24 b; b. Sot. 33 a, 48 b; San. 11 a; Sem. 8.
[2] Ab. i. 2, probably the High Priest Simon I, about 300 B.C.
[3] *Ant.* XIII. 10. 7.
[4] *Gram.* 31. Dérenbourg, *Essai sur l'histoire,* 66 f., 71, 74, 80 f.
[5] Bacher, *Agada der Tannaiten,* I. 234, 270.
[6] For the expression cf. Tg. Isa. xii. 1; Jer. iii. 14. Un-Jewish is Evang. Pal. *ṣebēt,* Peshito *eṣṭebēt.* Cf. also *W.J.* 226 f.

Transfiguration (Mk. ix. 7): *dēn hū berī ḥabībā shim'ūn lēh*: 'This is my Son, the beloved, hear Him'.[1]

The utterance of the voice heard by Saul of Tarsus on the way to Damascus was in 'the Hebrew language' (Acts xxvi. 14), i.e. in Aramaic, the language in which our Lord used to speak, and which was also that of Saul: *Shāūl, shāūl, mā att rādephinni.* The repetition of the name is frequent in the O.T. and also in Rabbinic literature.[2] The answer to the terrified Saul's question, *man att mārī*, 'Who art Thou, my Lord?', was: *anā jēshūa' nāṣerāyā deatt rādephinnēh*, 'I am Jesus the Nazarean, whom thou persecutest' (Acts xxii. 7 f.). The fact that Saul really persecutes *Him*, and not His *disciples*, is the goad, *ziḳḳetā*, against which it will not be easy for him to kick, *be'aṭ*.[3]

2. PRAYERS

The official formulae of Synagogue prayers which have come down to us are almost entirely in Hebrew, although, according to Rabbinic Law, not only prayers, but also the recitation of the Shema', the oath of witnesses and that of deposition of property, and the confession of sins, may be said in *any* language.[4] The Palestinian Joḥanan (in the third century A.D.) objected to praying in Aramaic, as the ministering angels were supposed to

[1] '*Shim'ūn*' in the Deuteronomic sense (Deut. xviii. 15) of *obeying*, as Him who proclaims the Divine will, and not merely in the sense of *listening* as to a teacher. In the Onkelos Targum (cf. Brederek, *Concordance to Onkelos*, 124), the Hebrew *shāma'*, 'to listen', is rendered by *shema'*, and *shāma'* in the sense of 'obeying' by *ḳabbēl min*, 'to accept from'. But *ḳabbēl* is not usual in other Jewish writings. Nebuchadnezzar heard a divine voice: 'Wicked slave, arise, destroy the house of thy master, whose sons are rebellious and *do not obey him*', *shāme'īn lēh* (Eccl. R. 12 (130 a)). A doctor of the Law is advised: 'And even when they (who wish that he should at the Synagogue reading from the Law make pauses not prescribed by the official text) tear off thy head, do not *obey* them', *lā tishma' lōn*. (p. Meg. 75 b; cf. Eccl. R. vii. 7; Evang. Pal. Mt. xvii. 5, John xviii. 8.) The Hebrew *shāma' le* for 'to obey', Gen. R. 42 end; Eccl. R. vii. 7 Aramaic *ishtema'*, 'to obey', is found in Onk. Gen. xlix. 10; Esther II. v. 1; cf. Dan. vii. 27; *shema'*, of listening to a teacher, p. R. h. S. 59 b; Bez. 62 b.

[2] Gen. xxii. 11; xlvi. 2; Exod. iii. 4; 1 Sam. iii. 10; Siphre, Friedmann's ed. 32; Exod. R. 2 (12 a); Num. R. 14 (125 a); Cant. R. ii. 14 (33 a); p. Pea. 15 c; cf. *W.J.* 186.

[3] Cf. Tg. Eccl. xii. 11; in Palestine, even now, it is called in Arabic *zaḳḳūt*. Of this it says in Lev. R. 29: 'I kick thee, *masḳēd lak*, like the goad of the ox kicks a young cow'.

[4] Sot. vii. 1; Tos. Sot. vii. 1, 7.

understand only Hebrew.[1] Yet even he did not intend to disparage Aramaic, since this language is used in the three parts of the Bible[2], and, in fact, he himself often used it.[3] Eleazar, when visiting the sick, sometimes prayed in Aramaic, because, so it was explained, the Shekina herself abides at the head of the sick, so that at the sick-bed the angels are not the interpreters of human prayers.[4] Moreover, the objection to praying in Aramaic referred only to private prayers of individuals.[5] Thus, Aramaic prayers must have been used in the Synagogue worship. A few remnants only of such prayers have come down to us,[6] and these, as it seems, are mostly of Babylonian origin; they prove, however, that the ruling of the Mishna was always recognised. But it is very probable that the introductory formula of the Aramaic *ḳaddīsh*, which resembles the first petition of the Lord's Prayer,[7] is of Palestinian origin. The Aramaic petitions of the synagogue inscriptions mentioned on page 14 show that even in the 'Holy Place' 'the holy language' did not have the sole prerogative. The donors of gifts for the synagogue who are 'remembered for good' 'may take their portion in this holy place', so runs the mosaic inscription of Naaran.[8] In this we find an echo of what, according to Neh. ii. 20, the rebuilders of Jerusalem claimed for themselves, namely, 'portion, right, and memory, in this city', and the wish: 'remember me, O God, to the good', with which words Nehemiah four times accompanied his own acts (Neh. v. 19; xiii. 14, 22, 31), and which is often written in Aramaic on the rocks in Petra.[9] Outside the Synagogue a stronger Aramaic influence can naturally be expected. The Midrash says of men in general, i.e. of non-Jews

[1] b. Sab. 12 b; Sot. 33 a. Human beings spoke Hebrew originally, like the angels, b. Hag. 16 a; Ab. d. R. N. 37.

[2] p. Sot. 21 c; Meg. 71 b; Gen. R. 74.

[3] Bacher, *Agada d. pal. Amoräer*, I. 251, collected all the occasions when Joḥanan used Aramaic.

[4] b. Sab. 12 b; Ned. 40 a.

[5] b. Sot. 33 a.

[6] Cf. Levisohn, *Sepher Mekore Minhagim*, 41 f., who puts it down that certain passages *must* be said in Aramaic.

[7] Siphre Deut. 132 b; b. Ber. 3 a; Gen. R. 13 (29 b); Midr. on Psalms, xviii. 12; cf. De Sola Pool, *The Old Jewish Aramaic Prayer 'Kaddish'*, 1909; the full later text see in *W.J.* 305.

[8] According to my reading, see Klein, *J.P.C.I.* II. 3 (read *le* for *be*); differently Clermont-Ganneau.

[9] Dalman, *Petra*, 96; *Neue Petrastudien*, 80 f.

(Hebrew *beriyōt*), that their prayers are concerned with agriculture only. They say (in Aramaic): *mārī ta'abēd ar'ā, mārī taṣlīaḥ ar'ā*, 'My Lord, may the land bring forth! My Lord, may the land prosper!' The Israelites, however, pray for the Sanctuary: *mārī yitbenē bēt makdeshā, mārī mātai yitbenē bēt makdeshā*, 'My Lord, may the Temple be built! My Lord, when will the Temple be built?'.[1] That the common people among non-Jews as well as among Jews prayed in Aramaic, is here taken for granted, as the narrative is in Hebrew and only the prayers are in Aramaic. But also Rabbi Levi ben Sisi (A.D. 200), when he saw from the roof of his house roving bands stream into the city, lifted up the scroll of the Law and prayed in Aramaic: 'Commander of the worlds! If I have broken (*baṭṭēlīt* = annulled) even *one*[2] word of this book of the Law, may they (the enemies) enter!' His bold prayer was answered with the immediate dispersal of the enemy; but when his disciples and their pupils endeavoured to imitate their teacher, they did not succeed.[3]

In the same language, although not in the same spirit, our Lord addressed God as *Abba*, 'My Father' (Mk. xiv. 36).[4] This appellation was to St Paul characteristic of the perfect relation of the Christian to God (Rom. viii. 15; Gal. iv. 6). It shows that this was the language in which our Lord conversed with His Father, and hence we are enabled to realise more or less the very sound of the words of His prayer in Gethsemane. As it stands in St Mark (xiv. 36), it must have been in Aramaic: *abbā, kullā yākhēl lak, a'bar minnī hādā kāsā, beram lā mā deṣābēnā anā ēllā mā deatt ṣābē*. (The active participle *yākhēl* is analogous to the Hebrew *yākhōl*—'possible'.) According to Targum on Zech. iii. 4, He might have used *a'dī* for 'take away', but παραφέρειν in Mark, παρέρχεσθαι in Matthew, point rather to a form from *'abar*. But also *a'bar min* must be taken in the sense of 'taking away'.[5] The simile of the cup for the approportioned

[1] Gen. R. 13 (27 b); instead of the Hebrew *mātai* there ought to be the Aramaic *ēmat*.

[2] Read *ḥadā* for *hādā*.

[3] p. Taan. 66 d.

[4] *Gram.* 198; *W.J.* 156 f.

[5] The words have a somewhat different meaning when used of the cup which 'passes from one to the other', e.g. Lam. iv. 21, the Targum on which mentions Constantinople as the final recipient of the cup!

destiny is based on the cup of wine which appertains to every participant at a meal (Psalm xxiii. 5); hardly on the double portion of wine which is presented to one after a bath.[1] In Jewish literature there is no parallel to this simile, although a number of passages deal with the Biblical application of the word.[2] Our Lord used this symbol also on other occasions (cf. Mk. x. 39 f., John xviii. 11), doubtless in exalted language, suggested especially by the style of the Psalms (e.g. Psalm xi. 6; xvi. 5).

Hence, the 'Lord's Prayer' (Mt. vi. 9 f.; Lk. xi. 2 f.), not being based on Biblical phrases, must have been in Aramaic, beginning with *abūnān debishemaiyā*.[3] According to Lk. xi. 1, it is the prayer by which the disciples of our Lord should be distinguished from the disciples of the Baptist. Moreover, according to Mt. vi. 5 f., it was meant for private prayer rather than for corporate worship, and certainly only as a pattern, as is also the Jewish prayer of the 'eighteen benedictions' which, according to Jewish tradition, was similarly prescribed for the individual.[4]

However, it must be assumed that the word from the Cross (Mt. xxvii. 46; Mk. xv. 34), taken from Psalm xxii. 2, and which will be dealt with later, was spoken in the original Hebrew.

3. RELIGIOUS DISCOURSES

The Synagogue homilies preserved in Pesikta and Pesikta Rabbati,[5] although the Aramaic colouring can often be detected in them, are in Hebrew. Yet, at the time when the translation of the Scripture lessons in the Synagogue service was necessary, the discourses and homilies must have been delivered chiefly in the people's language, i.e. in Palestine—either in Aramaic or in Greek. If, as is probable, the Aramaic *ḳaddīsh* brought such discourses to a close, this prayer would be an additional proof that the preacher spoke in Aramaic. A story is told in that

[1] p. Pes. 37 c; Gen. R. 51 (108 b); cf. Gen. R. 10 (20 a).
[2] p. Pes. 37 c; Gen. R. 88 (189 a). [3] *W.J.* 155 f.
[4] See the formula in *W.J.* 299 f., p. Ber. 8 a: the prayer should at least be *mīn*, 'of the kind', of the eighteen benedictions.
[5] Of the latter there is a German translation by Levertoff (Research Institute for Comparative Religion, Leipzig).

language of a Jewish woman who loved to hear a certain preacher, and who, on one Sabbath evening, remained later than usual in the synagogue, the sermon having been exceptionally long. Her husband allowed her to enter the house again only on condition that she should first go and spit in the face of the preacher![1] The story is told in Hebrew, with the dialogue in Aramaic, and so it is not probable that the preacher, who was the cause of the trouble, spoke in Hebrew.

It can be shown that, for instance, at public prayers for rain, when large gatherings stood outside the synagogue, and when an impression was to be made on them, the exhortations were in Aramaic. On one such occasion, Abba bar Zabda (i.e. son of Zebedee) interpreted in Aramaic the words of Lam. iii. 41 ('Let us lift up our hearts on (*el*) hands to God in heaven'), as follows:[2] 'Can a man take his heart and put it in his hand (in order to lift it up to God)? What then is the meaning of "lifting up"? Let us put our (sinful) hearts on the palms of our hands (in order to do away with them), and then turn to God in heaven!' On another occasion, when the fasting (for rain) brought forth no result, the last speaker, Berechya, began his oration (in Aramaic)[3] as follows: 'Our brothers (*aḥēnān*)[4], see what is wrong with us! Is it not that which the prophet (Micah vii. 3 f.) complains of against us: "Our hands are out for evil in order to do good?"'. The speech ended with the appeal: 'Therefore weep!' Shimon ben Yoḥai said once (the occasion is not recorded) in Aramaic: 'Had I stood on Mount Sinai when the Law was given to Israel, I would have prayed to the All-merciful that He should give man two mouths, one for the use of the Torah, and the other for things appertaining to this world'.[5] The purpose of our Lord, unlike that of the Rabbis, was "to save the lost sons of the house of Israel" (Mt. xv. 24; cf. x. 6), and in a much higher sense than they did He endeavour to come into contact with the life and the experiences of the common people.

[1] p. Sot. 16 d; Lev. R. 9 (24 a); Num. R. 9 (52 a f.).
[2] p. Taan. 65 a; Lam. R. iii. 41 (54 a f.).
[3] p. Taan. 65 b; cf. Yom. 43 d; Bacher, *Agada der pal. Am.* III. 347.
[4] Also St Peter and St Paul (Acts i. 16; ii. 29; xxii. 1) must have used this word. The preceding ἄνδρες is according to Greek idiom and cannot be imitated in Aramaic.
[5] p. Ber. 3 b; Sab. 3 a f.

Even assuming that He was able to speak Hebrew, it is unthinkable that He should not have condescended to express Himself in the language of those who gathered to listen to Him. Also the training of His disciples, who were men of the people (Acts iv. 13), as well as His whole intercourse with them, must have been in Aramaic. Hence we conclude that the teaching of our Lord everywhere: in the boat, on the mountain, or in the synagogue, could not have been in any other language than Aramaic.

IV. THE LINGUISTIC AIDS FOR THE STUDY OF THE ARAMAIC SPOKEN BY OUR LORD

He who wishes to re-think the words of Jesus in Aramaic is confronted with a considerable difficulty; these words, as we have them in our Gospels, were not slavishly translated from an Aramaic original, but were moulded into Greek, although into a Greek which has been influenced by the Semitic idiom and occasionally also by the O.T. style. A mere translation from Greek into Aramaic, as we have it in the East-Syriac Bible and in the Pal. Evang., does not therefore give us the certainty that herein we have actually gained a first-hand knowledge of the very words of our Lord. The difficulty is increased by the fact that we do not possess any Jewish-Aramaic literary documents going back to the time of Christ, from which we would have been able to conclude with the highest degree of certainty what the language of Jesus was. Generally speaking, Jewish literature offers for investigation only two kinds of Palestinian-Aramaic material: the Bible translations (Targums); and the more or less popular narratives which we find scattered in the Palestinian Talmud and in the Palestinian scriptural interpretations of the earlier Midrashim, which, in vocabulary and word-formation, differ from that of the Targums.[1] While the language of the Targums is often influenced by the exact imitation of the Hebrew original, the Talmudic and Midrashic narratives give the impression of naturalness, even in the sense of actually reproducing the dialect spoken by the Palestinian people. Of the

[1] See *Gram.* 11 f. for a more detailed account.

Targums it cannot be said with the same certainty where and when their idiom was actually in daily use.

As the above-mentioned narratives had their origin in Galilee, I designated their dialect as Galilaean. The language, however, by which Peter, as a Galilaean, and therefore a disciple of Jesus, was recognised (Mt. xxvi. 73; Mk. xiv. 70; Lk. xxii. 59), may, in some details, have been really somewhat different. But one can be certain that it was only in a few non-essentials, and that this Jewish Galilaean dialect was strongly tinged with the impress of that Galilee which, also linguistically, was the homeland of our Lord.

Schulthess[1] considers this attitude towards Jewish-Galilaean erroneous. He thinks that the Targum of the Samaritans and, above all, the Christian Palestinian Aramaic ought rather to be taken into consideration. According to him, the latter emanated from the descendants of the first Jewish Christians, and, consequently, from the circle to which our Lord Himself belonged. The famous editor of the Christian Palestinian texts, Agnes Smith Lewis, regarded the language of these texts as identical with the Galilaean dialect by which Peter was discovered as a Galilaean, and as being also the mother-tongue of our Lord.[2] But there is no proof that such was the origin of the Christian Palestinian dialect. Schulthess himself has to confess that nothing in this dialect is reminiscent of the Jewish past. This, in fact, is so little the case that even the Jewish Aramaic script was replaced by a script which must be designated as Eastern Aramaic, and when it was used in inscriptions in Palestine, it was concerned only with things Christian.[3] The vocabulary collected by Schulthess in his *Lexicon Syrio-Palestinum* (1903) shows such essential differences from the Jewish dialect (notwithstanding some agreements with it) that one can take either the one or the other of the dialects as a pattern for the language of Jesus. Should one decide for the Christian dialect, then the influence of the East-Syrian Bible on

[1] *Problem*, 30 f., 36.
[2] *Codex Climaci Rescriptus*, 1919, xvi.
[3] See the inscription of *umm rūs*, *P.J.B.* 1914, 28, and some inscriptions near Silwān which probably have not yet been published, but also all the manuscripts of the Christian Palestinian literature.

the Pal. Evang. would require a special examination, and, besides, the fact would have to be taken into account that both Syriac translations endeavour to render the holy original Greek text as literally as possible. The genuine dialects of Aramaic used by the people can be detected in some measure from such translations, but cannot directly be discovered in them. When, in the year 1890, I had to set up Franz Delitzsch's Hebrew translation of the New Testament in its final form, working on his material, and by his special request, I felt very acutely how the rendering of a book with a normative text compels one to make continually compromises between the linguistic form which the *thought* of the original demands and that which the *letter* of the original (which one is not permitted to change) forces upon the translator. Naturally, the result is a language which in fact never existed—outside the translation![1] The same is true of the Targum of the Samaritans, which, moreover, belongs to a religious sphere not that of our Lord. One cannot possibly make use of expressions taken from Christian or Samaritan sources, when it can be shown that the Jews used different constructions.

Nevertheless, in the Pal. Evang., especially where it differs from the Greek original, we can occasionally find hints for the reconstruction of the original Semitic idiom and syntax. It must, therefore, be carefully considered. But at the same time one has to examine in each particular case whether the Jewish dialect has an exactly similar construction. In the Samaritan domain, the not very ancient liturgic literature and those writings which are not merely translations contain some forms with which the Jewish religious idiom agrees. I have, therefore, also collected a great number of words and phrases from this source, which I always compare with and refer to when they promise any aid. But to me, the most important treasures are, apart from the literary Jewish sources, my own collection of Aramaic phrases (continually increased); my Lexicon of nouns; my grammar of the Jewish Palestinian dialects (supplemented by notes), and the dictionaries (of which my own has been

[1] Cf. my views on this translation in *Die Religionswissenschaft in Selbstdarstellung*, IV. 9 f.

increased, in the second edition, by more words from the Onkelos Targum). Schlatter's[1] comparison of the language of the Fourth Gospel with the style of the earliest Rabbinic scriptural interpretations has proved the great affinity in style and conceptions between them, even after deducting such sentences that are only similar in expression but not in content. Of course, scholars are aware that there are also essential differences (which Schlatter does not always point out). In consequence of the near affinity between rabbinical Hebrew and Aramaic it is not surprising that Burney, in his book *The Aramaic origin of the Fourth Gospel* (Oxford 1922), should have considered the Gospel of St John as a translation from an Aramaic original (although he was not able to prove it).[2] In a somewhat different sense we would reach a similar conclusion on comparing the style of the Synoptic Gospels with that of the Rabbis. Here it is less important to reconstruct the individual words of our Lord (although even this has a certain value), for each word has its own shade of meaning and special associations, and the sound of the words of our Lord as they were once heard is as essential a constituent of their reality as is the form and colour of the landscape which was the setting. This was felt also by St Mark, when he preserved certain words of Jesus in the original Aramaic. Of more importance than His use of individual words is the world of conceptions from which He drew those words and into which He poured His message, either in point of contact or opposition. This world, although not the purely Rabbinic, is yet the common Jewish one, and the same atmosphere prevails in it as in that of Rabbinic literature. It is characteristic of the Rabbis that to them the letter of Holy Scripture as that of traditional lore is the highest authority. The sound common sense of proverbs, the natural connexion of things in parables, and even experience itself, were, for casuistic purposes, at the service of this letter, and so, there was in this a certain contact with the purely human and ordinary religious life of the people. This is also the world from which our Lord derived His images and concepts, although for a different

[1] *Die Sprache und Heimat des vierten Evangelisten*, 1902.
[2] Cf. my review of this work in *Theol. Literaturzeitung*, 1923, 7 f.

purpose, i.e. for the presentation and proof of a Divine truth appealing authoritatively and directly. Because of this connexion, Rabbinic literature compels us at every step to compare the words of the Rabbis with those of our Lord. The Christian and Samaritan Aramaic literatures have nothing corresponding to this, and supply no aid to the understanding of the peculiar method of our Lord.

Together with the resemblance, however, the differences also must be pointed out, otherwise the investigation would be incomplete. As a matter of fact, these differences will eventually have to be considered as the most valuable result of the whole investigation. In them it will be seen wherein Jesus differed from the Rabbis, differed from the Jews in general and from their legal traditions; yea, differed, in His teaching, even from the O.T. In this 'otherness' lies His historic significance; or, more correctly, in it lies that which God wished, and still wishes, that He should be to humanity. The solution of this problem is therefore closely connected with the most vital work of theological study, namely, the elucidation of the content and essence of the Christian message to the world. It is impossible for one individual to accomplish this task; yet he would accomplish much indeed if his attempts should become the stimulus to others to improve on them.

V. TRACES OF THE USE OF HEBREW

Sure as it is that Aramaic was the common language of the Jews in the time of our Lord, it is also a fact that Hebrew did not entirely drop out of the life of the Jewish people. As the 'holy language' (*leshōn haḳḳōdesh*[1]), 'God's language' since the creation of the world,[2] the language of Adam,[3] of Abraham,[4] of Joseph,[5] and of the Law, Hebrew was still held to be the real language of Israel. Moreover, most of the personal names kept alive the memory of Hebrew antiquity. In Biblical times

[1] Sot. vii. 2, 4; viii. 1; ix. 1; Tos. Sot. vii. 7; p. San. 25 d; Eccl. R. 7 (108 b). In Aramaic this expression was probably unpopular. Only the Jerusalem Targum has *lishshān ḳudshā* (J. I. Gen. xi. 1), *lishshān bēt ḳudshā* (J. I. Gen. xxxi. 37), see *Gram.* 4.

[2] Gen. R. 18 (37 d).

[3] *Ibid.*

[4] Gen. R. 42 (87 b).

[5] Eccl. R. 7 (108 b).

every new-born child received a new name. Before the exile there was no second Jacob, Jehudah, Shimon, Joseph (Isaac is rare even in the first century; Abraham, Moses, Elia are unheard of); but later the custom arose of calling children by Biblical names as good omens.[1] Hence we have in our Lord's circle three James's (= Jacob), four Simons, two Johns (= Joḥanan), three Judases (= Jehudah), two Josephs, two Joses (= Joseph), four Marys (= Maryam), one Elizabeth (= Elisheba); all these strikingly in agreement with the names on the ossuaries of the neighbourhood of Jerusalem belonging to the same period and written in Hebrew script. We find in this connexion next in frequency to Jehuda, Jehoseph; then Joḥanan, Shimon, Jehoezer, and Eleazar; among the names of women—Maryam, together with a certain Elisheba. To the Hebrew circle belongs, perhaps as a shortening of Shelomit, the feminine name Shalom,[2] which is identical with Salome (Mk. xv. 40; xvi. 1).

While Biblical names do not in themselves prove the use of the Biblical language, we possess stronger evidence in the fact that the inscription on the tomb of the Bene Chezir in Jerusalem,[3] and a number of inscriptions on ossuaries, are written in Hebrew, as is evident from the introduction of *ze* in the former, and the addition of *ben* before the names of the fathers, *ēshet* before the name of the husband, and designations like *hassōphēr*, *hakkōhēn*, in the latter. It was thus occasionally considered of importance to use Hebrew on such inscriptions, and it was taken for granted that it would be understood. Among the disciples, the traitor Judas's surname, Iscariot (Mk. xiv. 10), or Iscariotes (Mt. xxvi. 14; Lk. xxii. 3; John xiii. 2), is of doubtful origin; the Syriac translators have evidently understood it to be a place-name (for which one might suggest Askarot, near Sichem[4]). Schulthess[5] suggests σικάριος, an assassin, which he supposes to have been developed, by way of an hypothetical aramaicised *iskaryāā*, into the Greek *Iscariotes*, the origin of the word having been forgotten. More probable is the derivation,

[1] Therefore only the names of the pious were used, Gen. R. 49 (102 a).
[2] Klein, *J.P.C.I.* I. 60; see also Shelamzion, p. 14 above.
[3] Klein, *ibid.* I. 8.
[4] *O.W.* 226, 357.
[5] *Problem*, 41, 55.

represented by Codex D, from ἀπὸ Καρυώτου, which presupposes the Hebrew *īsh ḳeriyōt*, 'the man of Kerioth', and reverting to an idiom frequently found in Jewish literature.[1] Iscariot would then be the original Greek rendering, and *iskariotes* a hellenisation, on the model of στρατιώτης. The Aramaic would have been, in that case, *diḳeriyōt*, 'the man of Kerioth'. Whether the traitor himself considered it of importance to use his surname in Hebrew, or whether his family had done it before him, we cannot know. Consequently, the conjectures built on his surname, as furnishing the key to his treachery are baseless, but it certainly can be deduced from it that Hebrew was in use.

Among the designations of Jerusalem localities[2] (of which the name of the Mount of Olives[3] has been preserved in its Aramaic form until this day), Gethsemani, or Gesamani (whether the first syllable is derived from *gat* 'wine press', or from *gē* 'valley'[4]) is the only one in Hebrew. This name was either preserved from ancient times or was formed later, suggested, e.g., by *gē shemānīm*, Isa. xxviii. 1.

That Hebrew benedictions should be inscribed at entrances to synagogues, for instance in 'Alma and Kefr Ber'im, probably also in Nebratēn in Galilee,[5] is natural. A memorial inscription in the same language is reported from Merom.[6] The synagogues were the most important centres of the Hebrew influence upon old and young. Of them we shall have to speak in particular.

The Mishna prescribes that besides the priestly benediction, certain declarations and formulae mentioned in Deuteronomy are to be spoken in the 'holy language';[7] but just this shows that Hebrew was only regarded as indispensable when Scripture itself seems to prescribe it, and the question is whether such ordinances were actually kept by all. It is not, for instance, likely that in Hellenistic synagogues the priestly blessing was spoken in Hebrew. Klein[8] thinks that Hebrew was generally

[1] *W.J.* 41 f.
[2] See above, p. 14.
[3] *Ṭūr*, 'mountain', for *ṭūr zētayā*; cf. Tg. Zech. xiv. 4.
[4] *O.W.* 340. Either word is pure Hebrew and not Aramaic.
[5] Klein, *J.P.C.I.* II. 6, 8.
[6] *Ibid.* II. 15. The inscription at Nawe (*ibid.* II. 14) might have been in Aramaic.
[7] Sot. vii. 2–7, viii. 1 f., ix. 1 f.; Jeb. xii. 6.
[8] *M.G.W.J.* 1925, 184.

used in the religious domain, and the fact that the phrases mentioned in the Mishna (Nedarim and Nazir) as common every-day expressions are given in Hebrew, is to him a proof of this. However, it is not the linguistic form which is here essential, but the meaning of certain common expressions, so that the question could arise concerning the difference between 'the language of the Law and that of men' (*leshōn ṭōrā* and *leshōn benē ādām*).[1]

'Αμήν, as used by our Lord (nowhere so applied in Jewish literature) when solemnly confirming a word uttered by Himself (e.g. Mk. ix. 1; x. 29; xi. 23; Mt. v. 18; Lk. iv. 24; doubled in the Fourth Gospel, e.g. John xiv. 12), is Hebrew. The corresponding expression in Aramaic would have been *min ḳushtā* or *beḳushtā*, 'in truth'.[2]

The Hebrew *āmēn* was habitual to every Jew as a confirmation—when listening to an uttered benediction; or of a prayer spoken by oneself—only in so far as it ended with praise.[3] But *āmēn* was also a confirmation of an oath, and of an accepted charge, or of a promise.[4] To end one's own prayer with *āmēn* was considered to be a sign of ignorance. When our Lord uttered it at the beginning of an affirmation, He gave it, under a conscious avoidance of an oath (Mt. v. 34), a religious character, as though it were something which one usually confirms with *āmēn*. Most probably the prayer in Rev. xxii. 20 ('Amen, come!') is also to be taken in this sense. The parallel to it suggested by Taylor[5] in the Akrostikon of an old Synagogue prayer is founded on a misunderstanding. It does not mean *āmēn bō*, 'Amen, come!', but *āmēn bārūkh attā*, 'Amen, be thou praised!'[6] It is almost certain that our Lord used the word in Hebrew and not in Aramaic. It shows how familiar to Him was the world to which this *āmēn* belonged.

[1] p. Ned. 39 c; b. Ned. 49 a.

[2] *Gram.* 211. The last word is used in the Targums for the Hebrew *ommām*, see Onk. Gen. xviii. 13; Num. xxii. 37; Tg. 2 Kings xix. 17; Isa. xxxvii. 18.

[3] Cf. Mt. vi. 13, where certainly the *āmēn*, as in Psalm lxxxix. 53 (cf. 1 Cor. xiv. 16), is meant to be spoken by the hearers of the prayer and not by him who says it. Ber. viii. 8; p. Ber. 12 c; Mo. k. 82 b; b. Ber. 47 a; Tos. Meg. iv. 27; Taan. i. 10.

[4] b. Shebu. 36 a.

[5] *The Teaching of the Twelve Apostles*, p. 78.

[6] See Maḥzor Vitry, 106.

VI. THE HEBREW INFLUENCE OF THE SCRIBES AND THE SCHOOL

Experts in the Hebrew language were naturally the *γραμματεῖς* (Mk. vii. 1), the *νομικοί* (Lk. vii. 30) or the *νομοδιδάσκαλοι* (Lk. v. 17), of the Gospels. Of these Greek designations only the first corresponds to the Hebrew term used by the Jews. It is identical with the *sōpherīm*,[1] Aramaic *sāpherīn*,[2] of Jewish literature. These were originally called so because they were the professional copyists of the Holy Scriptures, and, as such, acquainted not only with the art of writing but with the contents of the Book. In this double sense the designation is used also of Ezra (Ezra vii. 12). Even before the time of Christ it became the title of all those who were not only familiar with the *written* Law but also understood how to interpret it according to tradition. Knowledge of writing, knowledge of the Law, and knowledge of tradition, were closely connected, and formed the wisdom of the Scribes.[3] Moses was considered the greatest *sōphēr* of Israel,[4] who represented both the oral and the written Law. The doctors of the Law in the time of Ezra were, in a special sense, the *sōpherīm* of the past. To contradict them could, in certain cases, bring forth worse consequences than to contradict a commandment of the written Law.[5] That the knowledge and authority of the *sōpherīm* presupposes a thorough knowledge of Hebrew, is self-understood, since the oral legal tradition as well as the written Law were in Hebrew. When *bōr*, 'ignoramus', stands in contrast to *sōphēr*[6] or to an 'associate of scribes' (*ḥābēr*),[7] or when it is recommended to thank God for not having created one a *bōr*,[8] it does not characterise a person

[1] Siphre Num. 8 (4 a); b. Sot. 15 a; cf. Bacher, *Ag. d. Tann.* I. 31, 75. There were also Samaritan *sōpherīm*, according to p. Ab. z. 44 d; Yeb. 3 a.

[2] p. Meg. 70 c.

[3] Sot. ix. 15; b. San. 97 a; Der. Erez Zuta, 10, of the scribes, who are therefore also called 'the wise', *ḥakhāmīm*, Aram. *ḥakkīmīn*, Ab. vi. 9; Sot. ix. 15; p. Kidd. 59 a.

[4] Onk. Deut. xxxiii. 31.

[5] See San. xi. 3, according to which a dissenting doctor is guilty of death when he demands five phylacteries instead of the two prescribed by the *sōpherīm*; but not when he entirely breaks the ordinance (Deut. xi. 18) concerning the phylacteries.

[6] b. Ber. 45 b; Hal. 106 a.

[7] Lev. R. 18 (45 a); Eccl. R. xii. 2 (128 b).

[8] Tos. Ber. vii. 8; p. Ber. 13 b.

entirely ignorant of Hebrew, the basis of all Jewish religious knowledge. What was meant by 'ignorance' can be seen from the following definition:[1] 'He who reads (the Scriptures) but does not repeat (the traditional Law) is a *bōr*. He who "repeats" but does not read is a "man of the land" (*'am hā-āreṣ*).[2] He who reads and "repeats", even if he does not interpret (the oral legal tradition), is a sage. He who does the latter as well, is a man of judgment. He who neither reads nor "repeats"—it would be better for him if he had never been created'. In another passage the designation of a 'man of the land' is attached even to him, who, although a reader of the Bible and a repeater of the traditional Law, is a free lance, and does not join the school of an expert.[3] Our Lord as well as His disciples[4] would be considered 'ignorant' from the point of view of the above definition, although His discourses show that in intellectual maturity, in knowledge of the world, and in the power of the Word, He was certainly not behind the scribes. But He undoubtedly belonged to those who 'read', i.e. were familiar with the Scriptural text, and, above all, with the Law, and must have therefore understood Hebrew. The 'reading' of Scripture in its non-vocalised Hebrew text meant to the Jews more than a mere knowledge of the Hebrew consonants or the ability to read it as the result of a certain acquired knowledge of language; it implied acquaintance with the traditionally-fixed reading, especially in connexion with the Law. The minimum standard for competence in a reader (*ḳaryān*) was, according to one opinion, the ability to recite correctly three or four verses in the synagogue;[5] according to other opinions the minimum was the knowledge of the traditional translation or the reading of all the three parts into which the O.T. was divided: the Law, the Prophets, and the 'Scriptures'.[6] That certainly meant also the ability to chant in the traditional fashion, without which the reading was considered neither beautiful nor good.[7] All this

[1] Der. Erez Zuta, 10.

[2] This designation, which is always derogatory, here means most probably a person not as ignorant as a *bōr*, whilst in other places it designates the deepest grade of ignorance; see Sot. ix. 15; Tg. Cant. vi. 5; Gen. R. 78 (168 b).

[3] b. Sukk. 22 a.

[4] Acts iv. 13.

[5] b. Kidd. 49 a, *Barayta*.

[6] *Ibid.*

[7] b. Meg. 32 a, according to which the Mishna also had to be chanted.

could not have been acquired without the help of an expert, especially by one whose mother-tongue was Aramaic and not Hebrew, notwithstanding the affinity of the two languages. There were 'synagogues of the unlearned',[1] where the ordinances of the scribes were not considered to be authoritative. Yet, in one way or another, provision must have been made that there should be no lack of 'readers', if the Law was not merely to be read but really understood.

The Israelites were obliged, according to the Law, to instruct[2] their male children[3] in its ordinances. The father, therefore, taught his sons the Law and the Prophets. Even a Jewish mother could do it (2 Tim. iii. 15; cf. i. 5). Josephus considers it among the excellencies of his religion that the fathers were obliged to instruct their children in reading and in the Law.[4] A greater demand was made in the second century A.D. The father had to converse with the son in the holy tongue and teach him the Law as soon as he began to talk. The neglect of a father in this was deemed equal to his burying the child.[5] Rabbi Meir said:[6] 'He who lives in the Holy Land, recites, morning and evening, the *Shema*ʿ (Deut. iv. 10; vi. 4–8; xi. 13–21), and speaks the holy tongue, is sure to inherit the world to come'. The patriarch Juda I (A.D. 200) declared that in the Holy Land only the holy language or Greek ought to be spoken, but not Syriac[7] (= Aramaic). The study of Greek was considered permissible only to the family of the patriarch, because of his connexions with the Roman government.[8] Instruction in Greek wisdom was forbidden.[9] Of the four languages of high rank, Hebrew was considered to be suitable for (ordinary) speech, Latin for war, Greek for poetry, Syriac for dirges over

[1] Ab. iii. 10. Perhaps the Galilaean synagogues, the ornamental works of which are often rather strange (*O.W.* 151 f., 164).

[2] Deut. vi. 7; xi. 19; xxxii. 36.

[3] According to tradition (Siphre on Deut. xi. 19 (83 a)) not the *daughters*.

[4] *C. Ap.* II. 25, cf. *Ant.* IV. 8. 12, according to which the boys had to study the laws.

[5] Siphre on Deut. xi. 19; cf. Tos. Hag. i. 2.

[6] Siphre Deut. 333 (140 b); p. Sab. 3 c; Shek. 47 c.

[7] b. Sot. 49 b; Bab. k. 83 a; cf. *Gram.* 2.

[8] Tos. Sot. xv. 8; p. Ab. z. 41 a.

[9] b. Sot. 49 b.

the dead.[1] This renewal of Nehemiah's struggle against foreign languages meant the setting up of an ideal which corresponded only very imperfectly with reality. What actually happened, as far as it is possible to observe, was that a stronger emphasis was laid upon the erection of schools for the study of Scripture, and, therefore, also of its language.

Such schools Shimon ben Shetaḥ (about 70 B.C.) had already called into being.[2] Originally they were meant only for lads of sixteen and seventeen, but one of the last high priests, Joshua ben Gamla, brought the age down to about six and seven years, since the youths ran away from school when the teacher was angry. He is also supposed to have opened schools in all parts of the country; up to that time it was only Jerusalem that was so privileged.[3] In a later period elementary schools were considered to have been long-established institutions, so that it was said that every one of the four hundred and eighty synagogues of Jerusalem were supplied with a Bible-school and a Mishna-school,[4] and that the undoubtedly much smaller town Bittir had five hundred elementary schools.[5] It was also assumed that even a king's son had to attend school, for we read the following: A king said daily to his only son: 'Eat, my son! Drink, my son! Go to school (*bēt has-sēpher*); come back from school!'[6] If a child fell ill in school, he was obliged to be taken home before starting school again.[7] The Bible teachers in these schools were called *sāpherīn*,[8] because it was their business to instruct their pupils in the books of the Law (Hebrew *sephārīm*), in contradistinction to the teachers of the Mishna (*matneyānīn*).[9] The reading and rendering of the text into Aramaic had to be taught gratuitously; for God says of the Law: 'As I (gave you the Law) for nothing, so must ye (teach) for nothing;'[10] for 'one

[1] p. Meg. 71 b; Sot. 21 c; Esther R. iv. on i. 22. Midr. on Psalm xxxi. 7, with different texts.

[2] p. Ket. 32 c.

[3] b. Bab. b. 21 a.

[4] p. Meg. 73 d; Ket. 35 c; Lam. R. Peth.

[5] Lam. R. ii. 1 (43 b).

[6] Lev. R. 2 (5 b) (Shimon ben Yoḥai).

[7] Cant. R. ii. 5 (27 b) (Shimon ben Yoḥai).

[8] Sot. ix. 15; p. Hag. 77 b; Meg. 75 b; Num. R. 11.

[9] p. Hag. 76 c. Otherwise the Bible teacher, *ḳārāi*, 'reader', is also differentiated from *tannāy*, 'repeater', Lev. R. 30 (81 a), who had to teach orally.

[10] p. Ned. 38 c.

word of the Law is priceless (above all payment)'.[1] Yet the teachers did receive some reward for their time—or for the instruction in the proper way of separating the accent in chanting.[2]

A vivid picture of the mode of instruction in such schools is given in the Midrash on Eccl.[3] A Persian wishes to be instructed in the Law. The teacher (pointing to the letter): 'Say Aleph!' The pupil answers: 'Who says that it is Aleph?' The teacher: 'Say Beth!' He receives a similar answer. The teacher takes firm hold of the pupil's ear. The pupil in agony: 'My ear! My ear!' The teacher: 'Who says that it is thy ear?' The pupil shouts: 'The whole world knows that it is my ear'—at which the teacher replies: 'The whole world also knows that this is an aleph and that is a beth'. This demonstration had a convincing effect upon the pupil, and it is given as an example of the commendable patience of a teacher.[4] As a rule, the cane was liberally used, but it was recommended to let it rest in the Dog-Days, in which season also the pupils were to leave school as early as ten o'clock in the morning.[5] We read of a maid who cursed a teacher whom she saw beating a boy too hard.[6] It is related that the heretic Elisha ben Abuya once entered a house of study, and when he saw the children seated before the teacher, he exclaimed: 'What are these doing here? This boy ought to be a builder, that a carpenter, that a fisherman, that a tailor'. Hearing which the children 'left him (the teacher) and went out' (*hawōn shābeḳīn lēh weāzelīn lōn*).[7] Undoubtedly the method of instruction was then the same as it is to-day in the *ḥedārīm* (elementary schools) of the Jews: the teacher recites and the pupils repeat the Bible verses again and again until they know both the proper reading of the original and its meaning. Some Rabbis considered it permissible for the teacher to divide the verse into short portions.[8] Others again were rather doubtful

[1] Lev. R. 30 (80 b).
[2] b. Ned. 37 a; cf. Ned. iv. 3, where payment for instruction in the Bible is presupposed.
[3] Eccl. R. 7, 8 (104 b).
[4] A similar story is told of Hillel, b. Sab. 31 a; Ab. d. R. N. 15.
[5] Num. R. 12 (88 a); cf. Dalman, *Arbeit und Sitte in Pal.* I. 499.
[6] p. Mo. k. 81 d.
[7] p. Hag. 77 d. The expression at the end of the sentence corresponds exactly with Mk. xii. 12; Mt. xxii. 22.
[8] b. Meg. 22 a.

about this method. When the people of Tarbenet (south of Nazareth) demanded from the elementary teacher that he should, when reading, split up the Scriptural verses, in order that it should be easier for the children to repeat them, he received from Rabbi Ḥanina the advice—rather than do so to let his head be torn off, and the teacher was dismissed for not complying with the parents' wishes.[1] Occasionally an advanced pupil was allowed to read the verse word for word and the other children repeated after him in chorus.[2]

There is no documentary proof that Nazareth (a town scarcely smaller than the neighbouring place Tarbenet, now Tarbana, which lay in the valley of Jezreel, and which had a school) possessed a Bible school. Perhaps the boy Jesus did not sit on the beam which was shown in the year 570 as the school-bench on which He learnt the A B C,[3] but there can be no doubt that His pious parents took care that He should be instructed in the Torah, according to the ordinance, and therefore also in Hebrew. In a synagogue there were naturally people who were eager to read, and, therefore, also those who could instruct in the reading and in the interpreting of Holy Scripture, if it was not possible for the parents themselves to do it. Not everyone possessed a scroll at home, but every synagogue had it, and there the beadle instructed the children in reading.[4] They probably sat in a circle round the scroll, as even to-day the children of the South Arabian Jews do round the text book which they study, and which they can read from all sides. Even when a young boy, Jesus must have been drawn to the place where God's word was expounded, and the twelve-year-old who 'must be in things of His Father' wished to hear in the hall of the Temple-court what the doctors of the Law, at the centre of legal knowledge, had to say (Lk. ii. 46, 49). He sat in their midst, listening to them, asking them questions and answering their questions, and thus, corresponding to an old Rabbinic definition of a genuine student, He 'sat and asked and answered'.[5] When He said: 'Know ye not that I must be in the things of my

[1] p. Meg. 75 b.
[2] Tos. Sot. vi. 2; p. Sot. 20 c; cf. b. Sot. 30 b; Sukk. 30 b.
[3] Geyer, *Itinera*, 161; Dalman, *O.W.* 77.
[4] b. Sabb. i. 3.
[5] Ab. d. R. N. 40.

Father?' (Aramaic: *lā hawētōn yāde'īn diṣerīkh*[1] *anā lemihwē bideabbā*),[2] He did not refer to the Temple, but to the Law and to Scripture. That He did not learn in vain is seen from the fact that He stood up in the Nazareth synagogue to read the prophetic portion (Lk. iv. 16), which means that He was quite familiar with Hebrew. To the two languages which our Lord knew (Aramaic, His mother-tongue, and Greek, the language of the government and of the foreign inhabitants of the land), must also be added *as a third*—Hebrew, the language of His Bible.

[1] *Gram.* 209.

[2] For this use of the relative participle see *Gram.* 117; p. San. 29 a: *debāryākh 'abadt*, 'Thou hast done the business of thy Creator'.

PART TWO

IN THE SYNAGOGUE

VII. THE SYNAGOGUE SERVICE

To the Jew, the child as well as the adult, the best school for the study of Hebrew was the Synagogue (Aramaic *kenīshtā*,[1] originally *bē* (*bēt*) *kenīshtā*,[2] 'assembly house'). The institution of Divine service on Sabbath and Feast-days, which was ascribed to an oral ordinance of Moses or his contemporaries, directed the public reading from the Law for these days.[3] Every Jewish community was obliged to care for all the necessary arrangements in connexion with this service; it was the duty of the individual Jew to be present at the reading, and it was considered a meritorious act to take part in the same, and to co-operate thus in the community's obligations. The reading from the prophets as supplementary to that from the Pentateuch originated early.[4] That in course of time the Synagogue lessons became a part of a liturgical service[5] was not due to a desire to frame them appropriately, but rather to the connecting of this duty of reading from the Law with other duties. For this reason the service, in its individual parts, came to be considered an obligation in a peculiar sense.

The first duty connected with this reading was the recitation of the *Shema*ʻ (Hebrew, *ḳerīat shema*ʻ), which every individual Israelite was obliged to perform twice daily, and which consisted mainly of the Deuteronomic sections vi. 4–9; xi. 13–21, where a daily 'speaking' of the Commandments is enjoined.[6]

[1] p. Ber. 9 c; Sot. 22 a; Yom. 44 b.

[2] Lev. R. 32 (88 b). In my *Gram.* 149, I considered the *yōd* in *kenīshtā* to be short, but the ind. *kenīshā* shows that it is long.

[3] p. Meg. 78 a; Sopher. x. 1; Jos. *C. Ap.* II. 17 (Moses); Mech. 45 a; b. Bab. r. 82 a (Moses' contemporaries). Cf. Acts xv. 21.

[4] Acts xiii. 15, 27; Meg. iv. 1, 2.

[5] The expression is based on the analogy between the corporate community-prayer and the sacrificial service; p. Ber. 8 b; b. Ber. 15 a; cf. Acts xiii. 2.

[6] Ber. i. 1, 2; cf. Jos. *Ant.* IV. 8, 13.

This recitation meant both a literal observation of the Deuteronomic ordinance as well as a confession of faith in God's unity. The corporate recital of the *prayer*—which every Jew had to say daily in private, and which consisted of eighteen parts on week-days and of seven parts on the Sabbath[1]—was then joined to the *Shema'*.

In connexion with this prayer came, finally, the 'uplifting of hands' (cf. Lev. ix. 21), i.e. the Aaronitic blessing (Num. vi. 27).[2] Thus the Synagogue service was carried out in the following order:[3] first the *Shema'*, recited by all in unison, before and after which one of the congregation 'went in front of the ark of the Law',[4] in order 'to offer' (i.e. as a sacrifice),[5] in the name of all, the sevenfold prayer, each part of which was confirmed by the 'Amen' of the congregation. Between the sixth and seventh part of this prayer,[6] if priests were present, they unitedly 'lifted up the hands' to pronounce the Aaronitic blessing from the platform of the ark of the Law.[7] The additional prayer at the end, corresponding to the daily sacrifice of the Temple, dates probably from a later period.[8]

This 'Liturgy', which had in all probability some influence upon the order of the Church worship, was followed by the chief part of the service, namely the lesson framed in benedictions,[9] and probably read from the lectern, which stood at the forefront of the platform (p. 42). With the reading of the second lesson from the Prophets (also framed in benedictions), the congregation was 'dismissed'. The term 'dismissal' applied to

[1] Tos. Ber. iii. 10, 12; p. Ber. 8 a. For the text, see *W.J.*, German text, 299 f. The first three and the last three benedictions given there, with one prayer appointed for the Sabbath as the middle portion, formed the sevenfold prayer.

[2] Cf. Siphre on Num. 39 (11 b).

[3] It can be deduced from Meg. iv. 3; Cant. R. viii. 13 (78 b).

[4] Only of the precentor does it say that he 'went before the ark', Hebrew *'ābar liphnē hat-tēbā*, Ber. v. 4; Lev. R. 23 (61 a), Aramaic *'abar ḳummē tēbūtā*, p. Pes. 32 c. The reason is probably because he alone stood directly before the ark and facing it, while those who said the benedictions connected with the *Shema'*, and the readers, stood on the platform, but not near the ark, neither did they turn their faces to it.

[5] For the expression 'offer' cf. p. Ber. 8 b.

[6] *Ibid.* It is also understood so in Ber. v. 4; Schürer, *Geschichte*, II. 535, erroneously puts the priestly blessing at the end of the whole service.

[7] Num. R. 11 (83 a). [8] Meg. iv. 2; Sopher. xi. 5; p. Yom. 43 d.

[9] Meg. iv. 1, 2; Sopher. xiii. 8–10.

the prophetic lesson shows that the Law and the Prophets were not entirely of the same importance.[1]

The pronouncing of the benedictions connected with the *Shema*ʿ, the recitation of the prayer, and the reading of the prophetic lesson, could all be performed by the same person.[2] The reading from the Law on a Sabbath day was divided into seven portions for seven persons. The first and the last participants said the benedictions at the beginning and at the end respectively,[3] but every reader had to say a benediction for himself before and after the lesson.[4] Anyone who made a mistake in the prayer or in the reading had to be substituted at once by someone else.[5] Of regular singing nothing is reported. On festivals only was the Hallel,[6] i.e. Psalms cxiii–cxviii, which every Jew was obliged to chant, sung by the whole congregation, antiphonically, it appears.[7] Theoretically the *Shema*ʿ could be recited in the vernacular,[8] that is, in Aramaic, and even in the Synagogue service, though it is not probable that it ever was in any language but Hebrew. The priestly blessing had to be said in Hebrew.[9] As to the lessons—it was taken for granted in Palestinian Jewry, that they had to be read in the Hebrew original, and not in an Aramaic Targum. There is not the slightest proof that a written Targum[10] was in any way employed in Divine service. Even in the Synagogue of the Hellenists (Hebrew, *lāʿōzōt*), the text, at least at the beginning and at the end, had, if possible, to be read in Hebrew, or the whole section recited by one person.[11] Among the Hebraists the reading was

[1] This can also be seen from the treatment of the prophetic books; see p. Meg. 73 d f.; b. Meg. 27 a; Meg. iii. 1. The reading from the Prophets is attested also in Acts xiii. 15, 27; cf. Lk. xvi. 31.

[2] Meg. iv. 5.

[3] Meg. iv. 1, 2.

[4] Deut. R. xi. (38 a).

[5] *Ibid.*; p. Meg. 75 b.

[6] Tos. Sukk. iii. 2; p. Sukk. 54 b; b. Taan. 28 b; Arach. 10 a.

[7] p. Sot. 20 c; Tos. Sot. vi. 2; cf. b. Sot. 30 b; Sukk. 30 b.

[8] Sot. vii. 1; Tos. Sot. vii. 7. Yet, Jehuda I insisted on it being said in Hebrew.

[9] Siphre on Num. 39 (11 b) (Levertoff's Eng. ed. p. 28); Sot. vii. 2; b. Sot. 38 a; p. Sot. 21 c; Eccl. R. vii. 2 (102 a).

[10] Hänel, *Der Schriftbegriff Jesu*, 144, attempts to prove the contrary. But the polemics in Sab. xvi. 1; b. Sab. 115 a; p. Meg. 74 d, do not refer to a custom from which the existence of such a Targum could be derived, neither is it mentioned in b. Ber. 8 a.

[11] Tos. Meg. iv. 13. Strike the first *pōtḥīn* and add *ēllā* before *eḥād*, p. Meg. 75 a.

followed by an Aramaic translation; the Law—after each verse; the Prophets—after three verses.[1] The lesson was considered to be incomplete without a Targum, i.e. without the translation by one who was familiar with the traditional method of rendering.[2] In fact, the problem was, whether the mere reading of the lesson from the Law without translating it into the language understood by the people could even be considered a proper fulfilling of the Deuteronomic ordinance.[3]

The reader of the lesson was not to be the translator, otherwise the translation might be taken to be a part of the text. The translating had to be done reverently, without the use of a book, in order that the authority of the original text should not be shaken.[4] Any show of vanity in the translator was disapproved; beautiful chanting, for instance.[5] Even when the translator merely raised his voice above that of the reader, it was looked upon with disfavour. But neither was the latter to put the former into the shade.[6] The reader was not allowed to help the translator, in order that it should not seem as though the translation was part of the text.[7] As the benedictions and the Prayer, even the *Shema'*,[8] though consisting of Scriptural passages, were also to be said extemporarily, the lessons from the Law and the Prophets were thus stamped with a unique character.

There was no rubric concerning the sermon. It depended on whether there was a suitable person present at the service. The prophetic lesson could be shortened for the sake of the discourse.[9] It could, for instance, hardly have formed a constituent part of the proper service in connexion with the reading from the Law. According to the only existent suggestion, a discourse was given at the end of the service.[10] Still more frequently the discourse was entirely separated from the Sabbath morning service, and given instead on Friday evening.[11] The preaching was in the vernacular.[12]

[1] Meg. iv. 4; Tos. Meg. iv. 20.
[2] p. Meg. 75 a.
[3] p. Meg. 74 d.
[4] *Ibid.*
[5] Eccl. R. vii. 5 (102 b).
[6] b. Ber. 45 a.
[7] b. Meg. 32 a.
[8] Taan. iv. 3.
[9] Sopher. xii. 7; xiv. 2.
[10] b. Ber. 28 b.
[11] See above, p. 22.
[12] *Ibid.*

The chief of the synagogue, Hebrew *rōsh hak-keneset*, Greek ἀρχισυναγωγός (Mk. v. 22), was the master of ceremonies. It was not his office to perform any part of the Divine service himself.[1] His task consisted in inviting appropriate persons to pray and read (Acts xiii. 15) and in receiving applications to be allowed to perform these offices. The servant, Hebrew *ḥazzān*,[2] executed the orders of the chief, invited the appointed readers,[3] and took out the rolls from the Holy Ark, and put them back again after the reading.[4] Occasionally he also performed the office of reader.[5]

The synagogue was, as a rule, a simple hall, the roof of which was sustained by round columns or square pillars.[6] A platform, *bēmā* = βῆμα,[7] stood facing towards the direction of the Temple in Jerusalem; on it was the Holy Ark (Aramaic *arōnā*, *tēbūtā*), often in the form of a low cupboard with folding doors, so that its back was towards the Temple.[8] In front, at the edge of the platform, and facing the congregation, which sat before it, was the lectern, ἀναλόγειον.[9] The people, among whom was the beadle, sat on benches facing the ark (i.e. Templewards). Opposite the congregation, probably directly in front of the platform, the *zeḳēnīm*[10] had their seats. As *zeḳēnīm* must refer here, as elsewhere, not to the elders but to the scribes, our Lord's characterisation of them as preferring the πρωτοκαθεδρία (Mt. xxiii. 6) was taken from life. The priests stepped up to the platform[11] to pronounce the blessing, which they did facing the congregation.[12] The reader and the translator, both of whom stood whilst performing their offices, also faced the people, as did the preacher—who sat. The precentor, on the other hand,

[1] Tos. Meg. iv. 21.

[2] Yom. vii. 1; Sot. vii. 7, 8; cf. Tos. Sukk. iv. 61; b. Sabb. 35 b.

[3] p. Ber. 9 c; cf. Tos. Taan. i. 14, according to which he used also to call the trumpet-blower.

[4] p. Meg. 75 b.

[5] Tos. Meg. iv. 21.

[6] p. Ber. 9, 13 a; cf. *O.W.* p. 128 f.

[7] p. Meg. 73 d; Sukk. 55 a f.; b. Sukk. 51 b; Tos. Sukk. iv. 6; cf. Tos. Sot. vii. 13.

[8] Tos. Meg. iv. 21; p. Bikk. 65 c.

[9] p. Meg. 73 d; according to which *bēmā* and ἀναλόγειον stand in close relationship to the ark, although they were ordinary Synagogue utensils.

[10] Tos. Meg. iv. 21.

[11] Num. R. 11 (82 b f.).

[12] *Ibid.* Siphre Num. 39 (11 b f.) (Levertoff's Eng. edit. p. 30); b. Sot. 38 a; Siphre on Num. 44 d.

whose head, by the way, was veiled, had naturally to turn towards the ark, as he, like the whole congregation, must turn Templewards for prayer,[1] which was said standing, and the elders had, naturally, to turn round.

In the synagogue court, there was a laver[2] for the congregation to wash their hands before the recitation of the *Shema*ʿ and the saying of the Prayer.[3] In many places there was probably also a bath for ritual purposes.[4] The Synagogue was a house of prayer, a fact which is expressed in the designation προσευχή (Acts xvi. 13),[5] especially used by the Jews in Egypt, which has no Hebrew or Aramaic equivalent in Jewish literature. Prayer in the Temple is mentioned,[6] but we also read of the Synagogue being the place where prayers are especially answered by God[7]—God being present where ten people are gathered for that purpose.[8] An appointed place for prayer is recommended.[9] Nevertheless, the primal purpose of the Synagogue is kept to the fore, as prayers could be said in other places as well. The traditional conception of the Synagogue is that it is not to be used for anything but reading (of the written Law), repetition (of the oral Law), and research (the derivation of the oral Law from the written).[10] Thus, the Synagogue is designed to be a place for the study of the written, as well as the oral Law. What is occasionally connected with the 'house of study' (Hebrew *bēt ham-midrāsh*) is here attributed to the Synagogue—the proper house for Scripture-reading. Hence, the real purpose of that institution is more correctly expressed in a synagogue inscription found in Jerusalem, according to which it was built εἰς ἀνάγνωσιν νόμου καὶ εἰς διδαχὴν ἐντολῶν, 'for the reading of the Law and instruction in the commandments'.[11] Although we find no

[1] 1 Kings viii. 44; Dan. vi. 11; Siphre Deut. 29 (71 b); Ber. iv. 5, 6; Tos. Ber. iii. 16; b. Ber. 30 a; Cant. R. iv. 4 (48 b); cf. *O.W.* p. 130 f.

[2] p. Meg. 74 a.

[3] b. Ber. 15 a; cf. Judith, 12, 8.

[4] Ber. iii. 5; Tos. Ber. ii. 14; p. Ber. 6 c; b. Ber. 22 a. The 'water reservoirs' of the synagogue inscription of Jerusalem (Weill, *La Cité de David*, 186) possibly also served this purpose.

[5] Cf. Schürer, *Geschichte*, II. 500, 517.

[6] p. Ber. 8 b; Maaser, 56 a; Cant. R. vii. 2 (67 b); Gen. R. 81 (174 a); Lk. xviii. 10; xix. 46; Acts iii. 1.

[7] b. Ber. 6 a.

[8] *Ibid.* Mech. 73 b; cf. Mt. xviii. 20.

[9] p. Ber. 8 b.

[10] Cf. Tos. Meg. iii. 7; p. Meg. 74 d; b. Meg. 28 b.

[11] R. Weill, *La Cité de David*, 186.

certain suggestions that Jesus was instructed in the oral Law after the traditional manner, yet we realise that the original purpose of the Synagogue affected Him too. He came into contact there with 'the Law and the Prophets', and the submission under the letter of Scripture made an impression upon Him. Neither could the Synagogue prayers have failed to impress Him. By taking part in worship there He openly testified that for Him also Scripture contained the rule of life, and that the God who speaks in it is also His God. Yet, His prayer was bound neither by the place nor by the Synagogue formulae, nor was the Synagogue teaching the standard of His knowledge of the will of God. This is shown not only in the whole tenor of His teaching, but also in the manner in which He preached in the Nazareth synagogue (Lk. iv. 16 f.).

VIII. JESUS IN THE SYNAGOGUE OF NAZARETH AND THE FULFILMENT OF THE PROPHETIC WORD

When at a Sabbath service in the synagogue of Nazareth Jesus stood up in order to read a portion of the Scripture, the beadle 'delivered' unto Him the book of the prophet Isaiah. When He had opened the book, He 'found' the beginning of chapter lxi (Lk. iv. 16 f.). The atmosphere of the narrative suggests the usual reading from the Prophets at the conclusion of the service. At that time the prophetic lessons were probably not yet fixed, while the lessons from the Law were read (at any rate, later, in Palestine) in a triennial cycle, cursively, in fixed sections.[1] Yet it is worth noticing that of seven consecutive sections from the Law we know that (in later times in any case) the prophetic lessons for the last three of them were taken from Deutero-Isaiah.[2] The Sabbaths at the end of the Synagogue-year, when these lessons were read, were therefore called 'the consolation Sabbaths'. The last of these lessons was Isa. lxi. 10 f., while Isa. lxi. 1 f. is nowhere prescribed as a lesson. In any case, on that particular Sabbath our Lord was the 'dismisser' (Hebrew *maphṭīr*) of the congregation, and, as at that period the prophetic

[1] b. Meg. 29 b; cf. Elbogen, *Der jüdische Gottesdienst*, 160; Levertoff, *Commentary on St Matthew*, Introduction.

[2] See Pesikta de Rab Kahana, Piska 16–22.

lessons must have been taken from Isaiah, although He was free to select His own passage, He had to confine Himself to that book.

Perhaps when His eye fell on the beginning of chapter lxi, He put aside the appointed section, since this was more suitable to His purpose. He intentionally chose a lesson containing words of consolation. He *stood up* to receive the book, and remained standing during the reading.[1] The Evangelist, writing in Greek, speaks of the 'opening' and 'closing' of the book. But as Jewish literature always presupposes that the holy writings were written on rolls,[2] one has rather to think of 'unrolling' and 'rolling up', for which the usual word in Hebrew was *gālal*,[3] in Aramaic *gal*.[4]

The roll of the Law had to be unrolled behind the curtain (of the Holy Ark), and not in the sight of the congregation.[5] This could not have been the case with the prophetic roll, because in the prophetic lesson it was permitted 'to jump', i.e. to read bits of different portions unconnected with one another.[6] Another characteristic of the prophetic roll was that, unlike the roll of the Law which had twin rollers one at each end, it had but one fixed at the commencement, and therefore had to be rolled always towards the beginning.[7] It is not probable that the Evangelist intended to emphasise the fact that the roll used by our Lord contained only the book of Isaiah, but we do know that, as well as rolls containing all the prophetic books, there were also such which contained single books only.[8]

When our Lord had finished reading, He seated Himself. This was a sign that He wished to speak on the prophetic passage which He had just read; for the teacher *sat*.[9] There must have been a chair for that purpose on the platform,[10]

[1] Sot. vii. 7, 8; Yom. vii. 1; cf. Lk. iv. 16–20.
[2] Cf. Siphre Deut. 160 (105 b).
[3] Er. x. 3; Sot. vii. 7; b. San. 68 a; Meg. 32 a; Cant. R. v. 14.
[4] = *gelal*, p. Yom. 44 b; Sot. 22 a; Meg. 75 b. The Pal. Evang. and the Syriac have *kerak*, which, in the Jewish dialect, would mean 'to wrap up'.
[5] *Ibid.* [6] Meg. iv. 4. [7] p. Meg. 71 c; b. Bab. b. 14 a.
[8] b. Bab. b. 13 b; cf. Dalman, *Traditio Rabbinorum veterrima*, 28 f.
[9] p. Dem. 22 b; Shek. 47 a; Taan. 67 d; Yeb. 13 a; Lev. R. 32 (88 b); 34; b. San. 99 b; Tg. Judges, v. 9. Cf. Mt. v. 2; xxvi. 55; Mk. ix. 35; Lk. v. 3.
[10] A platform was specially made for the teacher, p. Yeb. 13 a.

similar to the chair (*ḳatedrā*), which, according to tradition, the provincials had in readiness for every Jerusalemite in order to hear his wisdom,[1] and like those of certain dying Rabbis, which, according to their instruction, had to be kept ready for their successors.[2] It was to this that our Lord referred when He spoke of the 'chair of Moses' (Mt. xxiii. 2).

Nothing is said in the Gospel narrative of an Aramaic translation following the reading of the Hebrew text. It might have been of no interest to the Evangelist. But it is also possible that our Lord incorporated the Aramaic translation in His discourse, which discourse is not recorded in its exact literal form. The Greek rendering of the prophetic passage, as preserved in St Luke, cannot but have an awkward appearance in a Hebrew New Testament. As the second task of the one who has been anointed with the spirit of God is left out, and, instead, something similar is inserted (in the fourth place) from Isa. lviii. 6, no credible Hebrew text can be constructed. Neither is there any evidence that the Isaiah scroll of the Nazareth synagogue had, like the LXX, 'blind' instead of the 'prisoners' of the Massoretic text. It is simpler to take the latter text for granted, and so it is rather interesting to see how Isa. lxi. 1 f. was understood in the existent Aramaic Targum on the Prophets. It runs there as follows:

rūaḥ nebūā min ḳodām adōnāy elōhīm 'alay, ḥalāph derabbī adōnāy yātī lebāssārā 'inwetānayā, shalḥani letaḳḳāphā litebīrē libbā, lemiḳrē ledisheban ḥērū ūleda-asīrīn itgelū linehōr, lemiḳrē shenat ra'wā ḳodām adōnāy.

'A spirit of prophecy from *before* the Lord God is upon me; because the Lord has appointed me to proclaim joy to the humble; has sent me to strengthen the broken-hearted; to proclaim liberty to the exiles and an opening towards the light to the captives; to proclaim a year of goodwill *before* the Lord'.

Genuinely Targumic is the here twice-repeated 'before the Lord', to avoid expressions which would suggest a too close connexion between God and the world. As our Lord Himself used similar expressions,[3] it is not impossible that, in translation

[1] Lam. R. i. 1 (19 b). Uncertain is the meaning of *ḳatedrā demōshe*, Pesikt. 7 b.

[2] p. Ab. z. 42 c.

[3] E.g. Mt. xi. 26; xviii. 14; cf. *W.J.* 172 f.

into Aramaic, He rendered it in the same way. He could not, however, have said, as does the Targum, 'the spirit of *prophecy* is upon me'; for the latter introduces the passage with the words: *amar nebiyā*, 'the prophet spake'. To the Targumist it is Isaiah who speaks here of himself and of his mission. Jehuda ben Simon concluded from the words 'the spirit of the Lord is upon me' that Isaiah's prophecy came directly from 'the mouth of the Power',[1] while the other prophets spoke 'one from the mouth of the other'.[2] Another Rabbi thought it was significant that the Holy Spirit is here closely connected with redemption.[3] Yet a third Rabbi found in this passage the suggestion that humility is the most essential characteristic of the pious.[4] Such are the sentiments which Jewish scribes connected with Isa. lxi. 1. The Nazaraeans might have expected from our Lord a discourse similar to that preserved in Pesikta de Rab Kahana, in the sections based upon the prophetic lessons for 'the Sabbaths of consolation'.[5] The first of these sections describes how twelve prophets attempted one after the other to comfort Jerusalem, but in vain, since all of them mingled future judgment with their message of salvation. When they complained to God of their failure, He said: 'I Myself must come with you to comfort Jerusalem!' (as it is said, Isa. xl. 1) 'Comfort ye, comfort ye *with me* (read '*immi* = with me, instead of '*ammī* = my people)! Comfort ye, comfort ye, that is, ye from below and ye from above, ye living and ye dead, concerning this world and concerning the world to come, concerning the ten tribes, and concerning Judah and Benjamin'.[6]

The expectation of such words of comfort must have been expressed in the eyes which (according to Lk. iv. 20) were intent upon our Lord when He was about to speak. The Gospel narrator mentioned it because he wished to lay stress on the personal concern of the Nazaraeans in what their countryman had to say. He made use for His purpose of the pause which takes place during the rolling up and putting back of the scroll

[1] Cf. Mt. xxvi. 64; see Levertoff's note on this verse in the one-volume *Commentary of the Bible*.

[2] Pesikt. 125 b; Lev. R. 10 (25 a).

[3] Lam. R. iii. 50 (55 a).

[4] b. Ab. z. 20 b.

[5] See above, p. 44.

[6] Pesikta, 128 a.

into the holy shrine. Our Lord's discourse is given in a condensed form and, in fact, was probably short. The phrase 'He *began* to say to them' (Lk. iv. 21) does not suggest that what followed was only the beginning of His speech, but is merely a narrative form often used by St Luke, and of which Jewish literature supplies many examples.[1] It was customary to say: 'He began to weep'; 'He began to knock'; 'He began to be angry'; 'He began to consider'; 'They began to beat'; 'She began to cry'; 'He began to speak'; 'He began to call'.[2] The Aramaic *shāri* or the Hebrew *hitḥīl* is in this case only a vivid introduction to a narrative, without suggesting any continuation. Thus, also here, it was merely intended by this phrase to give a vivid picture of how, by His words, Jesus put an end to the waiting of the congregation. He said:

'To-day is this scripture fulfilled in your ears'.

Aramaic: *yōma dēn itḳaiyam hādēn ḳerāyā be-udnēkhōn.*

Ḳerāyā is the usual Aramaic word for Scripture as a whole,[3] as well as for single Scriptural passages.[4] The word for 'to fulfil' (*ḳaiyēm*), which will be dealt with under IX, means *confirming* in contrast to *abrogating*. A prophetic word is confirmed when its content is realised.[5] Nothing less did our Lord's hearers experience at that moment. The Peshito puts *de* before *udnēkhōn*, and takes it thus as an addition to *ḳerāyā*. The word of Scripture which was *just heard* would, in any case, be the one that was fulfilled. But, according to the Greek text, the fulfilment took place in the ears of the hearers, i.e. in the fact that they were hearing Jesus at that very time. What is meant is, either that the prophetic word is fulfilled because He reads it as *His* word, or that the fulfilment consisted in the very fact of His pointing to Himself at this moment. In the message to John the Baptist (Lk. vii. 22), Jesus referred to His miraculous deeds and His gospel of joy to the poor, as a proof of His

[1] *W.J.* 21 f.

[2] p. Sanh. 23 c; Kil. 32 c; p. Bez. 63 a; p. Keth. 35 a; Cant. R. vi. 12 (67 a); p. Shebi. 35 b; p. Dem. 21 d; Shek. 48 d; p. Ab. z. 41 a; Eccl. R. vii. 13 (106 b).

[3] p. Shek. 49 c; Meg. 74 d.

[4] Indic. *ḳerā*, p. Yeb. 15 c; Naz. 54 b; plural ind. *ḳerāyīn* Lev. R. 24; det. *ḳerāyē*, Gen. R. 81; Lev. R. 19.

[5] Deut. xviii. 22.

mission. The narrator probably meant to convey this also here, but on this occasion our Lord simply let the prophetic word speak for itself, and confronted the listeners with His Person only, whom these words portrayed.

That there was no prophet in their midst, had long been the bitter cry of pious Jews (1 Macc. iv. 46). Tales were told of heavenly voices, heard at certain gatherings of Rabbis, proclaiming: 'Here is one who would be worthy of the Holy Spirit, if his contemporaries deserved it'.[1] They also thought they knew to whom among those present the voice referred. But God's Spirit descended on none of them. Had there been one who possessed it, they would have been prepared to 'hear him', i.e. to *obey* him[2] as one who, in regard to spiritual endowment, was equal to Moses.[3] According to tradition, he would have had to be obeyed even when he commanded transgression of any of the ordinances of the Law, like Elijah on Mount Carmel, who built an altar and sacrificed at a place not chosen by God, according to the 'demand of the hour'.[4] Only when advocating idolatry was he not to be followed, 'even if he should keep the sun in the midst of the heavens'.[5] And here stood before them one of their own townsmen and claimed to possess the Spirit of God, not in order to answer unsolvable problems of ritual and Law (cf. 1 Macc. iv. 46), but to announce that the time of bondage was now at an end, and that the year of grace had begun. He, whose task it was to accomplish this, was akin to the great Unknown of Isa. xl–lxvi, who comforted His exiled people by proclaiming salvation. He, Jesus, is taking up that prophet's work again, in order to bring it to fruition. What He proclaims is not that He is, or is to be, the King of Israel, but that it is His vocation not only to foresee the saving power of God, i.e. the reign of God (Aramaic *malkhūtā dishemaiyā*), as He understands it, but to introduce it into this world, as the full sunshine which announces, at the opened door of the prison, freedom to those who languish there in darkness.

[1] Tos. Sot. xiii. 3, 4; p. Ab. z. 42 c; Sot. 24 b.
[2] See above, p. 18.
[3] Cf. Tg. Yer. I on Deut. xviii. 15.
[4] Siphre Deut. 175 (107 b); b. Yeb. 90 b.
[5] b. Sanh. 90 a; cf. p. Sanh. 30 c.

The words of Jesus sounded to the hearers as 'words of grace' (Lk. iv. 22). The Aramaic for λόγοι τῆς χάριτος would probably be (cf. Pal. Evang.) *millaiyā deḥisdā*. Rabbi Ḥisdai once applied the hard saying of Ezek. xxi. 26 ('away with the head ornament!') to the Rabbis, and 'take away the "crown"!' (*ibid.*) to the nations of the world. He was praised for this in the words: 'Thou art *ḥesed* (a play on his name), and thy words (read *millākh*) are *ḥesed*, grace'.[1] However, in its formulation, the expression is neither pure Aramaic nor is it Greek, but Hebrew. It belongs to the Greek biblicisms of St Luke, and is reminiscent of the 'lips of grace' (*siphtē ḥēn*) of Prov. xxii. 11, and of 'the beautiful words of the wise' of Eccl. x. 12, which passages are quoted in the Midrash in connexion with the permission given by Cyrus to the exiles to return to their own land (thus also fulfilment of prophecy).[2] That the words of our Lord made such an impression upon the hearers, is natural. Until then they had heard the prophetic message only as a sound from olden times with an echo in a future of uncertain distance. But what they now hear seems to them like a fulfilment of the longing contained in the Aramaic prayer *yeḳūm purḳān*:[3] 'May your God set up to you, in your life and in your days, His great kingdom (*malkhūtēh rabbetā*), through the Messiah the son of David; as it is written in His holy words (Dan. ii. 44): "And in the days of these kings shall the God of heaven set up a kingdom which shall never be destroyed"'. But the Speaker in their midst did not seem to them to suit His message. They said with astonishment (Lk. iv. 22): 'Is not this the son of Joseph?' (Aramaic *lā hādēn hū berēh deyōsēph*). He is just like one of themselves. Of course, it would be excellent if redemption should come through a Nazaraean. But where are the proofs? Jesus read their thoughts when He said (verse 23 f.):

'Doubtless ye will say unto me this parable: Physician, heal thyself: whatsoever we have heard done at Capernaum, do also here in thine own country. Verily I say unto you, No prophet is acceptable in his own country. But of a truth I say unto you, There were many widows in Israel in the days of Elijah, when the heaven was shut up three years and six months, when there came a great famine over all

[1] Ruth. R. iii. (9 b); cf. b. Gitt. 7 a. [2] Eccl. R. x. 12 (123 a).
[3] According to Siddur Yemen, MS. Chamitzer.

the land; and unto none of them was Elijah sent, but only to Zarephath, in the land of Sidon, unto a woman that was a widow'.

Aramaic: *min kōl atar tēmrūn lī matlā āsyā assī garmākh. kōl mā dishema'nān da'abadtinnēh bikhephar naḥūm hawē 'ābēd uph hākhā bimedīnetākh. āmēn āmarnā lekhōn, delēt nebiyyā meḳabbal bimedīnetēh. min ḳushtā āmarnā lekhōn dahawayān saggīān armelān beyusrāēl beyōmōhi de-ēliyyā kid-it'aḥedūn shemaiyā telāt shenīn weshittā yarḥīn wahawā kaphnā rabbā 'al kōl ar'ā welā ishtelaḥ ēliyyā leḥadā minhēn ēllā leṣārephat dileṣaydānāē le-ittetā armaltā.*

The Greek πάντως ('at all events') which in Pal. Evang. occurs frequently in other connexions as well, is also represented in Jewish Aramaic.[1] But the Aramaic *min kōl atar* corresponds exactly to this.[2] παραβολή for 'proverb' is based on the Aramaic *matlā*, which stands for parable as well as for proverb.[3] This proverb, already known in a similar formulation from Sir. xviii. 20, runs in Jewish tradition as follows: *āsyā, assī ḥiggartākh*, 'physician, heal thy lameness'.[4] The Greek idiom 'What we have heard as having happened' is broken up in the Aramaic of the Pal. Evang., as much as it is linguistically possible, in the way used above. As to *āmēn*, see above, p. 30. One is inclined to hesitate concerning it, as this word is substituted by ἐπ' ἀληθείας, which might have only been used in order to avoid repetition. In this case our Lord Himself used *āmēn* both times. The Aramaic *ḳabbēl* for the *reception*[5] of guests as well as for the *acceptance* of a charge,[6] can be documented. The word concerning the 'prophet in his own country' was probably also a proverb, but it does not occur in Jewish literature. The three years and six months duration of the drought, which does not quite correspond to 1 Kings xviii. 1 (but cf. also James v. 17), is supposed to have been based on a Midrash.[7] But the only existent Midrash on 1 Kings xviii. 1 endeavours to lessen the duration of the dearth, by counting only three months for the first and third years, and so bringing the time down to eighteen

[1] p. Sanh. 23 b.

[2] Gen. R. 41 (84 a): 'When the barley is thine, then the wheat is mine. When the wheat is mine, then the barley is thine. At all events (*min kōl atar*), the wheat is mine'; cf. Eccl. R. x. 2 (120 b).

[3] p. Dem. 21 d; Sanh. 22 b; Gen. R. 48 (102 a); Num. R. 18 (146 b).

[4] Gen. R. 23 (49 b).

[5] p. Ḥag. 77 d.

[6] p. Shek. 48 d.

[7] Carlsson, *Aggadastoff i Nya Testamentets skrifter*, 96 f.

months only.[1] It evidently takes it for granted that there was no rainy season at all and that in the following winter the rain began only in January, so that the drought lasted from Tammuz (July) of the first year (beginning with Tishri), to Kislew (December) of the third year. However, from Jewish literature it can be seen that the compass of half of a septennial was a common phrase used to express a considerable period,[2] and can be inferred not from Dan. vii. 25; xii. 7 alone. For instance, an Athenian who wished to learn wisdom in Jerusalem stayed there for three and a half years.[3] The same number of years Jochanan and Shimon ben Lakish[4] spent on the study of one section of Scripture; and Joḥanan suffered from gallstones.[5] It took Nebuchadnezzar the same length of time to capture Jerusalem;[6] Hadrian to take possession of Bittir;[7] and Joshua ben Chananya made a sea-journey[8] which lasted the same period. 'So that', ὡς, before the mention of the consequence of the drought, could be rendered in Aramaic (as in Pal. Evang.) with *kide*; but the mere addition of *we*, 'and', is more probable. The manner in which Sarepta and the widow are mentioned, corresponds to 1 Kings xvii. 9, and may, therefore, be rendered according to the Targum. For the 'of', *lewāt*, of the Targums, the Pal. Evang., as well as of the Syr., would have to be avoided, as it is unusual in the Galilaean dialect.[9]

The Nazaraeans wished to see 'signs' (cf. Mt. xii. 38). When Jose ben Kisma was asked by his disciples: 'When cometh the son of David?', he answered: 'I fear that ye demand a sign from me'. When they denied and his answer seemed uncertain, they did say: 'Give us a sign!' He granted their request at last by saying: 'If my word is true, the water of the cavern of Paneas (near the source of the Jordan) will be turned into blood'. This is supposed to have actually taken place at the hour

[1] Lev. R. 19 (49 b); followed by Yalk Shim. i. 210. Windisch, *Die katholischen Briefe*, 32, erroneously takes it to mean three and a half years. Cf. Dalman, *Arbeit und Sitte in Palästina*, I. 195, 314, 519.

[2] Subsequently I find in G. Kittel's *Rabbinica*, 35, a similar explanation of 'three and a half'.

[3] Lam. R. i. 1 (22 a).

[4] p. Sab. 9 c.

[5] Cant. R. ii. 16 (35 b).

[6] Lam. R. Peth. (14 b).

[7] Lam. R. ii. 1 (42 b).

[8] Yalk on Psalm xciii; Midr. on Psalms speaks only of three years.

[9] *Gram.* 226.

of his death.[1] Our Lord refused to consider such desires, as His Father's directions pointed out to Him ways which had nothing to do with considerations of earthly conditions. By this refusal He brought into the open day the antagonism which had already gathered in the hearts of His hearers.

Therefore the decisive question, as to how far the promises of the liberation of the captives began to be fulfilled through Jesus, did not come up. After what He said in Nazareth, His very reciting of the passage was the beginning of the fulfilment. Proclamation and realisation are closely connected. To our Lord, he who speaks in Isa. lxi. 1 f. is undoubtedly the same person, who, according to Isa. xlii. 7, opens the eyes of the blind, and brings out the prisoners from the dungeons by bringing justice to the nations through His patient teaching (xliii. 1–4). The proclamation of the God who is a righteous helper (Isa. xlv. 21) is in itself redemption, or, at least, the beginning of it. Our Lord's understanding of the text which He read must have taken some such line. But it was just here that the stumbling-block lay which caused His countrymen's downfall. They expected quite a different redemption: one that was visible and tangible. To have believed this Bringer-of-Salvation would have meant grasping the invisible and entrusting oneself, with all personal and national wishes and hopes, for better or for worse, to this Messenger of God, and to His God. Such courage the Nazaraeans did not possess. Their initial enthusiasm was turned into antipathy. A prophet who did not wish to do anything for his native town, ceased to belong to them. A prophet who seemed to speak that which God had not given to Him to say, deserved death according to Deut. xviii. 20.[2] He alone can judge them who has never stumbled over that boulder.

In looking back on the manner in which our Lord appeared in Nazareth, it becomes clear that He was not, like the others,

[1] b. Sanh. 98 a.

[2] Cf. Sanh. xi. 5. According to Siphre Deut. 178 (108 a); b. Sanh. 89 a the false prophet had to be strangled. According to Tos. Sanh. xi. 7, he could only be judged in Jerusalem and executed on a festival (cf. Lk. xiii. 33). Deut. xiii. 2 f. speaks of misleading signs and wonders of a false prophet. Yet, according to p. Sanh. 30 c, a prophet appearing for the first time could be given a hearing only when he showed signs and wonders.

an interpreter of Scripture (Aramaic *dārōsh*).[1] *Derāsh* means 'to investigate the contents of the words of Scripture'. To the Rabbis the contents of a Scripture passage consisted less in the historical sense of the words than in their importance for religious practice and thought. What it 'intimates' (Hebrew *higgīd*), i.e. what 'suggestion' (Hebrew *haggādā*) it conveys, and what it contains for deduction (Hebrew *limmad*), what is its 'teaching' (Hebrew *talmūd*), is the result and content of such 'research' (*derāsh*, *midrāsh*).[2] The method applied to such research consisted, when dealing with law, in the use of certain fixed rules of interpretation; otherwise, chiefly in the construction of relationships between one passage of Scripture and another. In this art of the *derāsh*,[3] which often degenerated into artificiality, the Jewish *dārōshīn* were masters. Even when they introduced proverbs, personal experiences, parables (p. 26), it was all done to serve this method of interpretation. Our Lord, when necessary for His purpose, also did this. But He was not a haggadist. The Truth which He proclaims does not represent itself as Scriptural interpretation, nor is it such. It stands alone in independent majesty. Thus, also in the synagogue in Nazareth, He did not add an interpretation to the prophetic word, but pointed to a fact which was not meant to be an interpretation, but a fulfilment, and this fact was Himself.

Because this whole situation was foreign to Jewish theology, there was no category into which Jesus could be put. He was neither a doctor of the Law, nor a preacher in the Jewish style. Of His manner of speaking it was said that He 'taught', διδάσκειν, cf. Lk. iv. 31, and the Aramaic for it would be *allēph*, which is used of one who teaches the Law,[4] as well as of a master-craftsman.[5] What He did was really to 'call out' in public (κηρύσσειν, Lk. iv. 44), Aramaic *akrēz*, which is used of one who, as the *kārōz* (κήρυξ) in the Temple, called priests, levites, and Israelites to worship.[6] According to the content of the

[1] p. Sot. 16 d; Lev. R. 9 (24 a).
[2] See Bacher, *Die älteste Terminologie der jüdischen Schriftauslegung*, 25 f., 30 f., 94 f., 99 f.
[3] See the expression for instance in Lev. R. 32 (88 b).
[4] p. Mo. k. 82 d; Shebi. 36 c. [5] p. Ab. z. 40 c.
[6] p. Shek. 48 d.

proclamation, it was a 'communicating of good news' (εὐαγγελίζειν, Lk. iv. 43), Aramaic *bassar*.[1] If Jesus was a Prophet, as He, according to Lk. xiii. 33, claimed to be,[2] it was in the sense of the one who in Isa. xl f. points to a redemption manifesting itself in the present. What the Nazaraeans could have become, had they accepted the Gospel of Jesus, is suggested in the phrase used by Rabbi Meir: 'he is assured (Hebrew *mebussār*) of becoming a son of the future world'. According to this Rabbi, the conditions required for this assurance are: to live in the Holy Land; to speak the holy tongue; to consume one's fruit in purity; and to recite twice daily the Jewish confession of the Divine unity.[3] To Jesus, the decisive condition of salvation is the acceptance of His message, i.e. faith in Him. For this reason He considered the passage in Isa. lxi as suitable for His purpose. One speaks there who says twice of himself that he will 'proclaim', and thrice that he is 'to bring good news'. This was, in fact, the kind and essence of all the preaching of our Lord, according to the very foundation of His purpose. And in that prophetic word, then half a millennium old, lies the most important historic root of His gospel, as well as of ours.

[1] Lam. R. i. 5 (29 a); cf. *W.J.* 84 f.

[2] Only the Gospel of St John speaks of 'the Prophet' (i. 21, 25; vi. 14; vii. 40) of whose expectation Jewish literature knows nothing.

[3] p. Shek. 47 c; cf. above, p. 33.

PART THREE

THE PREACHER ON THE MOUNT

IX. THE FULFILLER OF THE LAW

In the synagogue of Nazareth our Lord sat in the seat of the exponents of the Law and wished to be accepted by His hearers as One, Who in His very self was the fulfilment of God's promise (Lk. iv. 16 f.). In the first Gospel (Mt. v) we see Him seated on one of the many basaltic rocks on the heights above Capernaum,[1] proclaiming Himself to be in truth—what the scribes, who sat in the chair of Moses, claimed to be—the Teacher of the Law according to the mind of God. In both passages the idea of fulfilment is the central point—the connexion between His work and teaching and the Divine Will revealed in the Old Testament.

St Matthew expresses this thought twelve times by the passive verb πληροῦσθαι, 'to be fulfilled' (found twice in Mark and thrice in Luke). Our Lord Himself used this term (Mt. xxvi. 54, 56; Mk. xiv. 49; Lk. iv. 21; xxii. 16; xxiv. 44); in Mt. xxvi. 54, 56 and in Lk. xxiv. 44, in connexion with His suffering; in Lk. iv. 21, as an expression of the relationship of His active mission to the Divine promise. Akin to this is τελεῖσθαι, 'to be accomplished' (Lk. xviii. 31; xxii. 37), also used by our Lord; on the other hand the τετέλεσται of the last Word from the Cross (John xix. 30) has a different meaning (see under xx). He also made use of the active sense when speaking of the πληροῦν 'of all righteousness' (Mt. iii. 15), which, however, is less in the nature of a principle. Moreover, he proclaimed (Mt. v. 17) that He did not come to do away with (καταλῦσαι), but to fulfil (πληρῶσαι) the Law and the Prophets.

According to a passage in the Talmud, when a 'philosopher' appealed to a new 'Law' purporting to replace the Law of Moses, Gamaliel answered: 'I have read at the end of the Book (of this new 'Law'); there it is written: "not to take away (*lemiphḥat*) from

[1] *O.W.* 137 f.

the Law of Moses, and not[1] to add (*le-ōsōphē*) to the Law of Moses, have I come"'.[2] Meyer[3] finds in this the authentic words employed by our Lord for 'doing away' and 'fulfilling'. But what is given here as a quotation from a Gospel is in reality coined from the phrase found in Deut. iv. 2. Thus, although it may in some way reflect Mt. v. 17, it cannot throw light on the actual words used by our Lord.

For 'fulfilling' and 'being fulfilled' the Pal. Evang. as well as the Peshito always have *mallī* and *itmallī*, 'to make full' and 'to have been made full', which words correspond exactly to the Greek πληροῦσθαι. There is a similarly near relationship between καταλῦσαι and *sherā*, 'to make loose', found in the Pal. Evang. and Peshito. Delitzsch and Salkinson render, in their Hebrew translations of the N.T., the first word with the biblical *hāphēr*, 'to break', and for 'fulfilling' they have *mallōt*, 'to make full', although a biblical word is to be found for τελεῖσθαι in Dan. xii. 7, namely *kālā*, and for τελεῖν *killā* (Ezra i. 1; 2 Chron. xxxvi. 22).[4] But the near relationship of these Aramaic and Hebrew words to the Greek is not in itself a guarantee that they were actually those of our Lord. In fact, whenever thoughts conveying this are to be expressed in Jewish Aramaic and in Hebrew, neither *mallī* nor *sherā* nor *hēphēr* are the words used.

In Jewish-Palestinian only the Hebrew *ḳiyyēm*, and the Aramaic *ḳaiyēm*, correspond to 'fulfil'; and the Hebrew *biṭṭēl*, and the Aramaic *baṭṭēl*, to 'annul'. The first is connected with the root *ḳūm*, but according to its meaning is rather derived from *kaiyam*, 'constant', it does not therefore mean 'to erect', 'to make to stand', but 'to make constant', 'to confirm'. *Baṭṭēl* can be derived directly from the root *beṭēl*, 'to cease', and means, therefore, to 'make to cease'. But one might also take the participle *bāṭēl*, 'ceasing, null, void, of no force', as the basis, and the meaning would be exactly the same. The latter expresses the denial of the constant validity of something; in the former this is affirmed or realised. Such expressions must have been floating also in the mind of St Paul, when he

[1] This is the correct reading.
[2] b. Sab. 116 b.
[3] *Jesu Muttersprache*, 80.
[4] Read *lekhallōt* for *likhelōt*.

contrasted *ἱστάνειν* with *καταργεῖν* (Rom. iii. 31), and the same is true of the author of the Epistle to the Hebrews (*ἱστάνειν* and *ἀναιρεῖν*, Heb. x. 9).

1. Scripture is either confirmed or annulled according to whether its ordinances are kept or not. When a prophet 'uproots' (Hebrew *'āḳar*) a certain ordinance of the Law by his prophecy, the case is postulated that he demands that one should 'annul' (Hebrew *biṭṭēl*) one part of the Law, and 'keep' (Hebrew *ḳiyyēm*) the other.[1] 'He who is upright in his dealings with his fellow-men, with him are men pleased, and it is counted to him (by God) as if he had *kept* (Hebrew *ḳiyyēm*) the whole Law'.[2] 'He who keeps (*meḳaiyēm*) the Law when poor (in poverty), will eventually keep it when rich (in affluence), and he who annuls the Law (*mebaṭṭēl*), when in affluence, will eventually leave it unfulfilled, through poverty'.[3] To the heathen, who expressed surprise at the Israelites carrying two shrines (that of the Law and that of Joseph's body) through the desert, Israel exclaims: 'We would not have achieved all this glory, had we not kept God's commandments; but ye wish us to leave the commandments unfulfilled' (Aramaic *mebaṭṭālā*).[4] Shim'on ben Shetah justified his flight from King Jannai with the words: 'I heard that my Lord was angry with me, and so I wished to fulfil this scripture (Aramaic *meḳaiyāmā hādēn ḳerāyā*): "Hide thyself for a little while until the anger shall pass away"' (Isa. xxvi. 20).[5] The words of a dying person must be 'fulfilled' (Aramaic *yitḳaiyemūn*) after his death.[6]

2. A Law teacher is a confirmer (fulfiller) of the Law when he gives the proper interpretation to the letter of it, according to the standard set by the Law itself, and hence, by God, so that the letter preserves its validity and is confirmed also by those who, in instruction or practice, follow the interpretation of that teacher. The Hillelites, who teach that everyone may recite the *Shema'* in an ordinary pose, 'confirm herewith two Scripture passages' (*meḳaiyemīn trēn ḳeraiyā*).[7] Concerning two Scripture passages which contradict each other, it is asked: 'How

[1] Tos. San. xiv. 13; b. Sanh. 90 a.
[2] Mech. 46 a.
[3] Ab. iv. 9.
[4] p. Ber. 4 c.
[5] p. Ber. 11 b.
[6] p. Ket. 29 b.
[7] p. Ber. 3 b.

can they be confirmed?' (reconciled, Hebrew *yitḳaiyemū*). And the answer is: 'the third passage will reconcile them'.[1] Levi ben Sisi was thinking of his own teaching, when he said that he never annulled (*baṭṭēlīt*) a word of the Law.[2]

3. God 'confirms' the words of man by allowing his decision to take effect. 'Praised be the God of the righteous, for He confirms (*meḳaiyēm*) their words'. To Elijah God says: 'All that thou decidest (*gāzar*), I confirm (*anā meḳaiyēm*)'. 'If the words of Moses were not confirmed (*ḳāmān*), should God confirm (*meḳaiyēm*) the words of Joshua?'[3] An untrue word of a prophet 'comes not to pass, and is not confirmed (*yitḳaiyam*)'.[4] Above all, God confirms His own words by fulfilling them. 'Not *one* word of all the good words which God spake to the house of Israel was made void (*beṭēl*); all was confirmed (*mitḳaiyam*)'.[5] Akiba said: 'I rejoice that the (threatening) words of Uzziah are being confirmed (Hebrew *nitḳaiyemū*), because then the words (of promise) of Zechariah will also be confirmed' (Hebrew '*atīdīn lehitḳaiyēm*).[6] In this the conviction is expressed, 'When those words stand (Hebrew *ḳaiyāmīn*) so will the others; when those are made void (Hebrew *yibbāṭelū*; by not being fulfilled), so will the others be'. Dreams can have the significance of a Divine decision, when they are 'confirmed' (Hebrew *mitḳaiyemīn*), i.e. when they come true.[7]

4. Human action or experience enters into the service of the Divine word when it is used by God to confirm this word, with or without the consciousness of the actor. Haman said to Mordecai: 'Come, ascend and ride this horse, in order that that which your Scripture foretells may be fulfilled (confirmed, *meḳaiyāmā*) in you (Jews) (Deut. xxxiii. 29): "And thou shouldst tread on their heights"'.[8] God's decision can be made ineffective, when man's prayer retards its fruition (*mebaṭṭelā*).[9]

A promise or threat is proved to be of Divine origin, when it

[1] Mech. 73 b.
[2] p. Taan. 66 d; cf. above, p. 20; see also p. Sanh. 28 b.
[3] *Ibid.*
[4] Onk. Deut. xviii. 22.
[5] Tg. Josh. xxi. 43.
[6] Lam. R. v. 18; b. Makk. 24 b.
[7] b. Ber. 55 b.
[8] Lev. R. 28 (78 a).
[9] Eccl. R. iii. 2 (81 a).

is confirmed by actually taking place. For 'not like the words of man are the words of God: man speaks and recalls—but what God says He does, and each word of His is confirmed (*mitkaiyam*)'.[1] The Divine origin of a Scriptural command is considered to be established, but whoso 'treats the Law impudently' (Hebrew *megalle phānīm bat-tōrā*)[2] prevents it from being realised, and thereby denies that origin, either for the whole Law or for a part. Even when a teacher's interpretation differs from the customary traditional one (Hebrew *shellō khahalākhā*),[3] it is considered to be an (unconscious) opposition to the Law. Neither the one nor the other can in reality make God's word void; but the sin of opposing, instead of promoting, the realisation of God's will, is great; it loses to a man his portion in the world to come,[4] and draws the sword over his contemporaries.[5] A 'rebellious teacher of the Law' (Hebrew *zāḳēn mamrē*) who insists upon holding to his own opinion, contrary to the decision of the majority of the teachers, should (according to the Rabbinic interpretation of Deut. xvii. 12) be brought before the highest tribunal in the Temple, and, when he himself acts according to his teaching, or instructs others to act thus, he should be strangled.[6]

What attitude Judaism takes to the O.T. as a whole can be seen from the following sentence of Jochanan (which, it is true, was not uncontradicted): 'The prophetic and the hagiographic writings will (in the Messianic Age) lose their validity (Hebrew *libbāṭēl*), but not the five books of the Law'.[7] In comparison with the latter the former writings are only 'tradition' (Hebrew *ḳabbālā*).[8] At any rate, no letter of the Law will ever lose its validity. Rabbi Shim'on relates:[9] 'Then (when Solomon bought twelve thousand horses) the *yōd* in *yarbe*[10] threw itself down

[1] Onk. Num. xxiii. 19.

[2] Ab. iii. 11; Tos. Sanh. xii. 9; b. Shebu. 13 a; Yom. 85 b; Kerit. 7 a; Sanh. 99 a.

[3] Ab. v. 8. This *shellō khahalākhā* in Ab. iii. 11; b. Sanh. 99 a, is wrongly inserted in the above-quoted phrase, as if it meant 'to disclose opinions relating to the Law'; cf. also Levertoff, *Siphre on Numbers*, 100.

[4] Tos. Sanh. xii. 9.

[5] Ab. v. 8.

[6] Sanh. xi. 1–4; Tos. Sanh. xi. 7; xiv. 12; Siphre Deut. 152–155 (104 b f.).

[7] p. Meg. 70 d.

[8] p. Hall. 57 b; Gen. R. 7 (13 b).

[9] Exod. R. 6 (21 b).

[10] Deut. xvii. 16: the king should not keep many horses.

before God and said: 'Lord of the world, hast thou not said that no letter of the Law should ever be made void (Hebrew *bāṭelā*)? Lo, Solomon now makes me void, and perchance since to-day he thus makes *one* void (Hebrew *mebaṭṭēl*), to-morrow he will also make another void, until, at last, the whole Law will cease to be!' 'Solomon has uprooted me', laments the Book of Deuteronomy, 'and made me a liar, for every will and testament of which two or three words are annulled, has become invalid in its entirety'.[1] God answered: 'Solomon and thousands like him will disappear (Hebrew *yiheyū beṭēlīn*), but not one tittle (Hebrew *ḳōsā*) of thee will I allow to become void (Hebrew *mebaṭṭēl*)'.[2] 'Even if all the inhabitants of the world should unite in order to blot out one *yōd*, the smallest letter in the Law, they would not succeed'.[3]

In, and in opposition to, this linguistic and conceptual nexus stands the Dominical logion, Mt. v. 17 f., which must have been in Aramaic as follows:

lā tihwōn sebīrīn da-atēt limebaṭṭālā ōrāyetā (ō nebīaiyā), lā limebaṭṭālā atēt ēllā limeḳaiyāmā. āmēn āmarnā lekhōn 'ad delā yibṭelūn shemaiyā we-ar'ā lā tihwē bāṭelā yōd ḥadā ō ḳōṣā ḥadā min ōrāyetā 'ad deyitḳaiyam kullah.

Literally: 'Do not be of opinion that I have come to do away with the Law (or the prophets). Not to do away with them, but to make them valid, have I come. Amen, I say unto you, before heaven and earth pass away, not one yod or tittle will be made void from the Law until the whole shall be realised'.

The γάρ behind the ἀμήν, which belongs to the Greek idiom, we have left untranslated. To render παρέρχεσθαι—'pass away' —with *'abar*, would not be in keeping with the saying concerning the *yōd*, which is determined by the contrast between *kaiyēm* and *baṭṭēl*. *Beṭēl*, 'to cease,' alone corresponds to this contrast. In a literal Aramaic re-translation the concluding sentence ἕως ἂν πάντα γένηται would be *'ad deyihwē kullā*, 'until all this takes place'. But the emphasised γένηται demands a more explicit rendering, and Onk. Gen. xxvi. 28 supplies it by translating the Hebrew *tehī*, 'let there be', with *titḳaiyam*. Also

[1] Lev. R. 19 (48 a).
[2] So according to Exod. R. 6.
[3] Cant. R. v. 11 (58 b).

the *yit'abēd*, 'it will be done', of the Pal. Evang. is due to the feeling that an elucidation is unavoidable. Hence, the most natural thing would be to connect the πάντα more closely with the 'Law', to which it refers, by adding to *kōl* the pronominal suffix. Thus we have the phrase constructed above: *ad deyitḳaiyam kullah*. It would also be possible to refer the verb directly to the Law, and so give it a feminine form (*titḳaiyam*), and let *kullah* follow as an apposition to the subject.

As the whole context deals with the permanency of the Law, it must be considered as probable that 'the prophets' in verse 17 is a later insertion. Moreover, the Law as a written entity is here the essential thing, as among the Jews a copy of the roll of the Law is simply called 'the Law'. Direction, for instance, is given as to what is to be done when, in a synagogue, there is only 'one Law' (*ḥadā ōrāyā*) or 'two Laws'.[1] In the 'Law' of Rabbi Meir (i.e. in his copy) a certain reading was found.[2]

To prove the truth of His words, our Lord does not draw attention to His actions, but, with a sixfold 'I say unto you' (verses 22, 28, 32, 34, 39, 44), to the manner of His teaching. From this it follows that *mebaṭṭālā* and *meḳaiyāmā* also refer to teaching. How important is right instruction to Him, can be seen from the consequences, for He adds in verse 19:

'Whosoever, therefore, shall break one of these least commandments, and shall teach men so, shall be called the least in the kingdom of heaven; but whosoever shall do and teach them, the same shall be called great in the kingdom of heaven'.

Aramaic: *ūman dimebaṭṭēl ḥadā min hālēn miṣwātā ze'ēraiyā umeallēph kēn libnē nāshā (biryātā)*[3] *hū 'atīd lemitḳerāyā ze'ērā bemalkhūtā dishemaiyā. Ūman dimeḳaiyēm yāthēn umeallēph kēn hū 'atīd lemitḳerāyā rabbā bemalkhūta dishemaiyā.*

No 'least commandments' were previously mentioned, to which Jesus might have pointed with 'these'. The word deals with commandments which were known as the 'least', and hence it is an expression which is frequently found in Rabbinic

[1] p. Yom. 44 b; Meg. 75 b; Sot. 22 a.
[2] Gen. R. 94 (203 b).
[3] For this designation of men as 'creatures' cf. p. Ab. z. 41 a; Gen. R. 60 (126 a); Ruth R. iii. 1.

literature.[1] One says, *hādēn sephar ōrāyetā*, 'this book of the Law';[2] *hādēn ta'lā*, 'this jackal';[3] *illēn galgelaiyā*, 'those drawing wheels';[4] without anything having been said about these things before. The clause would, in both cases, have to be introduced by *hū*, 'he'. As the 'being called' refers to the future, it is advisable to paraphrase the future tense with *'atīd le*.[5] According to examples in Hebrew and Jewish Aramaic,[6] it would also be possible to express the result, which would necessarily enter, by the insertion of *sōphēh*, with a participle, or with *de*, and a finite verb: 'his end is that' (without a preceding *hū*). Corresponding to the 'annulling' of the first sentence, one expects 'confirming' in the second. Instead of that, the Greek text speaks here of 'doing'. This could be literally rendered with *'abēd*. Yet, *meḳaiyēm*, the word which we naturally expect, is most probably the original one. It might refer to the knowledge which causes others to think and act accordingly. But the content of verse 20 makes it necessary to take it in the sense of the practical keeping or not-keeping of the commandments, which, in fact, the Greek text, in any case, presupposes with its ποιήσῃ. In that case, it contains a reminder that right teaching is not in itself the decisive factor in connexion with the place in the kingdom of God; the practice corresponding to it, in which the scribes often failed (Mt. xxiii. 3), is the essential thing. Thus, right teaching is valued only in so far as it results from right conduct. Right action but wrong teaching is considered to be an impossibility. Also the scribes insisted that fear of sin and good works are the foundation of wisdom,[7] and that to one who 'learns' for the sake of 'doing' God grants the gift of teaching.[8] Our Lord, however, would certainly have opposed the Rabbinic notion that the mere going to the house of study, even when it is not followed by 'doing', has its reward (although also according to the Rabbis only he who goes and 'does' can be called pious).[9]

[1] *Gram.* 113 f.
[2] p. Sab. 14 d.
[3] Gen. R. 78; in Hebrew, Ruth R. Peth.
[4] Eccl. R. xii. 6 (129 b); Lev. R. 18 (45 b).
[5] *Gram.* 268 f.
[6] p. Sanh. 29 a; Ket. 34 a; Lev. R. 12 (30 b); Lam. R. v. 21 (63 b); cf. Ab. ii. 4; iv. 9, 11; v. 17; Tos. Sot. vi. 8.
[7] Ab. iii. 9, 10.
[8] Ab. iv. 5.
[9] Ab. v. 14.

When the question was asked, Which was greater, study (*talmūd*) or action (*ma'ase*), it was only Rabbi Tarphon who answered: 'action'; Akiba and the others thought the opposite, since study leads to action, and, besides, the reward for study is greater than that for action.[1] Our Lord would have said that both are of value before God only when united, and, besides, He would have let it be undoubtedly known that the study and the work which Tarphon and Akiba had in mind did not express what is most essential in the Will of God.

The Rabbis did not differentiate between the smallest and the greatest commandments but rather between 'light' (Hebrew *ḳallīn*) and 'heavy' (Hebrew *ḥamārīn*). This distinction between commandments is made only in connexion with 'the words of the (Mosaic) Law', but not with 'the words of the scribes'.[2] Moreover, 'light' and 'heavy' commandments are not those which are in themselves easy or difficult to keep, but such that cause the keeping of other commandments to be either light (*ḳōl*) or heavy (*ḥōmer*). Yet Jehuda I, we find, did make a distinction between those that are easy to keep and those that are difficult.[3] Also Ben Azzai gives this warning: 'Pursue a light commandment'.[4] The pious receive their reward for the observance of these in the Age to come, but the wicked have theirs now.[5] Among such commandments the freeing of the mother bird (Deut. xxii. 6) is considered to be the 'lightest' of all; the 'heaviest' of all—the honouring of father and mother (Exod. xx. 12): in the Law the same great reward is promised for each of these.[6] Such a very 'light' commandment can be set aside when life is threatened, but never publicly, since that would be transgressing against the cardinal principle of the 'sanctification of the Divine Name'.[7] Therefore, in times of religious persecution life must be sacrificed even for the lightest of 'light' commandments.[8]

Our Lord's 'least' is of the category of these 'lightest'

[1] b. Kidd. 40 b; Siphre Deut. 79 b.
[2] p. Ber. 3 b; Ab. z. 41 c; Sanh. 30 a.
[3] Ab. ii. 1.
[4] Ab. iv. 2; Ab. d. R. N. 25.
[5] b. Taan. 11 a.
[6] p. Kidd. 61 b.
[7] p. Shebi, 35 a; Sanh. 21 b; b. Sanh. 74 a; cf. Siphra on Lev. xviii. 5 (86 b).
[8] Tos. Sab. xv. 17.

commandments of the Rabbis. The difference in expression is probably due to the fact that in the Dominical word the 'least' commandment must correspond to the 'least' position in the kingdom of God. Jesus is even more strict than the Rabbis; *He* permits of no exception at any time, not even for the smallest commandment. Although He does not entirely exclude anyone from participation in the kingdom of God, who deals differently, yet He assigns to him 'the least place' in that kingdom.

The thought of gaining positions of honour from God was remote from the mind of our Lord, but among the Rabbis ambition was closely connected with the idea of reward. It was a matter of great importance to them, even apart from future reward, whether a scribe was 'a great man' (*bar nāsh rab*), or 'a small man' (*bar nāsh ze'ēr*);[1] 'Why interrogate the small ones (*ze'ēraiyā*), when the great ones (*rabrebaiyā*) are present?' was asked with surprise.[2] But this differentiation between great and small was still more emphasised in relation to the age to come. We frequently read of gradations in the future age.[3] Each of the pious has his own paradise.[4] Each receives a world for himself, although all must 'taste death'.[5] Of the pious, occasionally seven groups are enumerated.[6] The place at the right hand of God will be taken by the faithful teachers of youth.[7] Gradations in the other world were conceived with such exactitude, that a certain Rabbi, returning from beyond the veil, could relate the order of rank of five well-known doctors of the Law there.[8] We read of the anxiety of a pious man's widow, lest the 'canopy of honour' of her husband in the other world should be behind that of his colleagues, because he had miraculously received his reward in this world in the form of a pearl of great price.[9] Thus concretely was the world to come fancied! The Disciples also were infected by these ideas. They spoke of

[1] p. Kil. 32 b; Ket. 35 a; cf. Eccl. R. ix. 10 (Hebrew *ādām gādōl*).
[2] p. Mo. k. 82 d.
[3] *W.J.* 113 f., 311 f.
[4] Lev. R. 27 (73 a).
[5] Lev. R. 18 (45 b); cf. Exod. R. 52 (116 a); Ruth R. iii. on i. 17 (10 b).
[6] Siphre Deut. 67 a, 83 a; Midr. on Psalms xi. 6; cf. Lev. R. 30 (81 a).
[7] Lev. R. 30 (81 a).
[8] b. Bab. m. 85 b; Eccl. R. ix. 10 (the latter text is corrupt).
[9] Ruth R. on i. 17 (10 b); cf. Exod. R. 52, where, instead of the 'canopy of honour', a banqueting table is mentioned.

the places of honour at the right and left hand of the Messiah (Mt. xx. 21), of the greatest in the kingdom of heaven (Mt. xviii. 1), and of the greatest among themselves at the time (Mt. xxiii. 11; Lk. ix. 46). Our Lord, not concerned at the moment with the emphasising of right motives, used their phraseology, in order to show them in their own language how important the keeping of the commandments was to Him. To be 'called' great or small means, according to the Biblical idiom (e.g. Isa. lxii. 4, 12), to *be* it; but the expression is not usual in later Hebrew or Aramaic.[1] The language of our Lord could not have been entirely unaffected by biblicisms.

Taken alone, the saying about the fulfilling and annulling of the Law (with the exception of the clause concerning acting and teaching) is quite within the range of Jewish legalistic conceptions; which also is true of others of His sayings. One might therefore be tempted to place it in the same category as Levi ben Sisi's conviction that he did not 'annul *one* word in the Law'.[2] Our Lord purposely claimed for Himself that which His adversaries, the scribes, were believed to possess; they were not to triumph in the consciousness that they were the only representatives of the Law in its entirety. He did not therefore make a point of the difference between them and Himself as a contrast between the letter and the spirit, as St Paul did (cf. Rom. vii. 6; 2 Cor. iii. 6 f.); what he wished them to realise was rather that *His* teaching it is that gives to the letter of the Law its full significance, and this to a much wider extent than they could claim for their teaching, and that to Him even position in the kingdom of heaven is dependent upon whether others treat the Law as He does. He assumed that the proud occupants of Moses' chair were unworthy of it. He would have to give a reason now for His conviction that it is He who puts the letter of the Law into the position which is due to it according to the will of God.

[1] It is different with the expression *mitkerāyā mehēman* (p. Gitt. 47 a), because the emphasis there is on 'to be called'.

[2] See above, p. 59.

X. THE RIGHTEOUSNESS WHICH IS BETTER THAN THAT OF THE SCRIBES

The transition to our Lord's declaration concerning His attitude to the Law is attained by a sentence which gives His point of view and at the same time expresses once for all how decisively important to Him is a conduct which is in harmony with His teaching.

Mt. v. 20: 'For I say unto you, that if your righteousness does not supersede that of the scribes and Pharisees, ye shall not enter into the kingdom of heaven'.

Aramaic: *de-āmarnā lekhōn de-in lā tehē zākhūtekhōn meyatterā yattīr min desāpheraiyā wedipherīshaiyā lētekhōn ʻatīdīn lemētē lemalkhūtā dishemaiyā.*

The central point here is the conception of *righteousness*. In O.T. Hebrew *ṣedāḳā* would be the word corresponding to it. The Pal. Evang. actually renders it here, and in Mt. v. 6, 10, with *ẓedēḳ*, det. *ṣidḳā*. The Targums, however, show that the Aramaic *ṣidḳā*, det. *ṣidḳetā*, similar in sound to the Hebrew, cannot be considered here. Onk. has it for the Hebrew *ṣedāḳā* only in Gen. xviii. 19, where it is coupled with *mishpāṭ* (cf. also Tg. Isa. lvi. 1). The sense in which it was taken is clearly seen from the frequent considerations of the question, how *ṣedāḳā* is to be practised in law-suits; for 'wherever there is justice (*dīn*), there is no *ṣedāḳā*, and wherever there is *ṣedāḳā*, there is no justice'.[1] Only when there is an agreement (*biṣṣūaʻ*) between the contending parties, so it is maintained, can it be said that both these contradictory principles are active;[2] for instance, the restoration of stolen property means practising *ṣedāḳā* towards both the lawful owner and the thief, as it is a benevolence to both, while at the same time strict justice, *dīn*, to both is accorded.[3] Right, *dīn*, as such, is not to be tempered with pity.[4] Abraham exercised first *ṣedāḳā*, then *right*, in so far as he first gave free hospitality to wayfarers, and then, when they refused

[1] See Tos. Sanh. i. 3; b. Sanh. 6 b, and the *Silluk* of Eleazar ben Kalir; Dalman, *Jesajah*, liii. 40 f., and *Die richt. Gerecht. im A.T.* 5 f.

[2] *Ibid.*; cf. b. Sanh. 32 b, where the double *ṣedeḳ* of Deut. xvi. 20 is referred to *right* (*dīn*), and *reconciliation* (*peshārā*).

[3] p. Sanh. 18 b, 20 a.

[4] Ket. ix. 2.

to praise God for His gifts, presented them with a bill for wine, meat, and bread.[1] *Ṣedāḳā* is always not exactly 'clemency'[2] in contrast to strict justice, but *benevolence*, the conferring of something good, with which this passage does not deal, but possibly Mt. vi. 1 does. Wherever the O.T. *ṣedāḳā* means righteousness it is rendered in the Targum by *zākhū*, det. *zākhūtā* (e.g. Gen. xv. 6; xxx. 33; Deut. xxiv. 13; Isa. ix. 7; x. 22; xlviii. 1; lviii. 2), and always in the sense of a righteousness, an uprightness, which is recognised by God, and resulting therefore in 'being in the right' according to His verdict. The particular meritorious act of a person, which tips the balance in his favour after death, is also called *zākhū*, in contrast to 'guilt', *ḥōbā*.[3] *Zākhū* means also a ground for acquittal in court,[4] as when the king asks the accused: 'Hast thou anyone who can announce a *zākhū* for thee (i.e. a ground for justification)?'[5] Hence, Deut. xxxiii. 21 ('the righteousness of Jahweh', Hebrew *ṣidḳat jhwh*, which Moses practised) is rendered by Onk.: 'deeds which are right before God' (*zākhwān ḳodām adōnāy*), as also St Paul (Rom. i. 17; iii. 21) seems to have done. The conception of 'merit' is closely connected with it, and is widely developed in Judaism, conjointly with the idea of reward. In the parable of the labourers in the vineyard (Mt. xx), in the saying concerning the worthless servants (Lk. xvii. 10), and also in the Sermon on the Mount (Mt. vi. 2, 5, 16), our Lord strove to eliminate this idea.

It is questionable whether Jesus actually ever used the word *zākhū*. According to Mt. v. 6, He spoke of those 'who hunger and thirst *after righteousness*'; but in Lk. vi. 21 'righteousness' is not mentioned. According to Mt. vi. 33 He exhorted His listeners to seek the kingdom of God and its *righteousness*; but in Lk. xii. 31 the word is not found. Even in Mt. v. 10 it is possible that 'for righteousness' sake' is a later insertion. The original word in Mt. vi. 1 might perhaps have been *ṣidḳā* (see above). 'The way of righteousness' (Mt. xxi. 32) and 'every righteousness' (Mt. iii. 15), where it means every *duty*, and

[1] Gen. R. 49 (103 a).
[2] In *Die richt. Gerecht. im A.T.* 1897, 5, I have over-accentuated this.
[3] p. Sanh. 23 c.
[4] p. Sanh. 21 c.
[5] Lev. R. 30 (82 b).

where the essential background of the conception is lacking, are probably due to the biblicism of the compiler. Our Lord would have had reason to avoid the use of this conception, as his adversaries spoke too much of it, and connected it too closely with the idea of reward. Besides, He usually avoided abstract terms. In our passage nothing else can be substituted for this word, and it occurs here in the nexus of the teaching of the scribes and Pharisees concerning it, and all that follows makes the meaning which our Lord attached to it sufficiently clear.

He, also, teaches the importance of righteousness for man's eternal destiny, i.e. for the Divine verdict which determines it. According to the Jewish manner of speech, this would refer to the 'entrance into the future world'. Tg. II. Esther ii. 5 (ed. David 1898) says of Simëi: *yizkē weyētē le-'ālemā de-ātē*, 'He deserves to enter into the age to come', similar to Lk. xx. 35, where it speaks of those who 'are worthy to enter that aeon'. Instead of this, our Lord uses His own characteristic expression 'the kingdom (sovereignty) of heaven', and speaks of 'entering into it'.

εἰσέρχεσθαι εἰς would, by the way, have to be expressed by *atā le*, not literally by '*al be*, or rather '*al le*,[1] as the Pal. Evang. and Peshito have it, as, to a Jewish audience, the latter would be too suggestive of the idea of 'entering into'. No stronger condemnation of the teaching of the scribes could have been uttered by our Lord. They believed that the followers of their ordinances, and they themselves, were sure to enter the future age. But Jesus knew that the kingdom of God makes other demands, and He excluded from even the most insignificant place in that future those who come short of this standard; while He left an open door to one who teaches erroneously about a less important point. They are not 'the justifiers of many' (Hebrew *maṣdīḳē hā-rabbīm*), who, according to Dan. xii. 3, will shine like the stars of the firmament.

Mt. v. 21: 'Ye have heard that it was said to the ancients: Thou shalt not kill, and he who commits murder, falls into justice'.

Aramaic: *shema'tūn de-it'amar leḳadmāyē lā tiḳṭōl uman deyiḳṭōl (yitmesar lebēt dīnā) hū yehē mitḥaiyab bēt dīnā.*

[1] See *W.J.* 95 f., 116 f.

Those whom our Lord addressed had 'heard' God's commandment during the reading of the Law in the Synagogue. But after what has been said before, the 'heard' refers not to the Law itself but rather to the scribal interpretation of it. The 'hearing' is, moreover, of great significance in Rabbinic Law, as the oral tradition concerning the meaning and practical observance of the written Law is its most important content. Shimon bar Wa explained the contradiction between his interpretation and that of the other Rabbis in the words: 'I speak what *I* have heard, they what *they* have heard'.[1] The judicial *sentence*, therefore, heard from the teachers (to be distinguished from the mere judicial *opinion*), which naturally cannot be altered, is therefore called *shemū'ā*, 'that which was heard',[2] especially when the communication of it is not by an individual but by the majority. Every teacher of the Law had to submit himself to such a tradition. Akabya ben Mehalalel, when about to die, advised his son to ignore the tradition which he, the father, transmitted to him, as he himself had heard it only from one individual, *his* father, although the latter again was convinced that he had heard it from the majority.[3] It always refers to the *oral* teaching, in contrast to the *written* Law. Our Lord had in mind here the oral instruction concerning the contents of the written Law, which instruction He presupposed His hearers to have received. Although the Scriptural text is the background, He did not quote it literally, since it is to that which had been said before, that He wished to put in opposition that which *He* has to say.

The passive construction 'it was said' is in keeping with the conventional mode of the period to avoid mentioning the name of God.[4] There can be no doubt that it refers to God. In a similar fashion *dibbūr*, 'speech', is used by the Rabbis for the speaking of God on Mount Sinai. 'Before the speech', *liphnē had-dibbūr*, means 'before the giving of the Law on Sinai'.[5]

[1] p. Ter. 47 b; cf. John xv. 15; xvi. 13.

[2] Det. *shemū'atā*, p. Ter. 45 c; Ab. z. 41 a; Gitt. 48 c; Yeb. 2 c; Kidd. 61 c; Sanh. 21 a. Another form is *shema'tā*, the det. *shema'tetā*, p. Yeb. 9 d; Bab. b. 14 b; Sanh. 18 c.

[3] Eduy. v. 7.

[4] Ab. ii. 15; iii. 5, 7, 8; iv. 4; cf. *W.J.* 183 f.

[5] Tos. Hag. i. 4; p. Hag. 76 b.

Those who heard it first were the people of Israel who stood at Mount Sinai. Our Lord certainly had no doubt that God's word was uttered just as His hearers perceived it. ἀρχαῖοι does not correspond to the Hebrew *zeḳēnīm*,[1] Aramaic *sābīn*[2] (which, in this connexion, could only mean the scribes), but to *rishōnīm*, 'the former ones', in contrast to *aḥarōnīm*, 'the later ones', by which the ancients are occasionally contrasted with those of the present day.[3] The Aramaic word for it is *ḳadmāīn*. 'If the ancients (*ḳadmāīn*) were sons of angels, then we are men; and if they were men, then we are asses', said Ze'era.[4] 'To kill' and 'to murder' (Hebrew *ḳāṭal* and *rāṣaḥ*) can be rendered in Aramaic only by the one word *ḳeṭal*, which also Onk. (Exod. xx. 13) uses, but with the addition of *nephash*, 'soul'.[5]

The phrase ἔνοχος τῇ κρίσει, 'to fall into judgment', cannot be rendered literally into Hebrew or Aramaic. One might, of course, suggest *itmesar*, 'to be delivered', for ἔνοχος. 'I am being delivered into the hands of the uncircumcised', *etmesar bīdā de-'arlaiyā* (Tg. Judges xv. 18); 'The wicked will be condemned to be delivered into hell for everlasting burning', *'atīdīn rash-shī'aiyā le-ittedānā le-itmesārā legēhinnām yeḳēdat 'ālam* (Tg. Isa. xxxiii. 14). Less suitable as a parallel is *dīnō māsūr lash-shāmaiyim*, 'his judgment is delivered to heaven (God)'.[6] The Pal. Evang. has *ḥaiyāb bedīnā*, 'guilty in court'; Peshito, *ḥaiyāb ledīnā*, 'guilty to court', which does not quite correspond to the Greek and, in any case, is without parallel in Jewish literature. There is a Hebrew phrase in Jewish legal terminology: *meḥuiyebē mītōt bēt dīn*, i.e. such who deserve punishment of death by a court of justice (in contrast to *meḥuiyebē kārētōt*, i.e. those about to be punished (by God) by being 'cut off',[7] or *ḥaiyābīn-kārēt bīdē shāmayim*, 'those deserving to be cut off by heaven (God)'), and *ḥaiyābin-mītōt bēt dīn*, 'those deserving capital punishment by a court of justice'.[8] In Aramaic we come across expressions

[1] So Wünsche, *Neue Beiträge zur Erläuterung der Evangelien*, 44.
[2] p. Bikk. 65 c.
[3] b. Yom. 9 b.
[4] p. Dem. 21 d; Shek. 48 c f.; b. Sab. 112 b.
[5] Suggested by Exod. xxi. 12; Lev. xxiv. 17, where tradition insists that only when life has actually been taken, must these laws be applied; Mech. on Exod. xxi. 12 (79 b); Siphra on Lev. xxiv. 17 (104 d); b. Sanh. 78 a.
[6] Tos. Bab. k. ix. 31.
[7] p. Meg. 71 a; Ket. 27 b.
[8] p. Yeb. 6 b f.; cf. Tos. Sanh. xi. 1.

such as *ithaiyab ketōl*, 'he would have been condemned to death';[1] *ithaiyab (ithaiyabat) ketōlīn*, 'he (she) was declared to be guilty of death (of murder);[2] *lēt lēh hōbat dīn diketōl*, 'he has no guilt of judgment of death (he is not guilty of murder)'.[3] One could, accordingly, assume *mithaiyab* for ἔνοχος; but the direct connexion of this word with the 'court' has no parallel in Jewish terminology. What is possible in this direction is suggested in the sentence of Onk. Num. xxxv. 21: *kid ithaiyab lēh min dīnā*, 'when he was condemned by the court (to death)'; but we cannot translate according to this. From the context it can be seen that our Lord undoubtedly meant to emphasise the fact that it is the court which gives the verdict, in order to make the import of the punishment clear. That it is only the ordinary court which has to deal with the offence is here the essential thing. Moreover, He is evidently not entirely influenced by the terminology of the scribes, even though He comes into contact with it. It would be rather venturesome to insert here and in verse 22 the word *mītat*, 'death', before 'court': 'death by the court'. But only thus would one get an expression entirely corresponding to the Jewish idiom. Our Lord speaks here of the 'court', thinking of 'punishment', which He afterwards designates as 'Gehenna'.

The mention of the 'court' is in keeping with the teaching of Jewish tradition, according to which 'being brought before the congregation' (Num. xxxv. 12) indicates, above all, the verdict of the court.[4] This must consist of twenty-three members, a so-called small Sanhedrin,[5] whilst for money and property cases a court of three is sufficient.[6] Our Lord is not concerned with such small details, nor with the question which of these tribunals had at that time the power to pronounce capital punishment. For His purpose it is sufficient to state the fact that in this case the Law appoints an ordinary court; for He intends to develop His argument from just this point. The scribes remain stationary on the outer circle of the Law and believe that thereby the letter of it is quickened, but our Lord knows that the whole depth of

[1] Onk. Exod. iv. 26. [2] Lev. R. 26 (69 b).
[3] Onk. Deut. xix. 6.
[4] Siphre on Num. xxxv. 30 (62 a f.); cf. Mech. on Exod. xxi. 12 (80 a).
[5] Sanh. i. 6; Tos. Sanh. iii. 7. [6] Sanh. i. 6; Tos. Sanh. i. 1.

God's will, as it is to operate in the kingdom of God, is not at all thus exhausted. He continues therefore in verse 22:

'But I say unto you, that everyone who is angry with his brother falls into judgment. But he who says to his brother "thou silly!", falls into the hands of the Sanhedrin; and he who says "thou fool!" falls into hell fire'.

Aramaic: *wa-anā āmar lekhōn dekhōl man dekhā'ēs 'al aḥūh yehē mithaiyab bēt dīnā; uman deāmar le-aḥūh rēḳā yehē mithaiyab sanhedrīn; uman deāmar shāṭyā, jehē mithaiyab nūrā degēhinnām.*

The contrasting of one's own opinion with that of others is not rare in the legal discussions of the Rabbis. Eliezer ben Jakob, in opposing the opinion of the majority in a Passover question, introduces his opinion with the words *ōmēr anī*, 'I say'.[1] Shimon ben Yoḥai asserted five times his opinion against that of Akiba, in the words *harē hū ōmēr*; *wa-anī ōmēr*, 'but I say'.[2] Our Lord does not place His authority in opposition to that of others; it is the Law-Giver on Sinai (i.e. God) who is on the one side, and on the other—Jesus; He being at the same time convinced that the same God is, in fact, in agreement with His, Jesus', purpose, which is to establish God's kingdom for ever. To traditional Judaism the God of Sinai is unchangeable.[3] Harold M. Wiener's[4] attempt to prove that in the Old Testament God is not static in His utterances would have awakened the same ire among the contemporaries of our Lord as did the speech of St Stephen (Acts vii. 2 f.), which started from similar premises. Even very insignificant deviations from the traditional interpretations of the Law were considered as *mīnūt*, 'heresy'. A disciple of our Lord, for instance, is said to have related in His name a certain interpretation of Deut. xxiii. 18, connecting it with Micah i. 7, and Rabbi Eliezar had qualms for having once enjoyed this interpretation of a 'heretic', and was sure to have been punished for it by God.[5] How much worse would his punishment have been, had he himself taught that heretical interpretation! A heretic (*mīn*) loses for ever his portion in the

[1] Tos. Pes. viii. 18. Other examples: Tos. Pes. viii. 21; Sot. vii. 7; p. Pes. 37 a.
[2] Tos. Sot. vi. 6–12.
[3] See however the Jewish tradition about the Law of the Messiah, p. 85 below.
[4] 'The Law of Change in the Bible', *Bibliotheca Sacra*, 1921, 73 f.
[5] b. Ab. z. 17 a; cf. Tos. Ḥall. ii. 24.

world to come, and is eternally damned in Gehenna, while an ordinary sinner's punishment lasts only for a definite period.[1] Our Lord did not set forth here His own Scriptural interpretation in opposition to that of the scribes; as a matter of fact, He did not interpret at all, but proclaimed, independently of the letter of the Law, the principle that is to prevail in the kingdom of God. His 'I say' and the 'I say' of a Rabbi have only a verbal resemblance.

Three sentences, formulated like legal paragraphs, present the new 'legislation' of our Lord. They contain ascending grades in the defining of the punishments, and also presume, therefore, corresponding grades of wrong-doing. All the three transgressions are very mild in comparison with murder, which of course is the most criminal act against one's fellow-man. Who 'the brother' is against whom these sins are committed, our Lord does not define. Jewish Law finds it possible to limit the protection which the court and the cities of refuge afford, to Israelites only, although at the same time it puts the life of the Gentile under Divine protection.[2] The warning given to one who is about to murder an Israelite begins with the words: 'Know that he is a son of the covenant!'[3] Our Lord, on another occasion, emphasised the fact that it does not matter who the person is who is in need of our help (Lk. x. 36 f.); and in Mt. v. 44 He teaches love to the enemy. Here, however, the emphasis is probably on the fact that it is one's own brother against whom one sins (see also verse 23), not having in mind the limiting of the brotherhood to a definite circle. Every sin against the brother is a crime, and deserves, therefore, the punishment meted to a criminal.

First comes anger. Because of the reading εἰκῇ, the Pal. Evang. adds *lemaggān* ('for nothing, without a cause'), suggesting thus the permission of reasonable anger; but probably this qualification is a later insertion. If to *be* angry is not as grave a sin as using angry words, the former must mean *silent* anger. Hence, none of those Aramaic terms can be considered

[1] Tos. Sanh. xiii. 5; b. R. h. S. 17 a; cf. b. Erub. 19 a.
[2] Mech. on Exod. xxi. 14 (80 b); cf. Siphre on Num. xxxv. 13 (61 a); Deut. xix. 3 (108 a); Makk. iii. 3; Tos. Makk. ii. 7.
[3] Tos. Sanh. xi. 4; p. Sanh. 22 d.

here which presupposes angry *words*, like *nezaph*, 'to scold',[1] *kattēsh, itkattash*, 'to quarrel',[2] *ḳanṭēr*, 'to tease', 'annoy',[3] *ge'ar*, 'to threaten';[4] but only *iḳḳephēd*, 'to get cross',[5] *regēz 'al*[6] and *ke'as 'al*, 'to be angry'.[7] The Pal. Evang. and Pesh. render it by the first of the last two, but, as it has no parallel in the Galilaean literature, *ke'as* is the most probable.

Our Lord could have based His teaching concerning anger on the prohibition of hatred in Lev. xix. 17. In Tg. Yer. I that passage is rendered: 'Ye should not have smooth speeches on your lips and at the same time hate your brother in your hearts'. Jewish tradition says concerning this verse:[8] 'Does it perchance mean only: "Thou shouldst not curse, strike, box thy brother on the ear?" It means more than that (literally: there is a teaching in the word), for it says: *in thy heart*. (God says): "I spoke of hatred in the heart"'. But our Lord did not quote; moreover, He avoided mentioning hatred even in this connexion, since He could not have given it as a suitable example of the 'lightest' transgressions against one's brother. He thought more of the kind of anger which is a passing mood, and of which the Jewish proverb says:[9] 'Where there is contempt, there is no hope, but where there is anger, there *is* hope, for he who is angry will be calmed by-and-bye (*kōl mān dekhā'ēs sōphēh le-itreṣāyā*)'. Jesus, in contrast to this, considers even such passing anger to be as punishable as murder.

To use unkind words in anger is a still greater sin. One of these words is ῥακά or ῥαχά. The Greek form has often been derived from ῥάκος or ῥάχος, 'a rag'. But most probably it is based upon the Jewish invective *rēḳā*, which cannot be separated from the Biblical *rēḳ'*[10] and which, like *rēḳān*, means 'empty'. The Targums render it always with *serīḳ*, which has the same signification, without defining the kind of emptiness. In the O.T. it has mostly an ethical meaning, and it could be translated

[1] Onk. Gen. xxxvii. 10; cf. Gen. R. 12 (26 a).
[2] Gen. R. 48 (99 a); Lev. R. 9 (22 b).
[3] p. Maaser, 51 a; Yom. 38 d; Hor. 47 d; Meg. 72 a.
[4] Gen. R. 56 (118 b f.).
[5] p. Mo. k. 80; Bab. k. 6 c.
[6] Onk. Gen. xl. 2.
[7] p. Ber. 5 c; 11 d; Shebi, 35 b; Kil. 32 b; Hag. 77 d.
[8] Siphra on Lev. xix. 17 (89 a).
[9] Lam. R. v. 21 (63 b).
[10] Judges ix. 4; xi. 3; 2 Sam. vi. 20; 2 Chron. xiii. 7.

'light-minded'. In later Jewish usage it seems to have been applied to intellectual poverty. 'Blockhead' would probably be the best translation of it. This word was once used, for instance, by a woman of a man whom she ridiculed, because he attempted to seduce her.[1] A Jew, who, not wishing to be interrupted in prayer, did not respond to the greeting of a high official, was called by him *rēḳā*.[2] A soldier, who was about to sell the High Priest's daughter as a slave, addressed the same word to a prospective buyer who wished to examine her beauty first.[3] A Rabbi, being respectfully greeted by an ugly man, said: '*rēḳā*, how ugly thou art!'[4] A disciple who once had doubts concerning the existence of the pearls of which the gates of the future Jerusalem is to be composed (Isa. liv. 12; Rev. xxi. 21), confessed later that he actually saw, on a sea-journey, angels preparing such pearls. When he related this to his teacher, Rabbi Jochanan (who preached on that subject), the latter said: '*rēḳā*, hadst thou not seen it, thou wouldst not have believed it! Thou scoffest at the words of the sages'. And the Rabbi looked at him, and he was turned into a heap of bones immediately.[5] Noah thus addressed his unbelieving contemporaries: 'Woe unto you, ye *rēḳaiyā*; to-morrow comes the flood!'[6] It is evident from the above examples that *rēḳā* was a popular expression of anger, deserving, according to our Lord, the judgment of the Sanhedrin.[7]

'Fool' expresses not so much anger, as scorn and slight. One who searched among the graves for his son who was lost, was called 'the greatest fool in the world' (Hebrew *shōṭe shebbā'ōlām*): 'the dead are sought amongst the living, but not the living among the dead'.[8] A Galilaean pedlar who, not being able to pronounce gutturals, and for this reason being misunderstood when calling his wares for sale, was dubbed 'foolish Galilaean!'[9]

[1] b. Ber. 22 a. [2] b. Ber. 32 b.
[3] b. Gitt. 58 a.
[4] b. Taan. 20 b; Ab. d. R. N. 41; Der Erez. 4.
[5] b. Bab. b. 75 a; Midr. on Psalms, lxxxvii. 2; cf. for the expression 'hadst thou not seen, etc.' John xx. 29.
[6] Eccl. R. ix. 15 (118 a).
[7] For a different interpretation, cf. Levertoff's notes on the passage in the *One Volume Commentary*, 1928.
[8] Lev. R. 6 (18 b); cf. Lk. xxiv. 5.
[9] b. Er. 53 b; cf. *Gram.* 57 f.

'Thou greatest fool of the world', were the mocking words addressed to a negro slave who said that her master was ready to cast away his wife because she had sooty hands, and would then marry her—the black one.[1] The same word (Hebrew *shōṭé*, Aramaic *shāṭē*) is used, in juridical terminology, of a lunatic. In discussing the latter's characteristics, the following definition is given: 'He who rambles at night, spends the night in the graveyard (cf. Mk. v. 2, 5), tears his garments, and spoils everything that is given to him, is a *shōṭé*'.[2] How this word was used in daily life, can be seen from the following riddle: 'He who says, "I give thee five, give me three", is a lunatic (*shāṭē*); he who says, "I give thee three, give me five", is a man; he who says, "I give thee three, give me three", is a spendthrift'.[3] Thus the word expresses an absence of sound common sense, and is more offensive than 'blockhead'. For this sin no punishment meted out by an *earthly* court of justice is severe enough.

These three gradations of punishment are characterised by three modes of punishment: (*a*) 'the judgment', (*b*) the Sanhedrin, (*c*) the Gehenna of fire. But the Greek expression makes it clear at the same time that these three modes are not entirely uniform. In the first two cases, therefore, where the decree of the judge is particularly thought of, ἔνοχος is connected with the dative; in the last case, where the punishment itself is mentioned—with εἰς and the accusative. That it cannot be properly imitated in Aramaic, can be seen from Pal. Evang. and Peshito, which have in all three cases *le* or *be*.[4] In the third place one might expect the mention of 'the upper court' (Hebrew *bēt-dīn shellema'alān*)[5], i.e. God, as the One who condemns to hell (Mt. x. 28), but this is purposely avoided[6] and only the punishment is mentioned.

From this it is evident that our Lord did not formulate a Rabbinic differentiation between the execution of punishments by human or Divine judicial decrees, but expressed the progression from earthly punishments of human courts to the other-worldly punishment which God alone inflicts. Hence it is not

[1] Cant. R. i. 6 (15 b).
[2] p. Gitt. 48 c; Ter. 40 b; b. Hag. 3 b; Tos. Ter. i. 3.
[3] p. Sanh. 26 b, 30 a.
[4] Cf. above, p. 69 f.
[5] p. R. h. S. 58 b.
[6] Cf. *W.J.* 220.

the same as the Rabbinic phrase 'death by heaven' (Hebrew *mītā bīdē shāmayim*),[1] by which premature death is meant, but is the equivalent of 'punishment of Gehinnom' (Hebrew *dīnāh shellegēhinnōm*),[2] the deep severity of which our Lord never attempted to soften; while Resh Lakish, for instance, thought that the very fire of Gehinnom could do no harm to Jewish sinners, for 'even the wicked among Israelites are as rich in works of the Law as the pomegranate is rich in pips'.[3] The addition of τοῦ πυρός is meant to emphasise the severity of the punishment, and does not imply the existence of a non-fiery hell;[4] still less does it suggest a contrast to the valley near Jerusalem by which name it is called. *Nūr gēhinnām*, 'the fire of hell' (cf. above), would be a more natural expression than 'the hell of fire'.

A certain distinction must also be made between the Sanhedrin and the (lower) court. The former was the highest administrative and judicial board of Judaea, familiar to us from the Gospels and from the book of Acts, as well as from Josephus.[5] According to Rabbinic tradition, 'the great Sanhedrin' was distinguished from other courts by having had its seat in a special hall of the Temple in Jerusalem, and by the large number of the members (71) of which it was composed.[6] Among other things, it had the sole right to pronounce judgment upon whole tribes, upon the High Priest, upon false prophets, and upon rebellious doctors of the Law; while verdicts of capital punishment were given by 'the small Sanhedrin' (see above). Occasionally, however, judicial pronouncements of the lower Sanhedrin were transferred to the highest tribunal for execution. The 'rebellious son' and false witnesses could not be executed immediately after the pronouncement of the verdict, but had to be brought to the Sanhedrin in Jerusalem, where they were

[1] p. Sot. 17 a; cf. Eccl. R. vii. 27 (109 b).

[2] b. Bab. b. 10 a; Sot. 4 b; Aramaic *dīn gēhinnām*, Tg. Eccl. v. 5.

[3] b. Erub. 19 a. See also above, p. 74.

[4] There are seven spaces in hell, b. Sot. 10 b. Rabbinic law differentiates also between the punishment of eternal death and a resurrection followed by punishment in hell. The latter is appointed for apostates and seducers, Tos. Sanh. xiii. 5; b. R. h. S. 17 a; the former for the 'generation of the desert', Sanh. x. 3; Tos. Sanh. xiii. 10.

[5] Schürer, *G.J.V.* 4th ed. II. 237 f.

[6] Sanh. i. 1; Tos. Sanh. iii. 9; Siphre on Num. xi. 16 f. (25 b).

kept for execution on the nearest approaching pilgrimage feast.[1] The purpose was to strengthen the intimidating effect of the punishment. Whether in our Lord's time the administrative bodies of the ten districts of Judaea could pronounce capital punishment is uncertain. It might be thought that our Lord conceived the gradation of the earthly punishments in the progress from monetary fines, or chastising, pronounced by the lower court, to the capital punishments of the highest; but, according to the preceding verse, even the 'court' (i.e. the lower court) could carry into effect the penalty for murder (i.e. death). Thus, since there can be no greater earthly punishment than this, the emphasis is here not on the penalty as such but on the tribunal which pronounces it. When the highest court operates, the crime and its punishment must affect the entire community of Israel: the criminal is to be blotted out from its midst. In contradistinction to this, the punishment of Gehenna means the exclusion of the sinner immediately after death from the community of the pious as well as at the general resurrection in the Messianic age.

Rabbinic casuistry, in order to establish a certain principle, occasionally classified definite cases of criminal acts. Naturally, when such cases occurred, they had to be treated exactly according to rule. Our Lord also meant to establish a principle, and yet it certainly was not His intention that human judges should deal literally according to His verdict, i.e. condemn a person to death for using abusive words. Similarly, He could not have meant that for one kind of abuse human punishment suffices, while another kind can only be expiated in Gehenna. His presentment, although expressed in the form of juridical casuistry, is not at all intended as instruction for the judge, which should, by the severity of its punishments, supersede that of the scribes. His wish is to teach the ordinary man concerning the essence of the 'righteousness' which he is to *practise*, rather than to instruct the judge who is to guard it.

The non-legal character of the sentence can be seen also in this, that in the original text it does not contain any important exception. Our Lord certainly did not mean to deny the fact

[1] Tos. Sanh. xi. 7.

that occasionally it may not only be legitimate but obligatory to be angry, and that this anger may even be expressed in words. He Himself called the Pharisees 'fools' (Mt. xxiii. 17), or 'un-understanding ones' (Lk. xi. 40), as, in the parable, God calls the selfish accumulator of treasures 'an un-understanding one' (Lk. xii. 20). The Pal. Evang. and Pesh., it is true, attempt to suggest a different shade of meaning in both of these words in the Aramaic; but, as a matter of fact, both words are really based on *shātyā* 'thou fool', the use of which our Lord considers sinful. Also in Lev. xix. 17 the prohibition of hating one's brother is followed by the command: 'Thou shalt in any wise *rebuke* thy neighbour in order that thou mayest not suffer any guilt concerning him'. Jewish tradition sees in the latter the duty of frequent reproving of a sinner. Jochanan ben Nuri testified before heaven and earth that, due to his denouncements of Akiba before Gamaliel, the former was punished by the Rabban more than four or five times, yet he knew that Akiba loved him the more for it.[1] That the same words can sometimes be an insult—which is sin, and sometimes a just rebuke—which is duty; that there is an anger aroused by selfish passion—which is wrong, and an anger for God's sake—which is right (cf. John ii. 17), our Lord could not have denied. Nor is He concerned with the important question as to whether some transgressions against one's neighbour are punished both by man and God, and if so, whether there is a way of escape from both these punishments.

According to Rabbinic conceptions, the Day of Atonement, in conjunction with the sinner's experience of punishment through pain and suffering, has the power to affect propitiation for him who deserves the penalty of death at the hands of men or directly from God—unless the sin involved an open profanation of the Divine Name.[2] Repentance is naturally a *conditio sine qua non*. On the way to his execution the culprit should express his penitence in the following words: 'May my death be the propitiation for all my sins!' This will save him

[1] Siphra on Lev. xix. 17 (89 a f.).

[2] Mech. 69 a; Yom. viii. 8; Tos. Yom. v. 8; p. Yom. 45 a; b. Yom. 86 a; cf. Siphra, 102 a.

from punishment in the world beyond.[1] Now, our Lord would certainly not have minimised the saving effect of repentance, nor would He mean to convey that God on His judgment-seat is not concerned with the sin of being angry with, or of using moderately offensive words against, one's neighbour. He only wished to accentuate the fact that malicious thoughts and insulting words against a brother are to Him sins which deserve the same punishments—yea, on certain occasions even severer—as murder does according to the Law of Moses. Thoughts and words against one's neighbour which no human judge would consider sufficiently serious to be dealt with in court and which everybody thinks permissible, without having the slightest qualms of conscience, or falling under the moral censure of public opinion, are here represented as transgressions which may result in the loss of one's life both here and hereafter. The impression our Lord intended to make was not that the question should arise in the hearer's soul: 'Who then is innocent?', and acknowledge: 'I am guilty'; but that he should realise that the righteousness in the Kingdom of God towers above that which is enjoined by the Law (as interpreted by the scribes).

It would not be fair to say of Rabbinic Law that it only safeguarded the *life* of man; for to cause harm in any form even to *oneself* was considered sinful. 'He who in anger dirties his face, pulls his hair, tears his garment, breaks dishes, throws away money, although he is exempt from human judgment (*pāṭūr mid-dīnē ādām*) is yet delivered up to heaven (God) for judgment; since it says (Gen. ix. 5): "Your blood which is like your soul (i.e. harm done to oneself) will I demand; of a man who is (his own) brother I will demand it"'.[2] In connexion with oppression (Lev. xxv. 17), the Rabbis differentiated between 'oppression' in words (*ōnāat debārīm*) and 'oppression' in a monetary sense (*ōnāat māmōn*), although it is not directly stated in the Law. By 'oppression in words' such offences as reminding a person of the unsavoury facts of his past, of old sins, of ancestral defects, was meant.[3] To insult a person in public

[1] Sanh. vi. 2; Tos. Sanh. ix. 5; p. Sanh. 23 b; b. Sanh. 44 b.
[2] Tos. Bab. k. ix. 31.
[3] Siphra on Lev. xxv. 17 (107 d); Bab. m. iv. 10; Tos. Bab. m. iii. 25; b. Bab. m. 58 b.

was considered to be on a par with murder; he who commits this sin, loses eternally his portion in the world to come; while the strangulation by which an adulterer, for instance, is punished is in itself an atonement for his sin.[1] This indicates tender consideration of the value of human personality, which also shows itself in the Rabbis' warning (based on Lev. xix. 16) against evil gossip,[2] a sin made equal to the greatest crimes,[3] and resulting in punishment both here and in the world to come;[4] one addicted to this, will, without doubt, one day deny a cardinal article of faith.[5]

Such glossary supplements to the fifth and eighth commandments of the Decalogue could not have been entirely unknown to our Lord, as they are akin to the prohibition of revenge and hatred endorsed by the Mosaic Law (Lev. xvi. 17).[6] He did not, however, refer to them, nor did He attempt to confirm His own words by pointing to suggestions for further developments contained in the Law itself. He only wished to show that the fifth commandment, with the threatening punishment attached to it, and as interpreted by the scribes, could not possibly express God's will in its entirety. That His struggle was not superfluous, is evident from a careful perusal of the Rabbinic law of homicide.

In dealing with the Decalogue, the Rabbis, in connexion with the fifth commandment, merely observed that the threat of punishment expressed in Gen. ix. 6 is supplemented here by a warning (a direct prohibition).[7] Further, from Exod. xxi. 12 it was deduced that only when 'the whole soul of the person had passed away',[8] is it murder, and that Num. xxxv. 30 insists upon the presence of at least two witnesses.[9] It was deduced also from the expression (Deut. xvii. 6) 'after the mouth of two witnesses' that capital punishment for murder could only be carried out when the witnesses, apart from being present at the crime, had warned the murderer beforehand of the punishment he might expect.[10] Thus, on this basis a law was formulated that

[1] b. Bab. m. 58 b, 59 a; Ab. iii. 11 (*gloss*).
[2] b. Ket. 46 a; cf. Siphra on Lev. xix. 16 (89 a).
[3] p. Pea. 15 d; b. Arah. 15 b.
[4] p. Pea. 15 d; 16 a.
[5] p. Pea. 16 a.
[6] See above.
[7] Mech. 70 a.
[8] Mech. 79 b f.
[9] Siphre on Num. xxxv. 30 (62 a); Deut. xvii. 6 (104 b).
[10] Mech. on Exod. xxi. 12 (80 a).

no homicide could be condemned to death unless there were two eye-witnesses of the actual murder, and also two who had warned him.[1] Moreover, he was only to be condemned when he had heard the warning and declared: 'I know (the punishment for murder) but nevertheless I will commit it'. Had he been silent, or had merely nodded, or simply said: 'I know it', he was not executed.[2] Under such conditions, and considering the method applied in the examination of witnesses, which aimed to prove, if possible, the non-validity of their attestation, a death verdict would be an impossibility. In order to prevent, to some extent, the evil effects of such legislation upon the community, the Rabbis, without any Scriptural basis, ordered, in cases where there were no witnesses, imprisonment for life for the homicide, and letting him die slowly from insufficient nourishment.[3] Capital punishment was often avoided also in other circumstances. When, for instance, a person should set a dog on someone and caused his death, or when he should push someone into the water and cause him to be drowned, or into fire so that he should be burnt to death, but in such a manner that it would have been possible for him to have saved himself, such a one is not condemned to death.[4]

Naturally, exemption from human retribution does not mean exemption from Divine. Onkelos' translation of the original text of Gen. ix. 6 is: 'He who sheds the blood of man before *witnesses*, his blood will be shed *according* to the word of the *judges*'. Targum Yer. I adds: 'He who sheds blood without witnesses, him will the Lord of the world punish on the day of the great judgment'. But Rabbinic criminal legislature, based on O.T. Law, means in fact a state of bankruptcy, both as to the applied methods of interpretation as well as to the pursued aim. The mere discussion of such legislation is in Pharisaic Judaism considered to be a most important religious activity for every individual Jew. He who, being 'unlearned', does not

[1] Sanh. iv. 1; Tos. Sanh. xi. 1; Makk. i. 9.
[2] Tos. Sanh. xi. 2.
[3] Sanh. ix. 5; Tos. Sanh. xii. 7; b. Sanh. 81 d. Also if an animal killed a person, the animal had occasionally to undergo the same punishment, Tos. Bab. k. v. 5; b. Sanh. 80 a.
[4] Sanh. ix. 1.

carry out this duty, neglects to fulfil a cardinal religious obligation, and is, moreover, bereft of this most vital aid to conduct; as judicial Law is at the same time also the highest *moral* Law. But this kind of jurisprudence could only divert the attention from the Divine purpose expressed in the Law; the conscience, instead of becoming tender for apprehension of the highest intention of the Law, was blunted. The fifth commandment could not operate under such interpretations and applications, but was made void, precisely by this eager attempt to protect its letter from being broken.

On another occasion our Lord pointed out how traditional Law deduced certain ordinances from the letter of Scripture, which were, in fact, in opposition to the intention of the Lawgiver (Mt. xv. 3 f.; Mk. vii. 9 f.); here, however, it was sufficient for Him to point out that righteousness as taught by Him supersedes that of the scribes, yea even that demanded by the Law given on Sinai. This contrasting of the new and the old Laws should have convinced of this all who had ears to hear, without any special arguments. Our Lord expected that the common sense and conscience of the hearers would be His allies in this, and He was certain that by His teaching He did not annul the letter of the Law but rather fulfilled it.

From earliest times the Rabbis had attempted to prevent the breaking of the Law by raising its demands above its literal meaning, which was called 'putting a protecting hedge around the Law' (*seyāg lat-torā*), and 'the men of the Great Synagogue', in the days of the last prophets, are supposed to have advised this.[1] Adam had already practised this method when he (so it was deduced from the words of Eve, Gen. iii. 3)[2] added to the injunction not to *eat* of the fruit of the tree (Gen. ii. 17) the warning not to *touch* it. What, according to the Law, would have been permitted until the beginning of daybreak, was by the Rabbis only allowed up to midnight, 'in order to keep man away from transgression'.[3] Such aids of a formal nature for protecting the Law were foreign to the mind of our Lord, but

[1] Ab. i. 1.
[2] Ab. d. R. N. 1; cf. Gen. R. 19 (39 a).
[3] Ber. i. 1; Mech. 6 b; cf. b. Seb. 57 b.

He was rightly convinced that whenever His teaching would be carried out, the fifth commandment would be properly kept. A man who is not wrathful and does not abuse his neighbour, will certainly not commit murder, and thus, the letter of the old Law remains unbroken. This is so obvious that it was not necessary for Him to enlarge upon it. What He says is in perfect accord with that which was said to the ancients: the God who spoke then, is the same who now proclaims anew, though in other words, His will to men.

Even Jewish tradition knows of 'the Law of the Messiah', which, notwithstanding the fact that according to some Rabbis it will only be of significance to the Gentiles,[1] has yet found entrance into the Jewish Prayer Book.[2] A scene is described where God teaches the pious in Israel, in the presence of His angels, and the sun, the moon, and the stars, 'the new Law which he will give through the Messiah' (Hebrew *tōrā ḥadāshā she'ātīd littēn 'al yad māshīaḥ*), after which the hymn of praise, sounded by Zerubbabel, is accompanied by the univocal 'amen', in which even the wicked in hell join.[3]

History has justified our Lord. Wherever the 'Law' of Jesus was accepted, the old Law also came into its own. With His 'Sermon on the Mount' the fifth commandment from Sinai marches through the world, and is being fulfilled among those who make His word the standard of their lives. On the other hand, the Mishna of the scribes, with its criminal Law, and all the acute discussions of the 'Amoreans', 'Saboreans', and 'Decisors', based on it, only serves as a dark background to the Gospel.

[1] Gen. R. 98 (212 a).
[2] Silluk on Par. Chodesh; Baer, *Siddur*, 702 (*lehinnātēn dāt ḥadāshā*); cf. 243 f. (*dāt ḥadāshā yeḥaddēsh*).
[3] Yalk. Shim. II. 296 on Isa. xxvi. 2.

PART FOUR

THE PASSOVER MEAL

XI. THE CONTRADICTION BETWEEN THE SYNOPTIC AND JOHANNINE PRESENTATIONS OF THE LAST SUPPER

THE proper understanding of the words of our Lord at the Last Supper is to a considerable extent dependent upon the conception of the character of this Supper. It is an undeniable fact that the Synoptists describe it as a Passover meal, while the Fourth Gospel presupposes that it was not, since, according to this Gospel, on the day of the Crucifixion the Passover lamb was yet to be eaten (John xviii. 28) and our Lord died on the Passover Eve (xix. 14 f., 31, 42). Two attempts have been made to solve this contradiction.

When, according to John xviii. 28, the Jews did not enter the Praetorium of Pilate that they might not be prevented, through defilement, from eating the Passover, we are not to think, says Zahn,[1] of the Passover lamb, as this had already been consumed on the previous evening, but of the further participation at the celebration of the Feast of the unleavened bread.

Now it is true that the Mishna and the Tosephta[2] speak of the '*pesaḥ dōrōt*', the 'Passover of generations' (i.e. all Passovers, in contrast to the 'Egyptian Passover' and the 'second' Passover, Num. ix and xi) having to be celebrated (*nōhēg*, practised) not only on one day, but on all the seven days. This, however, is connected with the Jewish custom of calling the Feast of the unleavened bread 'Passover'. 'Practising' the Passover means avoiding the eating of anything leaven, which, naturally, could not have been observed at the first, i.e. the Egyptian Passover, because of the Exodus, nor could it have had any reference to the 'second Passover', because it is of one day's duration only; which is expressly stated also in other places.[3] But sacredness,

[1] *Komm. zum Johannesev.* 621; *Einleitung zum N.T.* II. 523 f., 534 f.
[2] Pes. ix. 5; Tos. Pes. viii. 7; cf. 21.
[3] Mech. 19 b; p. Pes. 37 a; b. Pes. 96 b.

in the legal sense, is not attached to unleavened bread; it can, and must be, eaten also by the levitically impure, and therefore, also by those who, through entering a heathen house, have (according to Rabbinic, but not according to Mosaic law) become defiled for seven days.[1] A person levitically defiled was only forbidden to enter the inner courts of the Temple, and participate in sacrificial meals, which, in connexion with either obligatory or free-will offerings, could take place during the whole of the festival. To these offerings, according to the Jewish legal tradition,[2] that by which one fulfils the duty of not *appearing* empty before God (which is therefore called simply *re'iiyā*, 'appearing', or rather 'seeing', Exod. xxiii. 15) does not belong; for, according to the Rabbinic conception, this sacrifice was a burnt-offering, and thus dedicated entirely to God.[3] But, for instance, the sacrifice (deduced from Deut. xii. 7, 12; xvi. 14; xxvii. 7) of the 'festive joy' (*simḥā*), consisting of thank-offerings,[4] and above all, the 'celebration' sacrifice, the so-called *ḥagīgā*[5] (deduced by the Rabbis that it was offered on all the seven days of the feast from the commandment Exod. xii. 14, 'to celebrate the festival', *ḥāgag*), which could already have been eaten as a supplement to the Passover lamb, on the first Eve of the Feast, belong to them.[6] To such offerings, independent of the Passover itself, 2 Chron. xxx. 22 ('And they ate of the feast for seven days with *sacrifice of thank-offerings*') would refer, if the text there were not corrupt; but probably, instead of *wa-yōkhelū ham-mō'ēd* ('and they *ate* the feast') one should read—*wa-yekhallū ham-mō'ēd* ('and they *accomplished* the feast, by slaughtering thank-offerings'). So it is not possible to make use of this expression as an explanation of John xviii. 28.

No reader of the Johannine passage could have understood the words 'the eating of the Passover' to mean anything but

[1] Ohal. viii. 7; Tos. Ohal. viii. 11; cf. *O.W.* 333 f.

[2] Mech. on Exod. xxiii. 15 (101 b); Siphre on Deut. 102 b; Hag. i. 2; cf. Pea. i. 1.

[3] Tos. Hag. i. 4; p. Hag. 76 b.

[4] Siphre on Deut. 88 a; 89 a; 102 a; Tos. Hag. i. 4; p. Hag. 76 b.

[5] Mech. 8 a f.; Hag. i. 2; Tos. Pes. viii. 7; b. Pes. 69 b f.; p. Hag. 78 a; Siphre on Deut. xvi. 2 (101 a).

[6] Pes. vi. 3; ix. 9; Tos. Pes. v. 3; b. Pes. 70 a. For the introductory blessing to it, see Tos. Pes. x. 13; Ber. v. 22.

the Passover lamb itself; and no Jew, if the author of the Fourth Gospel was one, would have transferred an expression used of a definite legal duty to something else. Neither could the author have meant (in xix. 14, where he speaks of the day when Jesus died) by the expression the 'Eve of the Passover' anything other than the day which the Jews call in Hebrew *'ereb pesaḥ*,[1] and in Aramaic *'arūbat pisḥā*,[2] i.e. the day which preceded the Festival; never the Friday in the festive week, as Zahn suggests. But were it not for the Synoptists' statements contradicting those of St John concerning the relation of the Passover festival to the day of the Crucifixion, it would not have entered anybody's mind to explain the Johannine sentence as Zahn does. According to this Gospel, our Lord died on the day before the Passover, and the Last Supper could not have been a Passover meal, nor is it here described as such.

Nor is Chwolson's attempt to reconcile the contradiction of the two accounts acceptable, for according to his hypothesis the two narratives refer to two Passovers; the Synoptists' to an anticipatory Passover meal on the night of the 14th of Nisan, and the Fourth Gospel to the proper Passover meal on the night of the 15th; because the 15th of Nisan happened then to fall on a Sabbath, the Passover lamb had already been slain on the 13th, and some persons celebrated the meal on the 14th, others on the 15th. But, according to Rabbinic ordinance, the slaughtering of the Passover lamb had to take place in the afternoon of the 14th of Nisan, in this case on the Friday; merely the carrying home and the preparing of the lamb could thus have fallen on the Sabbath. That our Lord should have belonged to those who had scruples about it, is not probable. According to Jewish Law a postponement (but not an anticipation) of a 'celebration sacrifice' could well be possible, because it is not bound to any particular day of the feast, and, hence, does not abrogate the prohibition of the work of the first day of the festival, or of a Sabbath, especially as it is a private offering.[3] When Pentecost, consisting of one day, falls on a Sabbath, a postponement of the 'celebration sacrifice' to a time

[1] Pes. iv. 1; viii. 8; x. 1; Tos. Pes. ii. 18.
[2] Ruth R. iii. 1 (10 b).
[3] Tem. ii. 1.

after the feast was even a self-understood thing.[1] When through the death of David the whole of Israel had to mourn on the Pentecost, the 'celebration sacrifice' was offered up, according to the Rabbis, on the following day.[2] But for the Paschal lamb postponement was out of the question, because it is directly stated (Num. ix. 2 f., 13) that it had to be slaughtered on a fixed day.[3] The only exception mentioned there is that of a postponement for a whole month in consequence of defilement (Num. ix. 10 f.). The Rabbinic principle that the Passover abrogates the Sabbath,[4] i.e. makes the work in connexion with the duties of the Passover obligatory even when it falls on a Sabbath, harmonises, in this case, with the right purpose of the Biblical law. So Chwolson's theory lacks the necessary basis.

Some scholars find confirmation for the Crucifixion having taken place on the Passover Eve in the Talmudic tradition that a certain Jeshu[5]—who was a pupil of Jehoshua ben Perachya, and thus lived long before the Christian era!—was hanged on the Eve of Passover (Hebrew *'ereb pesaḥ*) for attempting to mislead the people. Previous to the execution, an announcement concerning it lasting forty days was made, in case anyone might wish to establish his innocence; but it brought no result. If this is meant to refer to our Lord, then it is evident that any knowledge of the intimate circumstances of His Death as well as of His Person and time is absent from this passage; but it would show a certain acquaintance with the Johannine narrative. If it does not refer to the Crucifixion, the reason for the Execution having taken place on that day was to give it the greatest possible publicity.

To other scholars again the Johannine chronology seems to gain credibility because of the story told in the Talmud of a certain orphan who was 'slaughtered' by his guardian on a Passover Eve.[6] It is clear that the motive of the crime was to obtain possession of the inheritance, and the reason that day

[1] Hag. ii. 4; cf. Tos. Hag. ii. 10, 13.
[2] p. Hag. 78 a; cf. Ruth R. 3 (10 a).
[3] Cf. Mech. 5 b; Jubil. xlix. 7, 8, 14.
[4] Pes. vi. 1; ix. 8; Tos. Pes. iv. 1, 2; v. 1; viii. 8; Siphre on Num. 17 a.
[5] b. Sanh. 43 a; cf. b. Sanh. 107 b; Sot. 47 a.
[6] Tos. Keth. xi. 4; b. Keth. 102 b.

was chosen was because people would abstain from entering a house where a corpse was, in order not to incur defilement for seven days (Num. xix. 14); furthermore, on the eve of the Feast the burial could be hastened, and thus the real circumstances of the orphan's death be kept secret. Moreover, Rabbenu Asher reads, instead of *'ereb hap-pesaḥ*, 'Passover Eve' (which might have been due to a copyist's misunderstanding of the abbreviation *he*; the article is in any case uncommon in the combination of these words)—*'ereb hā-rishōn*, i.e. on the very first evening of the orphan's arrival. If he is right, which is very probable, only the erroneous interpretation of this passage would contain a point resembling the narrative in St John, dealing with the behaviour of the Jews at the time when our Lord was delivered up to Pilate, but could not even then be considered as an analogy to it, since the condemnation and Crucifixion of Jesus took place openly, and was not influenced by any consideration of the approaching Feast.

Even those who accept the Johannine, as against the Synoptic, chronology, are convinced that the Words recorded by the Synoptists in connexion with the distribution of the bread and of the wine were actually spoken by our Lord, and that the Fourth Evangelist also knew of them (cf. John vi. 53 f.), but that he intentionally suppressed them in his account of the events of the last evening. He must have had a double reason for doing so. According to John vi. 35, 41, 48, 51, our Lord designated Himself the Bread of Life, and spoke (verse 53) of the necessity to eat His Flesh and to drink His Blood, and so He could not have expressed on the last evening such thoughts in connexion with material bread and wine, after having (vi. 26 f., 32, 58) consciously turned the minds of His hearers from earthly (although miraculous) bread, yea even from the manna, the bread from heaven. What this Evangelist desired to emphasise was, that it is the *Person* of our Lord (whose Flesh and Blood are the organs of His Spirit) that is of the greatest value to humanity (perhaps in opposition to a nascent tendency to over-emphasise the importance of the sign as such). As it was, the words seemed (according to vi. 60 f.), even to many of His disciples, a hard saying, because they could not distinguish between spirit and flesh (see vi. 63); but in their original form they could have led to an even more serious occasion for stumbling. Misunderstandings might have arisen which would put the teaching and behaviour of Christians in an unfavourable light.[1] To remove this and at the same time make clear the real purpose of our Lord, would thus have been the second motive of the Evangelist for suppressing the Words of the Institution. If this be the case, it is a serious warning to us not to put too much weight upon the Johannine presentation of the outward order of events of the earthly life of our Lord.

If then the words transferred by St John to another place originally were closely connected with the description of the Last Supper as a Passover meal, it was natural that once *they* were left out, the Passover meal itself (which, without the Words of Institution, had no purpose) had also to be left out. What our Lord had to say to His disciples on that last night, according to St John, had nothing to do with this Jewish rite. But to do away with the Passover character of the Last Supper would not be possible, if that evening was really the evening of the Passover festival, from the legally-ordered celebration of which our Lord and His disciples could not have excluded themselves. The simplest way of getting rid of this difficulty was, therefore, to push back this last evening for one day, so that the Passover meal would have taken place after the Death of Jesus. To the author, to whom the *spiritual* possession of God's grace and truth in Jesus was central, this method did not seem wrong.

Something else probably led the writer to this step. It is not a mere accidental form of style that the adversaries of our Lord are, in the Fourth Gospel, not the scribes and Pharisees, but 'the Jews'. The author was not anti-Jewish ('salvation is of the Jews', iv. 22), yet he realised that our Lord was not merely the flower of Judaism and of the Jewish people, but that He came from above (i. 14). The Jews had Abraham to their father, but Jesus is of a more ancient, and of a higher, origin (viii. 56, 58), and the forms of Jewish religious life are not to Him what they are to the Jews. The Evangelist speaks of 'the Passover Eve of the Jews' (xix. 42), of 'the Passover of the

[1] See under xv.

Jews' (ii. 13; xi. 55), of 'the feasts of the Jews' (v. 1; vi. 4; vii. 2), as though all this had only an external significance for our Lord, notwithstanding the fact that He goes to Jerusalem for these feasts (John ii. 13; v. 1; vii. 8, 10; cf. xi. 56). But Scripture, which the Jews search, testifies concerning Him (v. 39; xviii. 9; xix. 28). Thus, He is the Lamb of God of Isaiah liii, 'which takes away the sins of the world' (i. 29, 36); as the serpent in the wilderness must He be lifted up (iii. 14); as the real Manna must He be eaten (vi. 32 f.); He is also the real Passover Lamb. The passage quoted in xix. 36 'no bone in Him should *be broken*', although it does not quite correspond to the literal expression of Exod. xii. 36 ('one should not break a bone in him') and to Num. ix. 12, yet Codex A of the LXX has in both places the passive *συντρίψεται* and the position of the words with the concluding *αὐτῷ* reminds one of the *ἀπ' αὐτοῦ*, which in the LXX also stands at the end. There is no occasion, therefore, to refer to Psalm xxxiii. 21 LXX, where it is said of the bones of the pious 'not one of them shall be broken'. When, then, something that took place in connexion with the Death of Jesus had its antitype in what should be done with the Passover lamb according to the Law, it would have been appropriate to find a significance in the fact that Jesus died in the afternoon on which the Passover lambs were slaughtered in the Temple. But St John does not bring out this. He mentions the day and the hour of the Jewish time-reckoning, not in connexion with the Death of our Lord, but in xix. 14. It seemed to him of importance to note that the Jews at the sixth hour of the Passover Eve rejected their King and demanded that He should be crucified. Thus, to St John, although there was a connexion between our Lord and the Scripture concerning the Passover lamb, the relation was not to that which the Jews slaughtered and ate. This fact he did not wish to have obscured by a Passover meal on the Master's last evening, and the conscious ignoring by the Evangelist of the Passover does not mean an antipathy to the O.T., but rather to the Judaism which he knew. Those who are concerned with the central fact and its essential content, will acknowledge that the Evangelist was right. The outer process of what took place we shall hardly be able to learn from him; and although the Johannine account can in itself be considered as correct from the Jewish legal point of view, one has to ask whether it was clear to the Author that Joseph of Arimathaea and Nicodemus, by handling the body of our Lord (xix. 38 f.), made it impossible for themselves to partake of the Passover lamb; and that it might have been questionable whether they had the right to take upon themselves that duty, not being relatives of our Lord, who alone were legally obliged to care for His body.

XII. SUPPOSED DIFFICULTIES IN THE SYNOPTIC ACCOUNT

The fact that the Synoptists do not consider the day of the Crucifixion as having the festive character of the first day of the feast of unleavened bread, on which work is prohibited, is taken by most scholars as a proof that they themselves were conscious that it was not a festive day. Apart from this, our Lord's behaviour immediately after His Last Supper does not seem, at first sight, to harmonise with the Passover laws, and the details of the Synoptic presentation must therefore be examined in their proper order.

1. THE WALK TOWARDS GETHSEMANE

After the Passover meal, eaten within Jerusalem, Jesus went with His disciples to Gethsemane, at the foot of the Mount of Olives (Mt. xxvi. 30; Mk. xiv. 26; Lk. xxii. 39; cf. John xviii. 1).[1] That it was still full night-time is undoubtedly clear from Mt. xxvi. 34; Mk. xiv. 30; Lk. xxii. 34; John xviii. 3. According to tradition, the Passover meal should be concluded at the hour corresponding to that on which the Israelites left Egypt (Exod. xii. 29), i.e. at midnight,[2] although, according to the Law (Ex. xii. 10), it could be prolonged until the morning. In this way the Law was hedged about and the Jews protected from breaking it.[3] But, according to Ex. xii. 22, to go out of the

[1] Concerning the place, cf. *O.W.* 340.

[2] Pes. x. 9; Zeb. v. 8; Siphre on Deut. xvi. 6 (101 b); Tg. Yer. I on Deut. xvi. 6; cf. *P.J.B.* 1912, 132. Jubil. xlix. 12 considers the time for the meal open till two o'clock in the morning.

[3] Mech. 6 b; p. Ber. 3 a (p. Mishna).

house on the Passover night is forbidden. This prohibition was connected with the protection from the avenging angel which the Israelites enjoyed in their houses marked with the blood of the Passover lamb. Jewish tradition, therefore, rightly limited this prohibition to the Passover of the Exodus itself.[1] But, according to Deut. xvi. 7, the place of the God-chosen sanctuary might be left on the morning after the Passah. In itself, this merely means that presence in the Sanctuary is required no longer than is necessary for the duration of the Passover. On the other hand, Ex. xii. 16; Lev. xxiii. 7; Num. xxviii. 18 designate the first day of the feast of unleavened bread a day of rest, and seem to suggest that during the whole festival no change of place must be undertaken. Jewish tradition attempted to harmonise this contradiction in different ways. Either the law in Deuteronomy referred to the last day of the Feast (as the Targum Yer. I translates: 'And the morrow of *the last day of the festival* thou turnest and goest to thy city');[2] or, the 'tents' to which the pilgrims returned (Deut. xvi. 7) was taken to mean the lodging for the night, in contrast to the place where the Passover meal was consumed. The following ordinance seems to be based upon this latter differentiation, although no Biblical reference is given: 'At the Egyptian Passover the night was spent at the place where the Passover was eaten; but since then one may eat the Passover in one place and sleep in another'.[3] A third explanation—and it became the dominant one—was that the ordinance refers to the spending of the night (Hebrew *līnā*) in the city of Jerusalem, with permission to leave it in the morning; which, on the first day of the Feast, would mean that it is permissible to visit one's lodging outside the walls of Jerusalem in the nearest environment of the city. Rabbi Jehuda understood it in this sense in connexion with the so-called 'second Passover', to which the law of spending the night within the walls of the city was not applied; i.e. he considered it permissible for one to slaughter the Passover lamb in the afternoon in the Temple, and then immediately go to Bethphage and

[1] Tos. Pes. viii. 14, 17.

[2] So also Aben Esra on Deut. xvi. 7, while Rashi thinks of the second day of the Feast.

[3] Tos. Pes. viii. 17.

participate in the lamentation for the death of a father.[1] The majority of the Rabbis, however, would not allow this change of place even for the 'second Passover'; the duty of sleeping in Jerusalem was considered by them to be attached to every Passover, and extended even to other sacrifices.[2]

Our Lord, in leaving the city of Jerusalem immediately after the Passover meal, did not comply with the last-mentioned rule. Bethphage, however, was otherwise considered to belong ritually to Jerusalem, which consideration applied even to the eating of the Passover meal.[3] At all events, those pilgrims who lodged outside Jerusalem seem to have been used to return to their quarters after the Passover meal. The scribes probably justified it by an ideal extension of the environment of the sanctuary.[4] The common sense of the laity must have told them that, after all, the law of Deut. xvi. 7 referred only to the return journey to the native 'places' of the pilgrims, which would occur on the morrow; and was not intended to insist upon the pilgrims spending the night within the city walls. Our Lord must have interpreted this law similarly. In any case, He did not go that night beyond the traditional Sabbath 'journey', which, had He gone to Bethany, He would have done, for Gethsemane, lying at the western foot of the Mount of Olives, was within the permissible domain (Acts i. 12). Thus, also on that last night, He surely had shown Himself to have lived, according to His conviction, as 'one put under the Law' (Gal. iv. 4).

It was quite different in the case of the two disciples walking on the first day of the week (Lk. xxiv. 13). This was not a Sabbath, nor a Feast-day, when work is prohibited, but, being the third day of the festival, it was merely *ḥōl ham-mō'ēd*, 'an ordinary day of the feast', i.e. a half holiday, to which the Sabbath and feast-day laws did not apply.

[1] Tos. Pes. viii. 8.
[2] *Ibid.*; b. Pes. 95 b; Sukk. 47 b; Siphre on Deut. xvi. 7 (101 b).
[3] b. Pes. 91 a; cf. *O.W.* 269.
[4] Cf. Siphre on Num. xxix. 35 (55 a); Midr. Taan. on Deut. xvi. 8, according to which it is allowed to spend the night at Bethphage after having had a sacrificial meal in Jerusalem, except on Pentecost.

2. THE CARRYING OF ARMS

In the room where the Passover meal was eaten, there were two swords already at hand with which to defend our Lord against the destiny appointed for Him according to Isa. liii. 12 (Lk. xxii. 38). A sword was actually drawn for Him that night (Mt. xxvi. 51; Mk. xiv. 47; Lk. xxii. 50). The men sent out by the High Priests to capture Him were also armed with swords and staves (Mt. xxvi. 47, 55; Mk. xiv. 43, 48; Lk. xxii. 52). The night on which all this happened was the night of the 15th of Nisan, beginning with sunset, the Sabbath character of which is, according to Exod. xii. 16; Lev. xxiii. 7; Num. xxviii. 18, beyond doubt.[1] Only the permission to prepare food on the Feast (Exod. xii. 16) made the feast-day rest different from that of the Sabbath.[2]

The prohibition to carry arms on a Sabbath or feast-day was based on Neh. xiii. 19; Jubil. l. 8. The question whether arms were to be considered a burden was answered in the affirmative by pious Jews in the time of the Maccabees, and therefore the carrying of them on the Sabbath was forbidden, except for self-protection,[3] which prohibition has become an established thing since that time.[4] Rabbinic tradition explained the above-mentioned exception by the general principle, founded on Lev. xviii. 5, that when life is in danger, the Sabbath laws can be broken.[5] When a city is attacked by an enemy, the inhabitants, and also those who wish to help them, may use arms on a Sabbath to protect themselves; and at the frontier, even when there was no danger to life but only of robbery, this was permitted.[6] Also an individual, pursued by an enemy, may break the Sabbath laws in order to save his life. Otherwise, it was considered sinful to carry a sword, a bow, a shield, a stave, or a lance, on a Sabbath day; and when done unintentionally, it had to be propitiated by a sin-offering (Lev. iv. 27; Num.

[1] Cf. Mech. 9 b; Siphre on Num. 54 b. [2] Mech. 9 b f.

[3] 1 Macc. ii. 41; Jos. *Ant.* XII. 6. 2; XIII. 1. 3; XIV. 4. 2; XVIII. 9. 2; Jubil. l. 12; cf. Schürer, *Gesch.* 4th ed. II. 560. The fact that the Jews were not taken by the Romans for military service (*Ant.* XIV. 10. 6) was, however, not based upon Jewish ideas of the Sabbath.

[4] Cf. Jos. *C. Ap.* II. 22.

[5] Tos. Sab. xv. 11; p. Sab. 14 d, 15 a; b. Yom. 84 b.

[6] Tos. Er. iii. 5, 8; p. Er. 21 d; b. Erub. 45 a.

xv. 27);[1] when intentionally, Divine extermination (Num. xv. 30 f.) was considered to be the punishment; and if done in the presence of witnesses who had duly warned the transgressor, the latter would have to be stoned.[2] The question, however, was raised as to whether arms should not be regarded as ornaments, and thus belong to ordinary attire.[3] The Mishnah commentator, Bertinora, took it for granted that for martial purposes arms could be carried on the Sabbath, probably because they belong to soldiers' attire. These are the directing lines given by Jewish tradition to Jews who wished to live according to Pharisaic principles. The Mosaic Law is silent concerning the point, and the O.T. historical narratives do not suggest anywhere that the Israelites did not attack their enemies on the Sabbath, or that they put aside their arms on that day. It is not probable that the Sadducaic High Priests would have considered the carrying of arms on the Sabbath (not for offensive purposes but for the sake of public order, which could not have been looked upon as a burden, to be prepared for possible resistance against a task which they had to accomplish) as law-breaking. Galilaean pilgrims probably took their arms to be a part of their attire, as they would to-day, and, in reply to any Pharisaic objection, they would have pointed out that in such times danger to life made arms as indispensable during festive seasons as on other days. In any case, soldiers had to have their arms ready at hand on the Sabbath, if the permission to defend oneself on that day was to be of any practical value. A scribe, when told of the imprisonment of our Lord, would have remarked that 'the demand of the hour' justified the carrying of arms by the agents of the High Priest, and that Peter did not break the Law by drawing his sword to protect his Master. We cannot expect the Evangelists themselves to have had any legal scruples concerning this point, nor to have thought the readers of their narratives would have any.

[1] Cf. Sab. vi. 4.

[2] Sanh. vii. 8; Ker. i. 1, 2; Tos. Sab. ii. 9; b. Sab. 4 a; Mech. on Exod. xxxi. 14 (104 a).

[3] Sab. vi. 4.

3. THE JUDICIAL PROCEDURE

The most serious difficulty presented by the Synoptic chronology was found in the fact that the examination (Mt. xxvi. 57; Mk. xiv. 53) should have taken place in the night of a feast-day, when work was prohibited, and in the morning the judicial procedure (Mt. xxvii. 1; Mk. xv. 1; Lk. xxii. 66), which resulted in the death verdict. But the Sabbath-breaker in Num. xv. 33 was apparently brought before the congregation on the Sabbath, and would have even been condemned on the same day, had the Divine decision already been known. Rabbinic Law prohibits judging on a feast-day,[1] yet not without stating that it was only a scribal enactment. According to Schürer,[2] Augustus exempted the Jews from appearing at courts of justice on the Sabbath; but it refers only to acts which the Jews considered as belonging to pecuniary affairs,[3] and it does not prove the sitting in judgment on a feast-day to have been prohibited by Jewish Law. In any case, it was permissible to go to theatres and circuses on the Sabbath, in connexion with questions of public interest.[4] A rebellious teacher of the Law could even be *executed* on a feast-day.[5] Moreover, it was permitted to break even a Mosaic Law if 'the hour demanded it'.[6]

Here the situation was such that Judas' treachery came at an unexpected but opportune moment, because the delivery of Jesus into the hands of the High Priest would at this time create no stir. It was imperative to act as quickly as possible, in order that He could be delivered to the Romans before His adherents gathered round Him. They could not have known that our Lord Himself would bind the hands of His friends (Mt. xxvi. 52 f.; Lk. xxii. 51; John xviii. 11). It was already an agreed thing among them that Jesus had to be done away with (Mt. xxvi. 3 f.; Mk. xiv. 1 f.; Lk. xx. 19; xxii. 2). Originally the reason for the postponement of the decisive step to the time after the Feast (Mt. xxvi. 5; Mk. xiv. 2) was to avoid publicity, and not because they could not have condemned Him at the Feast. This post-

[1] Bez. v. 2.
[2] *History*, 4th ed. II. 263.
[3] Jos. *Ant.* XVI. 6. 2, 4.
[4] b. Keth. 5 a.
[5] Sanh. xi. 4; cf. Siphre on Deut. xvii. 13 (105 a).
[6] p. Hag. 78 a.

ponement was, thanks to Judas, now made unnecessary, and so, that which had already been decided, had to be executed. The fact that the councils which were held for that end in an unusual time did not quite correspond to all the regulations of the judicial practices, and ought not perhaps to have been described in the Gospels as *official*, would not subsequently cause any serious objection. The hair-splitting casuistry of Rabbinic Law would not have prevented a man like Caiaphas from executing something which the interest of the people and religion seemed to have demanded. Why then should we expect the Evangelists to have had any scruples concerning it? If the traditional Law be taken into consideration here, the difficulty would not disappear even when what happened was a day earlier, for traditional Law forbids not only verdicts of decisions of capital punishments at *night*, but also on the first day of the judicial examinations, and therefore all judicial councils dealing with capital crimes, on the day before a Sabbath or a feast-day.[1] Only the Johannine presentation would not contain a contradiction to this, since, according to it, the delivery to Pilate was a private affair of Hannas and Caiaphas and not preceded by an official Jewish decision, which, according to xviii. 31, was even actually declined.

In fact, the Crucifixion on the Feast was really a forbidden act, since, although it was not carried out by the Jews, it was *caused* by them. According to Jubil. i. 12, the taking of life belongs to acts prohibited on a Sabbath. When the question concerning judicial proceedings in connexion with capital transgressions on a Sabbath or a festival is discussed, it is not because the verdict of death is forbidden on these days, but it is due to the fact that the execution, which has to take place on the very same day as the verdict, cannot abrogate the day of rest.[2] The prohibition of an execution on the Sabbath was artificially derived from the expression 'in your dwellings', which occurs in connexion with the Sabbath law (Exod. xxxv. 2), as well as with verdicts (Num. xxxv. 29), and because (according to Exod. xxxv. 3) 'burning'

[1] Sanh. iv. 1.

[2] A postponement of the execution would be 'a grieving of justice', '*innūy had-dīn*, as it aggravates the agony of the criminal. Sanh. xi. 4; p. Sanh. 22 b; b. Sanh. 35 a; Ab. v. 8.

being prohibited on a Sabbath, execution by burning (and consequently by any other method) was also forbidden.[1] From this it is again evident upon what feeble foundations the scribal Law, supposed to have been seriously considered by Caiaphas, rests; and how precarious it is to derive from it important conclusions concerning the Gospel history. It is scarcely necessary to point out that even Pharisaism would in this case, as in similar cases, only have praised Caiaphas for having taken energetic steps to do away with the 'enemy' of the Law and of the Temple. The great scribe Shim'on ben Shetaḥ gave the verdict for eighty witches to be hanged, although, according to traditional Law, only two criminals could be judged on one day, and women were not to be hanged at all.[2] This at first astonished the Rabbis, but 'the hour demanded it'.[3] One riding a horse on a Sabbath day (only a Rabbinic prohibition)[4] was condemned to be stoned by a court of justice; another who was found with his own wife under a fig tree, was punished with 'forty less one' lashes, 'not because he deserved it, but because the hour demanded it'.[5]

4. THE COMING FROM THE FIELD

According to Mark (xv. 21) and Luke (xxiii. 26), the Cross was put upon Simon of Cyrene when he came 'from the field'. This is usually interpreted to mean that Simon had been working in the field on the feast-day—an act prohibited by the Law. A man was not allowed even to *inspect* his field on such a day.[6] There is a reference made in the Talmud in connexion with the time of the evening *Shema'* to one who comes from 'the field' in the evening, and he is advised to fulfil his religious duty in the synagogue before going home to his meal.[7] There the expression 'from the field' may (but not necessarily) mean *working* in the field; but in the Gospel narrative, it was not in the evening but in the morning before nine o'clock that Simon

[1] p. Sanh. 22 b; b. Sanh. 35 b; Mech. 80 b; 105 a.
[2] Sanh. vi. 3.
[3] p. Sanh. 23 c.
[4] Bez. v. 2.
[5] b. Sanh. 46 a.
[6] b. Erub. 38 b; Maimonides, H. Sabbat, 24, 2 bases it on Isa. lviii. 13. Also according to Jubil. i. 12 it is prohibited to inspect an estate on a Sabbath day.
[7] b. Ber. 4 b.

came (cf. Mk. xv. 25), a time when no one goes home from work in the field. What it really means, however, is that he came from *outside the city*. The disciples in Emmaus went, according to Mk. xvi. 12, 'to the field'; he 'who is on the field', i.e. outside, should not, on the Day of Judgment, go after his clothes, i.e. go home (Mk. xiii. 16). 'The field' (*sāde*) often means also in Hebrew, 'the free country', or 'the heath' (cf. Gen. xxiv. 63; xxvii. 3; Isa. xl. 6; lv. 12).[1] The Targum renders it, Gen. iii. 1, vi. 14, by *bārā*, 'outside'. In Galilaean Aramaic one might also think of *ṭūrā*, as, apart from 'mountain' its chief meaning, it is also used for 'field'.[2] There is no reason given why Simon came back so early from outside Jerusalem, but it is possible that, like our Lord Himself, he lived outside the city walls, and on the first day of the Feast, about the ninth hour, he intended to go to the Temple for prayer (Acts iii. 1).[3]

5. THE INTERMENT

If the Last Supper was a Passover meal, then our Lord died on the afternoon of the 14th of Nisan. If this first day of the Feast was a Friday, as it is presumed in the Synoptic tradition as well as in the Fourth Gospel, then two days on which work was prohibited followed one another. The Synoptists state that the burial took place before the following Sabbath (Mk. xv. 42; Lk. xxiii. 54; cf. Mt. xxvii. 62), and also that (because of the Sabbath) the usual anointing of the Body was postponed (Lk. xxiii. 56; cf. Mk. xvi. 1). Matthew is silent concerning the anointment, and the women accordingly went, when the Sabbath was over, only to see the grave, as it was officially sealed (Mt. xxviii. 1; cf. xxvii. 66). The wrapping-linen was already bought *before* the Sabbath (Mk. xv. 46), the spices *after* the Sabbath (Mk. xvi. 1), while according to Luke (xxiii. 56; xxiv. 1), the latter also were perhaps already prepared before the Sabbath; in any case, they were brought to the sepulchre only after the Sabbath. That, in this case, work could not be done on the Friday either, it being a feast-day, does not seem to have concerned the narrators.

[1] Cf. also p. Sab. 3 b; Kil. 31 c; Ter. 46 a.
[2] p. Kil. 31 c; Ter. 46 a; Sab. 3 b, d; Taan. 64 b, 66 d.
[3] Cf. Dalman, *Arbeit und Sitte in Palästina*, I. 618.

It is necessary here to understand the teaching of Jewish Law concerning the interment on a day of rest, and it should be remembered first of all that the temperature of Palestine makes a quick burial imperative. The rule is to bury the body on the very day of death if it occurred at night or in the morning, but on the following day if it occurred in the afternoon or evening. The Law does not directly state that to bury on the Sabbath is not allowed, but it is almost certain that when death takes place on a Sabbath, the grave must not be dug on that day, although it is conceivable that, from the point of view of the Mosaic Law, the body may be laid in a grave which was already prepared; for the prohibition to carry on the Sabbath is most probably a later innovation. According to traditional Law, burying on the Sabbath is of course forbidden. To move even one member of the body on that day is not permissible.[1] Even the body of King David, it is said, could not be buried on the Sabbath; while in order to save the life of a one-year-old child the Sabbath can be broken.[2] To perform on the Sabbath all the necessary preparations for the interment, as, for instance, the washing and the anointing of the body, is permitted, on condition that the body itself is not moved. Other business, such as procuring the coffin and shroud, may be done,[3] and one could walk on a Sabbath evening the maximum allowable distance in order to prepare these things.[4] Even the preliminary arrangements in this connexion were permitted, e.g. the consideration of place and price; but the actual buying and even mention of the sum was not allowed on the Sabbath.[5] For a Jew to dig a grave on the Sabbath or a festival is quite out of the question, even a Gentile was not allowed to do this for a Jew;[6] but the latter could prepare for burial such graves as had already been made in rocks.[7] In this way everything could be prepared

[1] Sab. xxiii. 5.
[2] b. Sab. 151 b; Midr. on Ruth R. 3 (10 a).
[3] Sab. xiii. 4, 5.
[4] Tos. Sab. xvii. 13; p. Ber. 5 d; b. Sab. 151 a.
[5] Tos. Sab. xvii. 13; b. Sab. 151 a.
[6] Sab. xxiii. 4; Tos. Sab. xvii. 15. Yet a Gentile may close the grave by putting a stone against its opening, p. Mo. k. 82 a.
[7] Mo. k. i. 6; if the Hebrew *bemō'ēd* really means a feast-day, and not merely a half-holiday which has not the Sabbath character.

on a day of rest for the burial to take place immediately after sunset.

Many complications arose when two days on which work was prohibited followed one another. The body could not remain unburied for such a long time, and in an oriental house, often consisting of one room only, there could be no special place where it could be kept. If there should happen to be an upper chamber (Acts ix. 39), the body might not be carried there. The Talmud mentions a case of this kind happening on a Sabbath followed by a feast once only, and Rabbi Joḥanan then advised that the care of the dead should be transferred to Gentiles;[1] by this he probably meant the whole preparation and execution of the interment. Later, this care of the dead was understood to mean the preparing of the coffin and the grave: while the Jews themselves had to wash the corpse, dress it, and perform the actual burial.[2] It is not stated what should be done in cases where there was no Gentile willing to do it. But as using Gentiles for this purpose was in itself something irregular, and the later practice allows a Jew to perform the interment, everything speaks for the fact that, Jewishly expressed, the dutiful care for the dead abrogated the Sabbath; and when there was a ready-made grave to be found, the burial could take place on the Sabbath or feast-day. It is also conceivable that when a Sabbath should follow a feast-day on which, by the way, work was only partially prohibited, such a day was of less importance than the Sabbath, and in relation to it considered but an ordinary work-day in regard to such a matter as a burial, so that Sabbath rest would be strictly observed. One could even argue that, according to Deut. xvi. 7, the first day of the Feast of unleavened bread was not a day of rest at all, as one could go back 'to the tents' on that day. Jewish tradition probably had long since harmonised this with the non-Deuteronomic law.[3]

In agreement with such theories and usages are the Gospel narratives dealing with the interment of our Lord. Even Jewish traditional Law would have had nothing to say against the legality of this interment, if the purchase of the grave clothes

[1] b. Sab. 139 a f.
[2] Shulchan Arukh, Orach Chayyim, 526.
[3] See above, XII, 1.

was in accordance with the Jewish enactments. One should not, without proof, accuse the Evangelists of having changed an earlier account, according to which the Last Supper was not a Passover meal, to suit their new chronological order, without noticing that here were difficulties which could at least have been cleared up by a word of explanation or excuse. But, as a matter of fact, they did not feel any difficulty themselves, nor did they presuppose it in their readers. They were convinced that the burial of the Master was according to the Jewish usage of the time, although, perhaps, not altogether in accordance with the judicial theories of the scribes.

Moreover, it has also to be kept in mind that here was an extraordinary case. According to Deut. xxi. 23, a criminal who had been hanged had to be buried before nightfall, in order that the land should not be defiled longer than necessary. John xix. 31 is probably based upon this, although the consideration of the holiness of God's Land is there turned into that of the holiness of the Sabbath; perhaps the Fourth Evangelist, out of reverence, avoided mentioning the real motive of the law. Although Jewish Law, as we have seen, implies the permission to execute on a feast-day (see above), it says nothing concerning the interment on that day; but there can be no doubt that the rule would be that if a person has been hanged on a feast-day, the body must necessarily be also buried on that day, especially when it is followed by a Sabbath. The prohibition not to let the body hang over-night on the wood, and the command to bury it,[1] would, in this case, certainly have annulled the prohibition of work on a festival. The fact that there was a ready-made grave near (John xix. 42) made the performance of the interment simpler. A coffin, which even to-day is only used in Palestine for the carrying of the corpse to the grave, was, in the case of a rock grave, still more superfluous. The grave clothes alone could not be done without, since all the clothes of Jesus had been taken away from Him (Mt. xxvii. 59; Mk. xv. 46; Lk. xxiii. 53; John xix. 40). That according to St Mark these were bought, may be due to an inaccurate account of the Evangelist. Yet it is not impossible that St Mark was not aware

[1] Cf. Siphre on Deut. 114 b; Sanh. vi. 4.

of the prohibition concerning working on the first day of the Feast, or, it may be, he was not quite certain when this day terminated. According to Mk. xiv. 12 (similarly Lk. xxii. 7), the Passover meal was prepared 'on the first day of the unleavened bread, when the Passover was slaughtered'. In Mt. xxvi. 17 the last half of the sentence is missing; but even so, the expression is extraordinarily strange. No instructed Jew could have called the eve of the Feast 'the first day of the Feast'; only a Gentile could possibly have thought of the day of the offering of the Passover lamb and the night of the Passover meal as the first day of the Feast.[1] When I was editing Franz Delitzsch's Hebrew New Testament, I felt strongly what a difficult task was that of a translator of a Biblical text, a text which he is not allowed to alter, however awkward it may sound in the language into which it is being transferred, in this case Hebrew. Perhaps the Synoptists considered the day of the Crucifixion as the second day of the Feast of the unleavened bread, in that case only a half-festival, on which work was not prohibited.

In one point alone is the Burial of our Lord an unreconcilable contradiction to Jewish traditional Law. Criminals had to be buried in special burying-places of the court of justice, and not in family graves; the beheaded and the strangled by themselves, and the stoned and burned also by themselves:[2] as the pious and the wicked could not be buried together, so neither could different classes of criminals.[3] Even to take part in the burial of those condemned to death was not allowed.[4] But Joseph of Arimathaea put Jesus in a sepulchre which he probably had prepared for himself (Mt. xxvii. 60; Lk. xxiii. 53; John xix. 41); which means that he did not consider Him to be a transgressor. This was an act of protest against the condemnation of our

[1] Even Josephus suggests it, when he apparently supposes that (*Ant.* III. 10. 5; cf. II. 14. 6) the Passah was not only slaughtered, but also eaten on the 14th of Nisan, and when, in accordance with Ex. xii. 6, 14 f., he lets the Feast of the unleavened bread, lasting seven days, follow this entire celebration of the Passover lamb, the chaos is still more increased, because at that time the Feast of the unleavened bread was simply called 'Passah'; *Ant.* XIV. 2. 1; XVII. 9. 3; XVIII. 2. 2; *Bell. Jud.* II. 1. 3; VI. 9. 3; Lk. xxii. 1; Pes. ix. 5; Tos. Pes. viii. 21; Shek. iii. 1; cf. Ned. viii. 2, 5; p. Ned. 44 a; Sanh. 21 b; Tg. Yer. I. Exod. xxxiv. 25; Lev. xxiii. 15.

[2] Sanh. vi. 5.

[3] b. Sanh. 47 a; p. Sanh. 23 d.

[4] Sem. ii. 7.

Lord, and thus an unconscious contradiction to the prophetic word (Isa. liii. 9), according to which, the Servant of the Lord would be rejected even at His burial and treated like a transgressor, and this honourable interment was, from the point of view of the Jewish authorities of the time, given to a 'criminal'.

XIII. THE LAST SUPPER AS A PASSOVER MEAL

After what has been pointed out, the Synoptists' account, carelessly as it slides over certain points which might have appeared dubious to Pharisaic Judaism, can be well harmonised with their chronology. When we consider, for the above reasons, their presentation, as compared with that of the Fourth Gospel, as more in keeping with the words and facts which they describe, we cannot avoid doing it also in reference to the time and the character of the Last Supper. Just the fact that the Words of the Institution do not necessarily imply a Passover meal shows that they would not have subsequently changed an ordinary meal to that of a Passover and furnished the narrative with the details which are connected with such a meal. And, had they, consciously or unconsciously, reconstructed the scene in order to emphasise its Jewish connexion, it would have been easy for them to have presented a closer relationship of the words and actions of Jesus to the Passover lamb. That they did not do it shows the objectivity of the account, which we prefer to that of the Fourth Gospel. But even supposing that the presentation of the Synoptists (which in Lk. xxii. 15 has been strengthened by a saying of our Lord relating to the Passover) was not true to fact, it is important to show how the Last Supper was conceived by those whose tradition they represented.

I. THE PREPARATIONS

That the Last Supper was to have been observed as a Passover meal, our Lord Himself expressly stated (Mt. xxvi. 18; Mk. xiv. 14; Lk. xxii. 11). That was the reason why it was not held in the usual place where Jesus lodged, but in the 'city' (Mt. xxvi. 18; Mk. xiv. 13; Lk. xxii. 10), i.e. in Jerusalem, in accordance with the rule, founded on Deut. xvi. 7, that the Passover should be celebrated in the place chosen by God. Originally this meal was consumed in the fore-court of the Temple,[1] but when the multitude of the Passover lambs increased,[2] there was no room for all the participants. Moreover, the quarrels and disorders which were unavoidable at sacrificial meals, when wine was consumed, certainly also contributed to the reflexion that, after all, the Deuteronomic passage does not state that the meal had to be consumed in the Sanctuary, and so the words, 'in the place which the Lord will choose', were interpreted to refer to the whole of Jerusalem;[3] and the whole area within the walls (with the exception of the outer court of the Temple), which was taken to be equal to the camp of the Israelites in the desert, was considered as the place for the Passover meal, as well as for all sacrificial meals of the lower degree (Hebrew *ḳodāshīm ḳallīm*),[4] while Bethphage was considered to be outside this area.[5]

In Mt. xxvi. 18; Mk. xiv. 14; Lk. xxii. 11, it is taken for granted that the owner of the house would be willing, without much ado, to prepare a place for the Passover meal. *This is in keeping with the teaching of the Jewish tradition that the houses of Jerusalem were the common property of the people and should not therefore be let for money.*[6] A house might be sold, but not the ground.[7] Even for the divans and bolsters no payment was to be asked; the only compensation was the skins of the sacrificial animals. It is stated that no one in Jerusalem looked in vain for an oven (*tannūr*) in which to roast the Passover lamb, or for a lodging for the night;[8] no one ever said: 'I cannot spend the night in Jerusalem, there is not enough room for me'.[9] It appears that it was a charge upon the estates of Jerusalem to keep places for the pilgrims, and so there was nothing extraordinary in the fact that the owner of the house granted

[1] 2 Chron. xxxv. 13; Jubil. xlix. 16 f.
[2] According to Jos. *Bell. Jud.* VI. 9. 3, there were 256,000 Passover lambs; according to another tradition (Tos. Pes. iv. 3), 1,200,000.
[3] Kel. i. 8; Seb. v. 8; Makk. iii. 3; Siphre on Num. 69 (18 a).
[4] Num. R. 7 (36 b); Tos. Kel. Bab. k. i. 12; b. Seb. 116 b; Siphre on Num. i. (1 b).
[5] Cf. above and *O.W.* 269 f.
[6] Tos. Maas. Sh. i. 12; b. Meg. 26 a; cf. concerning the claims of the Tribes on Jerusalem, Dalman in *Graf Baudissin-Festschrift*, 116.
[7] Ab. d. R. N. 35.
[8] *Ibid.* b. Meg. 26 a.
[9] Ab. v. 5.

the request of the Disciples; it was more surprising that they encountered one who still had a free place to offer.

According to Mk. xiv. 15; Lk. xxii. 12, the room given for the Passover meal would be 'furnished and ready' (ἐστρωμένον) for the purpose. In fact, not every room could be used for it. Although it is commanded in the Law (Exod. xii. 11) that the Israelites should eat the Passover with girdled garment, staves in hands and sandals on feet (i.e. prepared to start in haste on a long journey), this referred to 'that time' only, i.e. to the time of the Exodus, but not to 'all generations'.[1] The Jews differ in this from the Samaritans, who even now swallow down the Passover lamb in great haste, as if preparing for a sudden journey;[2] but the former consider it essential that the eating of the Passover should have the real character of a festive meal, in which free men, not slaves, take part. The slave eats standing; the Israelite, reclining at the Passover meal, demonstrates that his people had attained freedom from Egyptian bondage.[3] This, even the poorest Jew is obliged to show forth; he partakes of the meal to this day neither standing nor sitting, but reclining.[4] For this attitude at a meal post-Biblical Hebrew uses the term *hēsēb*, 'to make a round',[5] i.e. to curl up. The partakers of the meal were called *mesubbīn*, 'those united for the round'.[6] In the Targums we find another word, describing the same pose—*asḥar*, or its reflective form, *isteḥar*.[7] In the Galilaean Aramaic idiom the word *reba'*, 'to lie down', corresponds to this.[8] In a parable a king commanded each of his guests to bring with him something on which he could *lie* at table (*'al mā deyirba'*).[9] This word is also used in the Pal. Evang. (Lk. xxii. 14 and in other places), while the Peshito has *istēmēkh*, 'leaning', instead.[10] The

[1] Tg. Yer. I. to Exod. xii. 11 in agreement with Pes. ix. 5; Mech. 7 a; Siphre Deut. 130 (101 a).

[2] Linder, *P.J.B.* 1912, 119; Dalman, *ibid.* 129; Whiting, *Samaritanernas Påskfest*, 42 f.

[3] p. Pes. 37 b.

[4] Pes. x. 1.

[5] Pes. x. 1; Ber. vi. 6; Tos. Ber. v. 21; Eccl. R. vii. 12 (105 b). It has this meaning perhaps also in 1 Sam. xvi. 11, where, instead of *nāsōb*, it ought to be *nāsēb*.

[6] p. Ber. 10 a; Pes. 37 b.

[7] Onk. Gen. xxxvii. 25; xliii. 33; Exod. xxxii. 6; Tg. 1 Kings x. 5.

[8] p. Ber. 12 b; Taan. 66 a.

[9] Eccl. R. iii. 9 (82 b).

[10] With this corresponds the Syr. *semākā* for συμπόσιον, Mk. vi. 39, Pesh.; which occurs in the same meaning in Petra, cf. Dalman, *Petra*, 61.

room prepared for this reclining at a meal is called in the Targum *bēt asḥārūtā*, 'the place of the table-round',[1] and the table itself is called *asḥārūtā*.[2] In daily life they used in Palestine the Greek designation τρικλίνιον, in the Aramaic form *ṭriḳlīn*,[3] i.e. the reclining place for three. Such a room had to be, according to Rabbinic Law, ten ells long, broad, and high;[4] this height seems to be rather extreme, but in the East airy spaces are a necessity.

When, in 1900, I was present in Jerusalem at a Passover celebration of South Arabian Jews, the mattresses for the participants were spread, according to the usual custom of the East, on the floor. But according to Jewish tradition it seems that they were formerly put upon wooden stands; for the guests, who had already gathered in the dining-room, had to 'ascend' (Hebrew '*ālā*)[5] for the festive meal.

Mention is made of the table on which the dishes stood[6] and of the food which remained, therefore the expression was used 'to eat at the table' (Hebrew *ākhal 'al shulḥān*, Ab. iii. 3; Aramaic *akhal 'al pātūrā*, Lev. R. 9), and the fallen crumbs (Hebrew *pērurīn*) could be collected from under the table.[7] We find illustrations of these table customs in Petra. Triklines and stibads are cut in the rock, and the reclining place (either cornered or round like a horseshoe) rises to about 90 cm. above the ground and usually slopes a little in the direction of the feet. At the headside, i.e. on the inside, there is a somewhat deepened edge, which takes the place of the table.[8]

Among the Nabataeans, that is to say, also in Petra, thirteen persons were considered to be the normal number of participators in a banquet,[9] so that about five persons must have taken their places on the right and on the left of the three reclining-places of the *triklinium*, three persons remaining to seat themselves on the

[1] Tg. on 1 Sam. ix. 13 f., xix. 25.
[2] Tg. on 1 Sam. ix. 22; 1 Kings x. 5.
[3] p. R. h. S. 59 b; Lev. R. 16 (41 b). [4] Bab. b. vi. 4.
[5] Tos. Ber. iv. 8; v. 20; Eccl. R. vii. 12 (105 b).
[6] Tos. Sab. xvi. 6; Pes. v. 3; b. Pes. 100 b.
[7] Tos. Ber. vi. 4; p. Mo. k. 81 b; Sanh. 26 b; cf. Mt. xv. 27; Lk. xvi. 21.
[8] Dalman, *Petra*, 89 f.; *Neue Petraforschungen*, 28 f.; Bachmann-Watzinger-Wiegand, *Petra*, 1921, 91.
[9] Strabo, XVI. 4. 26.

centre narrower one;[1] *and thirteen is exactly the number of those who took part at the Last Supper* (Mt. xxvi. 20; Mk. xiv. 18; Lk. xxii. 14). According to the Law (Exod. xii. 3 f.), the house-party should, when necessary, be increased by neighbours, so that the Passover might be entirely consumed; later ten persons were considered to be the necessary minimum of participants.[2] Traditional Law ordered that for each person there should be at least a portion as big as an olive, i.e. perhaps about ten grams,[3] and it also allowed an extension of the table-fellowship to a number at which the consumption of the Passover lamb would, according to our ideas, be almost merely symbolic. The Apostolic company did not, in any case, exceed this number. It corresponded also to the traditional ruling in so far that it was not a house-gathering as described in Exodus, but a casually-composed offering-fellowship, kept together by the fact that in its name and with its knowledge (as adults)[4] the lamb was bought and then slaughtered in the Temple.[5]

From Exod. xii. 27 it was deduced that only at the 'first Passover' was the family the nucleus of the Passover company.[6] It was not permissible to join such a company of sacrificers (*ḥabūrā*) after the lamb had been slaughtered, at any rate, not after the blood had been poured out at the altar;[7] nor was the distribution of a part of the Passover meal to non-members permitted.[8]

That the Last Supper presupposes a preceding Paschal sacrifice is suggested in Mk. xiv. 12; Lk. xxii. 7, since they allude in a general way to the slaughtering of the Passover lamb. But the narratives do not directly state that a lamb was ordered, thus saying nothing of the buying of the lamb, which, according to Exod. xii. 3, ought to have been done already on the 10th of Nisan, that is, four days before the Feast; but according to tradition this was not obligatory in later times.[9] As every adult

[1] Cf. Dalman, *Petra*, 90.
[2] Tos. Pes. iv. 3; Jos. *Bell. Jud.* VI. 9. 3.
[3] Mech. 5 b; Pes. viii. 3, 7; Tos. Pes. vii. 6; b. Sukk. 42 b; cf. *P.J.B.* 1912, 122 f.
[4] Tos. Pes. vii. 4.
[5] Pes. v. 3; vi. 6.
[6] Mech. 18 a; Tg. Yer. I. on Exod. xii. 47; cf. Tos. Pes. viii. 12, 13.
[7] Pes. viii. 3; cf. ix. 8–11.
[8] Tos. Pes. vi. 11.
[9] Mech. 4 a, 5 b; Pes. ix. 5.

Israelite had, according to Num. ix. 13, to keep the Passover, i.e. to take part in the slaughtering of the Passover lamb (unless he be at a long distance from the sanctuary), the neglect of which incurred Divine punishment, there can be no doubt that it was observed in our Lord's circle. Hence it need not be asked whether Jesus fulfilled this duty: not only in the last year of His life on earth, but as often as He was present in Jerusalem at Passover time, from His twelfth year onward (Lk. ii. 41 f.), the Passover lamb was also offered in His name.[1] Our Lord's going to Jerusalem for the Passover was (although not mentioned in the Synoptic narrative, for according to Mt. xx. 17 f.; Mk. x. 33; Lk. xviii. 31, He went only to die there; it is different in St John),[2] primarily, not so much in order to participate in the festivities, but a pilgrimage to the God-chosen spot for the sake of slaughtering the Passover lamb at the prescribed time in the evening of the 14th of Nisan (Deut. xvi. 6). It was not, however, necessary for our Lord Himself, as the 'Paterfamilias' of His disciples, to buy the lamb. The slaughtering of it in the Temple on the 14th of Nisan, at the north side of the altar, together with the thousands of the people who had come for a like purpose, while the *Hallel* (Psalms cxiii to cxviii) was being sung and the priests offered its blood and its pieces of fat,[3] could be performed by someone else in the name of the whole company; even an Israelitish slave might be entrusted with that task.[4]

The Law fixed the time for the slaughtering of the Passover lamb (Exod. xii. 6; Lev. xxiii. 5; Num. ix. 3, 5) as 'between the two evenings'. Tradition understood this to mean the time

[1] According to Beer, *Pesachim*, 48, 174, a minor was excluded from participation in the Feast. However, only the levitically impure were excluded, Num. ix. 6, 10. A minor could even become a member of a sacrificing fellowship if he were old enough to consume a piece not smaller than an olive of the sacrificial meat, Pes. viii. 7; Tos. Pes. vi. 4; Hag. i. 2. The duty of participating in the sacrifice undoubtedly began with puberty, Tos. Hag. i. 3, with which must be connected Lk. ii. 41 f.; but for the appearing at the festival it is put back to the earliest age at which any kind of co-operation is possible. None of these duties refers to a woman. See Hag. i. 1; p. Hag. 75 d, 76 a; Mech. 101 b; Siphre Deut. 102 b.

[2] See above.

[3] 2 Chron. xxxv. 11 f.; Jubil. xlix. 20; Pes. v. 6, 10; Tos. Pes. viii. 14.

[4] Pes. viii. 2.

between the afternoon and sunset.[1] As the hour of the daily evening sacrifice is fixed by the same phrase (Exod. xxix. 39; Num. xxviii. 4, 8), the time of slaughtering of the Passover lamb was set to occur after the evening sacrifice.[2] Eventually, 2.30 p.m. was considered to be the boundary between the two, although the validity of a Passover lamb slaughtered earlier but after noon was not questioned.[3] That this was also the practice in the time of our Lord, can be gathered from Jubil. xlix. 10, 12, where the time between two and six o'clock was considered to be the offering time; and from Josephus,[4] who limits it to the time between three and five p.m. The Samaritans, however, think (and probably rightly) of the time as being between the reddening of the sun before setting and the fading of the sunset glow.[5] The large number of the sacrificial animals probably occasioned a different understanding of the Biblical phrase.

The Evangelists, in narrating the 'preparation' of the Passover by the two disciples sent out by our Lord (Mt. xxvi. 17, 19; Mk. xiv. 12, 15 f.; Lk. xxii. 8 f., 12), thought exclusively of the room for the celebration, taking it for granted that the Passover lamb was there and that only the question concerning the place where the meal was to be held had to be settled. The whole emphasis is on the manner of appointing this place; our Lord's direct indication (Mt. xxvi. 18) or circumstances (Mk. xiv. 13; Lk. xxii. 10) would determine it. The narrators probably wished to show forth herewith the miraculous power of our Lord in perceiving and directing coming events; the real purpose of our Lord, however, was probably to prepare a place for an undisturbed meal. It was known only to a few because it was found late in the day; the traitor must have got to know of it only when he was led there with the others. We are thus left without information concerning the person who slaughtered the lamb in the Temple and of him who, after the animal had been

[1] Mech. 6 a; Siphra, 100 b; Pes. v. 3; p. Pes. 31 c. Beer (*Pesachim*, 47) speaks erroneously of the Pharisaic fixing of the time between the third hour (decline of the sun) and the sixth hour (setting of the sun). Cf Dalman, *Arbeit und Sitte in Palästina*, I. 596.

[2] Siphre Num. 53 b.

[3] Pes. v. 1, 3.

[4] *Bell. Jud.* VI. 9. 3.

[5] Dalman, *P.J.B.* 1912, 123; cf. Linder, *ibid.* 111; Whiting, *Samaritanernas Påskfest*, 35.

skinned,[1] carried it on his back to the banqueting-house,[2] the owner of which house finally receiving the skin. In the court of this house, at any rate in the open air,[3] was the baking-oven in the form of a cylinder (*tannūr*), inside of which the lamb was laid upon a spit in the form of a cross;[4] for, according to Exod. xii. 9, the Passover lamb was to be roasted, not boiled.[5] But the unleavened bread, the bitter herbs, and a certain kind of sauce, had to be taken into account. It is possible that house-owners in Jerusalem had such additional articles appertaining to the Passover celebration in readiness; but it is hardly conceivable that this extended also to Passover *lambs*, so that additional guests could, against tradition, subsequently join the supper-fellowship of their host. And so our Lord's messengers would only have had to see that everything necessary was offered to them for the celebration, and that, in the right proportion and in its proper place in the chamber. Probably the Evangelists supposed it to have been somewhat in this fashion; but it is equally possible that in reality things turned out to be different, and that the reason why the disciples merely asked concerning the place where the meal should be held was because all the rest would then follow in its natural order. In the latter case, the proceedings must have been somewhat like this: first, the messengers ascertained the place and made arrangements that the room should be put in order; then one of them would go to the market to purchase the things necessary for the Feast (John xiii. 29), while the other would repair to the Temple to slaughter the lamb (also bought at the market) and bring it to the banqueting-place, where it would be prepared. One, finally, would return to the Master, to report that everything was ready and lead Him and the others to the place.

The afternoon would be filled with these preparations. It is not recorded when the meal actually began. From the fact that the time of the slaughtering of the lamb was to have been 'between the two evenings' (Exod. xii. 6), i.e., as we have seen,[6]

[1] Pes. v. 9. [2] b. Pes. 65 b. [3] p. Taan. 66 d.
[4] Cf. for this Linder, *P.J.B.* 1912, 113 f.; Dalman, *ibid.* 125 f.; Whiting, *Samaritanernas Påskfest*, 39, pictures 46 to 52.
[5] Pes. vii. 1; Mech. 9 a; p. Pes. 34 a; b. Pes. 74 a.
[6] See above, p. 111.

according to Rabbinic interpretation, between afternoon and sunset, and, in fact, only after the offering of the daily sacrifice at half-past two in the afternoon,[1] it was concluded that the meal, which, according to Exod. xii. 8, was to be eaten at night, could begin with 'the second evening', i.e. about sunset.[2]

If, however, through the tremendous pressure of the slaughtering at the Temple, one's turn came shortly before sunset (and the roasting of the lamb would take about three hours or even more), it would be about nine o'clock in the evening that the company could settle down at table.

The great hall in which the meal took place was, according to Mk. xiv. 15; Lk. xxii. 12, an ἀνώγαιον, i.e. a room added to the top of the house proper. A hall on the first floor is shown in Jerusalem, since the end of the fourth century, as the place of the Last Supper, although it would appear that the tradition that it was a part of old Jerusalem refers merely to a building which once had been there.[3] We find also in other sources that sometimes a *triklinium* was situated on the upper floor. A Rabbi who studied in such a room summoned a street-hawker to 'ascend' to him.[4] An upper room (Aramaic '*illītā*), in which one could be undisturbed and hidden,[5] was a favourite meeting-place for scholars,[6] as it was also for the Disciples of our Lord (Acts i. 13; cf. xx. 8). That even three-floored houses were not infrequent, is implied in a later narrative concerning Jerusalem,[7] and is directly recorded of Troas (Acts xx. 9). Probably the uppermost floor of the house often had the largest room, which was even provided with windows (Acts xx. 9), and in which there was no lack of air and light, should the moonlight-night of the Passover-festival make lamps (Acts xx. 8) superfluous.

In such an upper hall Jesus 'reclined' with the Twelve for the meal (Mt. xxvi. 20; Mk. xiv. 18; Lk. xxii. 14). We possess an ancient direction of the procedure for such a banquet.[8]

[1] Pes. v. 1.

[2] Jubil. xlix. 12; Pes. x. 9; Seb. v. 8; Mech. 6 b; Tg. Yer. I. on Exod. xii. 8; on Deut. xvi. 6.

[3] *O.W.* 333 f.

[4] Lev. R. 16 (41 a).

[5] p. Sanh. 23 c; Ab. z. 14 a; Acts x. 9.

[6] p. Pes. 30 b; Sanh. 21 b; Hor. 48 b; b. Sab. 13 b; Men. 41 b; Kid. 40 b

[7] Lam. R. i. 1 (18 b).

[8] Tos. Ber. iv. 8; p. Ber. 10 d; b. Ber. 43 a.

First, the guests were offered (on a special table) a kind of 'hors-d'œuvre', for which they sat on simple seats and couches. During this preliminary meal each participant was considered as a unit and had to say the benedictions in connexion with the food, individually. At the Passover meal this *apéritif* was probably joined to the proper meal, and the guests ascended to the *triklinium* right away, forming a closed corporate table-fellowship, which became, as it were, *one* before God, so that the benedictions and the 'table-prayer' were duties to be carried out in unison. The consideration of rank was almost unavoidable at the apportioning of the places, and this explains why, according to Lk. xxii. 24, even at the Last Supper the Disciples could occupy themselves with this question. Generally the scribes wished to sit at the head of the table, even to the exclusion of the host (Mt. xxiii. 6; Mk. xii. 39; Lk. xx. 46).[1] Of the three reclining seats (which number can be considered as normal) the first seat of honour was at the 'head' of the middle one; the second 'above', i.e. on the right of it; the third 'below', i.e. to the left of the first.[2] If the head of the middle reclining seat was at its left end, then the second place must have been on the same seat; the third at the right end of that seat, standing at the left, where, among the Romans, the house-father reclined. Yet the different order of the second and third places would probably correspond better with the terminology of the Jewish regulation. Jesus had at table John 'at His breast' (John xiii. 25; xxi. 20), or 'in His bosom' (John xiii. 23). A disciple of the Rabbis thus described the Passover meal of his teacher: 'We lay on one another's knees.'[3] As it was always the custom to lean upon the left arm,[4] in order to keep the right arm free for the food, one had the neighbour at the right, in front of the breast, and lay behind his back. Therefore, if John was in this position, he was at the second place of honour after the Master, if our Lord occupied the first place; Peter, who, according to Lk. xxii. 8, prepared the meal together with John, probably sat at the third place, i.e. with legs outstretched behind our Lord.

[1] Cf. above, p. 65 f.
[2] Tos. Ber. v. 5; p. Taan. 68 a; b. Ber. 46 b.
[3] b. Pes. 108 a.
[4] *Ibid.*

Every meal, especially when bread was used, was looked upon as sacrificial and had, according to Rabbinic ordinance, to begin and end[1] with the rite of the washing of hands (Hebrew *neṭīlat yādayim*),[2] so that even 'common food' (Hebrew *ḥullīn*) should be consumed in 'purity'. Especially the 'associates of the scholars' took it upon themselves to practise this rite.[3] The disciples of our Lord and He Himself did not usually observe it (Mt. xv. 1 f.; Mk. vii. 1 f.; Lk. xi. 38),[4] but the Passover meal was actually a sacrificial meal in those days, and the Passover lamb, slaughtered in the Temple, belonged to the 'holies of a lower degree', which, according to Num. ix. 6, 10 (cf. Lev. vii. 19), had to be consumed in purity, as it is also presumed in the Fourth Gospel (xi. 55; xviii. 28), and, as one had to be particularly careful concerning purity at a festival,[5] it can be assumed that our Lord and His disciples adhered to it. It is not probable that He neglected to conform to a Biblical ordinance. He, as well as the Disciples, came to Jerusalem, according to John xii. 1, 12, five days before the Passover, so that they had ample time for the purification with the ashes of the red cow (Num. xix. 12, 19).[6] (Even one whose near relative died on the Passover Eve and had not yet been buried, was obliged to take a bath in order to be enabled to 'eat the Passover'.[7]) Perhaps they also used on that occasion the famous trough of Jehu.[8] And there can scarcely be any doubt that they also washed their

[1] Tos. Ber. v. 5; p. Ber. 12 a. In case of necessity, the performance of the rite in the morning (or in the case of a donkey-driver on a journey wherever he finds water) can hold good for the whole day; p. Ber. 12 a; b. Ḥull. 106 b.

[2] Concerning the manner in which it was to be done, see Yad. ii. 3; Tos. Yad. ii. 2, 4; b. Ḥull. 106 a.

[3] Tos. Dem. ii. 2.

[4] Apparently this refers to immersion, which, however, could not have taken place in a strange house. Hence W. Brandt's (*Jüdische Reinheitslehre*, 34 f.) reference to p. Ber. 6 c, according to which a certain person put himself in danger in order to bathe before food, is wrong. That case had probably to do with pollution.

[5] b. R. h. S. 16 b.

[6] The conception of the defilement by a dead body was extended to heathen dwelling places; Ohal. xviii. 7; Tos. Ohal. xviii. 11; John xviii. 28; cf. *O.W.* 298.

[7] Pes. viii. 8; p. Pes. 35 a; Hoz. 48 a. This bath abrogated even the law of he Sabbath rest when the Eve of the Passover was a Sabbath; Bez. ii. 2.

[8] Mikw. iv. 5; cf. *O.W.* 298.

hands before eating the Passover meal (forks were not used), in order to consume the sacrificial meat in undoubted purity.

According to the Jewish rite, the hands were not washed in a basin, but with elevated hand affused from above;[1] but it is not certain whether it is only the fingers as far as the second knuckle that had to be rinsed.[2] A basin for the catching up of the water was deemed unnecessary at the washing of hands before a meal,[3] but probably it was not lacking in a well-ordered household. The servant had to carry the water-jug, basin and towel, from one person to the other. The washing of the feet[4] was not a religious rite, but was appropriate when, like the disciples of our Lord on the Passover Eve, someone came from out-of-doors[5] with dusty or tired feet;[6] for this a basin must have been necessary.[7] The servant would for such an occasion gird himself with an apron, as Haman was supposed to have done when attending at Mordecai's bath,[8] and as our Lord presupposed it for him who serves at table (Lk. xvii. 8).

This washing, as well as the diluting of the wine, and the fetching of the dishes of food, required a servant (Aramaic *shammāsh*). When there was none, one of the company had to serve the rest. It happened that a Rabbi 'stood up and served the others', *ḳāēm umeshammēsh ḳummēhōn*, but that was felt to be something unusual. When a guest once criticised the behaviour of such a scholar-servant, the former was told: 'Is it not enough that thou reclinest, whilst he stands and serves? Let him now recline, and stand thou up instead of him and serve'.[9] Even Gamaliel once served his guests, and was said to have acted like Abraham, who served angels, although at the time he took them to be idolaters.[10] When disciples of Rabbis served,[11] they were expected to be particularly careful about the crumbs of bread falling from the table; a fragment of at least

[1] Tos. Yad. ii. 2.
[2] p. Ber. 12 a; b. Ḥull. 106 a.
[3] b. Ḥull. 105 a.
[4] *shazzēg riglaiyā*, p. Pea. 15 c; Kidd. 61 b; Meg. 74 a.
[5] p. Pea. 15 c.
[6] p. Ber. 5 b; Mo. k. 82 d; Yom. 44 b; Taan. 64 c.
[7] Yad. vi. 1; Kel. xx. 21.
[8] Lev. R. 28 (78 a); Pesikt. 72 a; cf. Esther R. vi. 11.
[9] p. Ber. 12 b.
[10] Mech. to Exod. xviii. 12 (59 a).
[11] Such a case is also reported in p. Ber. 11 c.

an olive size had to be picked up before the actual sweeping of the room (cf. Mt. xiv. 20; John vi. 12);[1] they were not allowed (as servants often were) to wipe with the crumbs their oily hands.[2] When our Lord stood up to serve (since no one else offered himself) He, in like manner, girded Himself with a towel only, as a servant, and washed the feet of His Disciples (John xiii. 4 f.). At the washing of hands the water was brought first to the youngest of the company;[3] if our Lord used this procedure, Peter (John xiii. 5 f.), whom He probably served last, must have been the oldest of the company.

This must have occasioned the Logion concerning the service of the greatest (Mt. xx. 26 f.; Mk. x. 43 f.), which Luke (xxii. 26 f.) connects with the Last Supper, thus demonstrating that the conventional idea that those who recline at table are of a higher rank than those who serve at it, was wrong, as was shown by His example. In Matthew and Mark it is connected with the death of our Lord: 'the Son of Man came not to be ministered unto, but to minister, and to give His soul as a ransom for many'. In Aramaic: *bar nāshā lā atā deyishtammash ēllā dīshammēsh weyittēn naphshēh purḳān ḥulāph saggīīn.*

The symbol of service was also a reminder of the fact that the personal rendering of service, i.e. the renunciation of one's rights for the sake of others, was the essential thing in His life-work. The motive of it was absolute devotion to others. The concluding sentence shows that He was willing to renounce even life itself, the highest earthly good; but not without mentioning the purpose. Ransom (Hebrew *pidyōn*; Aramaic *purḳān*) is, according to Exod. xxi. 30, substitute for the forfeited life. Rabbinic tradition thinks here of death decreed by God, from which the ransom frees. According to Akiba ransoms were paid for the life of the owner of the ox who killed a man, but not for the life of the man who was killed by the ox.[4] In the saying of our Lord it could only refer to the life which had been forfeited

[1] Tos. Ber. vi. 4; cf. p. Ber. 12 a (text corrupt).
[2] Tos. Ber. vi. 5; p. Ber. 12 b; b. Ber. 43 b.
[3] Tos. Ber. v. 6; p. Ber. 12 a.
[4] Mech. 87 a; Tg. Yer. I. on Exod. xxi. 29, according to which the Synhedrion defines the sum of the ransom. Concerning the whole legislation in connexion with the ransom, cf. Bab. k. iv. 5; Tos. Bab. k. iv. 6, 8.

through man's own sin, for which the Son of Man gave His soul as a ransom. It is significant that the acceptance of a ransom, as well as its amount, depended on the goodwill of him to whom it was offered. It belonged thus not to the domain of strict justice, with its forced executions of definitely settled performances, and was not applicable to murder (Num. xxxv. 31 f.),[1] but entered where the application of justice was declined. The 'many' whose life the service of the 'One' saves, gives an impression of the far-reaching significance of this service; the expression has most probably its Biblical background in Isa. liii. 10 f. The figure of the ransom has its counterpart there in the substitutive payment (*āshām*), and the 'many' refers to the Gentile world which will benefit by the suffering of the Servant of God. As 'redemption' is an important conception, it must be remembered that *purḳān* (ransom) also means redemption,[2] and the Redeemer is called in Aramaic *pārēḳ* or *pārōḳ*.[3] The Hebrew word for 'ransom' (*kōpher*) yields yet another relation, for it permits the following transition: *kuphrā kappārā*, 'ransom is propitiation',[4] namely 'like sin-offerings and guilt offerings'.[5] This connexion is already found in Exod. xxx. 12, 15 f., where the ransom (*kōpher*) of the half-shekel which was to be paid at the counting of the people is applied to the soul (i.e. to the life), for which in this way propitiation is made (*lekhappēr*).[6] The ransom, therefore, in verse 16 can be simply called 'propitiation money', *késeph hak-kippūrīm*. As our Lord, according to Mt. xvii. 24 f., had paid the half-shekel for Himself, it would be conceivable that this well-known tax caused the application of the figure; but it cannot be proved that the idea of the ransom was at that time directly connected with the Temple tax. We find however the following sentence pointing to Exod. xxx. 16: 'The Israelites should be pledged for their (unpaid) shekels, in order that the community-offerings should be bought with them; for the community-sacrifices

[1] Tg. Yer. I. renders here the Hebrew *kōpher* with *purḳān*; Onk. with *māmōn*, money.

[2] See Onk. Gen. xlix. 18.

[3] Cf. Lev. R. 32 (89 a); Lam. R. i. 16 (37 a).

[4] b. Bab. k. 40 a, 41 b; Makk. 2 b.

[5] b. Bab. k. 40 a.

[6] The ransom in connexion with the first-born (Num. iii. 46 f.) has a different background.

reconcile the Israelites with their Father in heaven, and so we find it written, "Thou shalt take the money of the propitiation from the sons of Israel"'.[1] Yet, the conceptions of 'redeeming' and 'reconciling' were not used by our Lord in connexion with His Death. Although the 'redemption of Jerusalem' which Hannah looked forward to (Lk. ii. 38), and the 'redemption' which our Lord's disciples will one day experience (Lk. xxi. 28), are also *purḳān* in Aramaic, as is the 'eternal redemption' of Isa. xlv. 17 Targum, and the 'recovery' in Lev. xxv. 26 Onk., which is the duty of him who 'recovers' (*pārēḳ*), these thoughts were not a part of our Lord's conception of ransom in that instance.

2. THE MEAL

At that time spoons and plates were not used; it was the custom that all should eat from a central dish. Bread, when in soft flat cakes (its natural form in the case of unleavened bread), was used as a spoon, as it is to this day in Northern Palestine. With a piece of bread broken off from the cake a bit of vegetable would be held, and thus dipped into the dish of broth. Good breeding demanded that the one who pronounced the benediction over the bread was to be the first to dip into the dish, and no one commenced eating before him.[2] It could happen that one person should dip into the dish at the same time as others, but be prevented from eating;[3] nevertheless, in ordinary circumstances, the dipping was followed by the eating of the morsel.[4] Exceptionally it once happened on a fast-day that some person dipped (*ṭeba'*) his morsel (*pissetēh*) into ashes.[5] Rabbi Meir, when fleeing from heathen persecution, sought to hide among Gentiles at a butcher's. When those present murmured: 'It is a Jew! Observe, how he will not eat pig', Rabbi Meir dipped his finger into the pig-blood, but very cleverly put another finger into his mouth.[6] A certain person saw in a dream that lettuces (*ḥassīn*) grew in his vineyard. It was interpreted to him as follows: 'Thy grapes turn to vinegar (*besīm*) and thou

[1] Tos. Shek. i. 6.
[2] Tos. Ber. v. 8; b. Ber. 47 a.
[3] Eccl. R. vii. 12 (105 b); Tos. Ber. v. 20.
[4] It is presupposed in Tos. Pes. x. 9.
[5] p. Taan. 69 c; Maas. sheni, 55 c.
[6] Eccl. R. vii. 12 (116 a); cf. b. Ab. z. 18 b.

takest lettuce and dippest it therein'.[1] Ruth was invited by Boas to dip her morsel into the vinegar (Ruth ii. 14), which last word Midrash and Targum take to mean *food prepared with* vinegar, since it was not customary to dip a morsel into vinegar alone.[2]

At the Passover-feast the prescribed bitter herbs could, of course, not be left out (Exod. xii. 8; Num. ix. 11). There was a choice of five different plants[3] for this purpose; there were two kinds of lettuce;[4] the *Eryngium creticum* (a kind of thistle); endive; and cress. As a sauce (as well as the customary vinegar or salt water) there was also one that was made from mashed fruit with vinegar (*ḥarōset*)[5]. The fruits used (according to Maimonides) were dates, figs, and raisins. It was the custom of Hillel, carrying out literally the command of Num. ix. 11, to take together as one morsel a little of each of the following: the meat of the Passover lamb, the unleavened bread, and the bitter herbs.[6] The dipping into the dish by each one of the company at the Passover meal (as in Mt. xxvi. 23; Mk. xiv. 20) fits in exactly with these table customs, as does John xiii. 26, that Jesus, through bestowing a morsel that He had dipped into the dish, indicated the traitor, and, by the same act, also showed His love for him.

The whole Passover meal centred round the roasted lamb, to which the name Passover really clung. The idea that the animal appeared absolutely whole at the meal is incorrect. It is true that the Jews, unlike the Samaritans, did not lay aside a portion for the priests,[7] but the wool was removed, the stomach opened, the lower joints loosened, and the fat burnt on the altar. Yet, in order to fulfil the commands in Exod. xii. 9, the head was not loosened, and the lower joints were laid with the bowels in the rump for the roasting;[8] at any rate, it was to be roasted whole.[9] It might arrive on the table, however, divided up, and,

1 p. Maas. sheni, 55 c.
2 Ruth R. 5 (15 a); cf. Lev. R. 34 (93 a); Tg. on Ruth ii. 14.
3 Pes. ii. 6.
4 *P.J.B.* 1912, 130. Cf. Dalman, *Arbeit und Sitte in Palästina*, I. 346 f., where all the plants in connexion with the Passover meal are dealt with.
5 Pes. ii. 8, x. 3; Tos. Pes. x. 9.
6 Tos. Pes. i. 34; p. Ḥall. 57 b; b. Pes. 115 a; Zeb. 79 a.
7 *P.J.B.* 1912, 125; Whiting, *Samaritanernas Påskfest*, 38, picture 49.
8 Pes. vii. 1; Mech. 9 a; Tos. Yom. Tob. ii. 15; *P.J.B.* 1912, 125 f.
9 Tos. Pes. vii. 2; p. Sab. 4 b.

indeed, in the process of roasting it often fell to pieces.[1] Each one then took from the meat-dish the piece he desired, unless the head of the house himself apportioned the meat, which, in the case of a large Passover gathering, was necessary. Care had to be taken that during the eating no bones should be broken, as is prescribed in Exod. xii. 46; Num. ix. 12; for that passage refers, according to the traditional interpretation, to the eating of the lamb, not to its handling before the roasting;[2] it was even thought that it referred only to bones to which meat clung.[3] For the loosening of the joints a knife could be applied,[4] but care had to be taken that none of the bones should be bitten through or broken to take out the marrow.[5] That greediness, which might lead to the breaking of bones in order to suck out the very marrow, was not to be expected at a Passover meal.[6] Besides, before the 'Passover lamb' the lamb of the 'festive-offerings' was eaten, so that the former would be partaken of by those whose appetite was already satisfied.[7] How small a portion of the Passover lamb was sufficient, has already been stated.[8]

It need not seem strange that our Lord did not use the Passover lamb as a symbol of His approaching Death, which He could, for instance, have done when distributing its flesh. Apart from the fact that there existed no rite in connexion with the distribution of the lamb which could have served Him as a starting-point for a symbolic interpretation, it is of significance that the post-Egyptian Passover-offering was not officially considered to be a means of propitiation. In Egypt the blood saved the Israelites from threatening destruction; the side-posts and the upper door-post of their houses (Exod. xii. 7) were, so to say, three altars on which the blood testified for the Israelites.[9] The Samaritans even now smear the entrances of their tents, put up on Mount Gerizim, with the blood of the Paschal lamb,[10]

[1] Among the Samaritans, Linder, *P.J.B.* 1912, 118; Whiting, *Samaritanernas Påskfest*, 41 f.

[2] Pes. vii. 11; Mech. 21 b; p. Pes. 35 a; b. Pes. 84 b; *P.J.B.* 1912, 131 f. Differently in Jubil. xlix. 13, where it is connected with the roasting. The transgression of this law was punished with 'forty less one' stripes, Tos. Pes. vi. 8.

[3] b. Pes. 84 b.

[4] Pes. vii. 12.

[5] Tos. Pes. vi. 10; Tg. Yer. I. on Exod. xii. 46.

[6] p. Pes. 33 c.

[7] Tos. Pes. v. 3.

[8] See p. 110.

[9] Pes. v. 5.

[10] *P.J.B.* 1912, 124; Whiting, *Samaritanernas Påskfest*, 36.

because they consider it as an ordinance for all time.[1] In the book of Jubilees (xlix. 15) we find an echo of the ancient idea of the protective significance of the Passover. Its observance, it is stated, protects Israel from plagues for a whole year. Of this conception, which in popular sacrificial customs prevails in Palestine until this day,[2] one can find no trace in later Judaism. The absence of the domestic blood-rite, which is recognised also in the book of Jubilees, is considered in Rabbinic literature to be one of the characteristics of the post-Egyptian Passover.[3] Yet the night of the Feast is a time of happiness, for, while praise and thanksgiving ascend to God, angels pour out the treasures of the dew upon the earth.[4]

The blood from the Passover lambs was caught by the priests, at the slaughtering place in the Temple, in a golden bowl. On this occasion the priests stood up to their knees in the blood,[5] and they would come in a long queue bringing it to the altar,[6] where in one jet it was jerked towards the north-eastern and south-western corners of the altar,[7] or, maybe, into the gutters which surrounded its base.[8]

None of the sacrificial blood was to come on to the horns of the altar, for the Passover was not a propitiatory sacrifice, not even according to Jubil. xlix. 9, 15, where the passage, interpreted by Beer[9] to mean an appeasing of God, merely speaks of 'well-pleasing' to God, which, according to Lev. xix. 5; xxii. 19, 20, is true of all burnt- and thank-offerings brought according to ordinance. Traditional Law classes the Passover sacrifice with the first-born and tithe-offerings.[10] According to the idea connected with it, the slaughtering and eating of the Passover lamb signified a remembrance of the redemption from Egyptian slavery: 'In every generation each one must consider that he himself went out from Egypt'.[11] But this remembrance, which

[1] Marka in *Bibliotheca Samaritana*, III. 33 b.

[2] Dalman, *Arbeit und Sitte in Palästina*, I. 30 f., 432.

[3] Pes. ix. 5; Tos. Pes. viii. 15.

[4] Tg. Yer. I. on Gen. xxvii. 1.

[5] p. Pes. 32 c.

[6] Pes. v. 5.

[7] 2 Chron. xxx. 16; xxxv. 11; Pes. v. 6, 8; Zeb. v. 8; Tos. Pes. iii. 11; Zeb. vi. 15; cf. Dalman, *Neue Petraforschungen und der heilige Felsen von Jerusalem*, 139 f.

[8] b. Pes. 121 a; Zeb. 37 a; p. Pes. 32 a; cf. *P.J.B.* 1912, 125.

[9] Pesachim, 49.

[10] Zeb. v. 7, 8; cf. *P.J.B.* 1912, 132.

[11] Pes. x. 5.

is ordered in Exod. xii. 26 f.; xiii. 8, is, together with all the rites connected with it, not merely a pious custom, but a duty, the negligence of which leads to Divine punishment (Num. ix. 13).[1] Before the Passover was eaten, it was said eucharistically: 'Blessed be He who sanctified us with His commandments and ordered us to eat the Passover'.[2]

The description of the unique significance of the Passover Eve would lack completeness without the mention of the relationship to the future Messianic redemption which it warrants and proclaims. Every thought of the redemption from Egypt, of which it is a memorial, must have led to a comparison between what had taken place and the present. Everything imperfect in the latter and not quite in tune with that redemption from slavery, must have awakened the hope of a future new redemption. The reality of God's act at the Exodus, in so far as it was believed and perceived as the foundation of the character of Israel as a People of God, was an assurance of the fact that the second Divine act could not but take place, when the success of the former one seemed to have been made void through human sin. The idea that the carrying out of the observance of the memorial feast according to the Law would affect the coming of this redemption, was not remote, and generated the hope that God would again assign the same chosen day for the exhibition of this still greater redemptive act. Thus it came about that the dawn of the future redemption was expected upon this day. The expression 'night of observance' (Hebrew *lēl shimmūrīm*), used in Exod. xii. 42 of the night of Exodus, was interpreted according to this idea: 'In it (in this night) they *were* redeemed, in it they *will* be redeemed'. Hence Onkelos (Exod. xii. 42) designates this night as *neṭīr* ('noted' and 'worthy of notice'). Targum Yer. I speaks even of 'the keeping (of this night) for redemption'; Yer. II refers the passage to the coming of the Messiah from Rome, the 'hiding place' (where he is kept) where he suffers before his appearance.[3]

[1] Jubil. xlix. 9; Siphre Num. 18 b; Kerit. i. 1.

[2] Pes. x. 9; Tos. Pes. x. 13.

[3] That Nisan is a month of redemption is accentuated in b. R. h. S. 11 d; Pesikt. 47 b; Tanch. on Exod. xii. 2; Exod. R. 15 (33 a); Sopher. xxi. 2; Sepher Zerubbabel, Jellinek, Beth ha-Midr. II. 55 f.

Kalin says in his Passover hymn 'Omez geburothekha':[1] 'Those two (barrenness and widowhood) Thou wilt suddenly bring on "Uzyt"[2] (Edom = Christendom) on Passover;—Thy hand will prevail, Thy right hand will be uplifted in the night when the Passover sacrifice will be sanctified, and ye speak again (as in Exod. xii. 27): "A Passover sacrifice (it is for God)"'. As Elijah was looked upon (according to Mal. iii. 1; iv. 5) as the herald of the coming Messiah,[3] it is natural that his appearance also was expected on this day,[4] and that the custom arose (it cannot as yet be traced to Talmudic times) of having at the Passover meal a cup of wine ready for him. Even now, after the pouring out of the third cup, the door is opened; which can only mean that on this night, as the 'night of safety' (*lēl shimmūrīm*), there is no need to fear that anything evil would enter; on the contrary, Elijah may appear.[5]

When our Lord wished to celebrate the Passover with His disciples, it was indeed the Passover of the Law that He had in mind. Its bread, bitter herbs and lamb were to Him primarily what they were meant to be in this celebration. The memories which were bound up with it did not exclude thoughts of a future redemption; but just the Passover flesh of the meal was a scarcely appropriate bearer, or medium, of such thoughts. When St Paul writes in 1 Cor. v. 7: 'For also our Passover has been slaughtered, Christ', and when St John sees the 'lamb' that was slaughtered stand in the midst of the throne of God (Rev. v. 6), they do not refer to the flesh of the Passover meal, but to the animal just slaughtered as a sacrifice, the violent death of which can be considered as a symbol of the Death of our Lord. That which stood ready on the table at the Passover meal, was not the lamb led to be slaughtered, with which our Lord could have compared Himself according to Isa. liii. 7; but it was a tasty roast which had probably already dropped apart, a toothsome dainty for a festive banquet, though probably

[1] Machzor Cremona (1560), 97 b (German rite); Machzor Bologna (1540) (Roman rite); Siddur Kolbo, 394 a; Schulchan Arukh, Orach Chaiyim, 480, 1 and Baer heteb; Landshuth, *Hagada*, p. xvi f., 44; Schick, *Siddur Minhagim*, 69 b, 72 b; Horowitz, *Mincha chadasha*, Jerusalem, 1867, 15 a f.

[2] Cf. Lam. iv. 21.

[3] Dalman, *Der leidende und der sterbende Messias*, 28 f., cf. Moore, *Judaism*, II. 357 f.

[4] Exod. R. 18 (48 b).

[5] *Ibid.*

the fat tail which the Samaritans eat with the lamb (according to Lev. iii. 9) had been burned on the altar. Anyone who has ever seen the Samaritans sit round the dish, ravenously munching their Passover meat,[1] understands how impossible it would have been to connect words meant to refer to a higher antitype of the Passover lamb, with the formless remnants of a sheep, surrounded by people thus eager to consume it. That our Lord did not connect the words of the Institution with the Paschal lamb cannot therefore be considered to be a proof that the Last Supper was not a Paschal meal.

3. THE WORDS OF OUR LORD CONCERNING THE PASSOVER MEAL

According to Lk. xxii. 15, our Lord, before the commencement of the Supper, spoke the following words: 'With desire I have desired to eat this Passover with you before I suffer'.

Aramaic: *meḥammādā ḥammēdt denēkhōl hādēn pisḥā 'immekhōn 'ad delā nēḥōsḥ.*

These words, not found in Matthew and Mark, are intensely Hebrew in form, the conception of the verb being strengthened by the corresponding abstract form (ἐπιθυμίᾳ ἐπεθύμησα), similar to the Hebrew use of the infinitive for the same purpose. Apart from O.T. quotations, this form of speech is found only in Acts iv. 17, E. P. Syr. v. 28; and xxiii. 14 (where, in Hebrew, an addition of a noun would be more appropriate). The Targums follow the original Hebrew in this, but to Biblical Aramaic this style is foreign; in the Galilaean dialect it is a rare exception; but in the Babylonian Jewish-Aramaic it is more frequent.[2] It is different when the word used for emphasis is an adjective, as in 'He loved them with perfect love' (Hebrew *ahābām ahabā gemūrā*).[3] Luke evidently presupposes a solemn expression, based on Biblical style, in the reproduction of which he follows the Septuagint. A suitable parallel is Gen. xxxi. 30, which passage Onkelos renders *ḥammādā ḥammēdta*, 'thou hast desired greatly'. However, it is uncertain whether this Biblicism was actually used by our Lord. One might suggest, as rather more

[1] See *Samaritanernas Påskfest*, picture 52.
[2] *W.J.* 34 f.; *Gram.* 2nd ed. 280.
[3] Lev. R. 2 (7 a).

idiomatic, *hawēt mitḥammad saggīn*, 'I have greatly desired', and point to p. Sab. 8 c, where we find the expression *hawō mitḥam-medīn miḥwe*, 'they desired to see'.

Of the eating of the Passover the phrase 'eating it' is used in (with the direct object) 2 Chron. xxx. 18; 'eating of it' (Hebrew *bō*, i.e. of the participation in it) in Exod. xii. 48. Only the former can be assumed in Mt. xxvi. 17; Mk. xiv. 12; Lk. xxii. 11; John xviii. 28. In Lk. xxii. 15 one should expect 'of it', but it is not there. Instead of an infinitive, the Pal. Evang. has the imperfect connected with *de*, but the Galilaean Aramaic demands first person plural (instead of singular).[1] One says in that dialect *habēh lī nishteyēh*, 'give it to me that we may drink it'; and even in Hebrew *'ad shennāphūg et yēnī*, 'until we dispel my intoxication (from wine)'.[2]

The words 'before I suffer' are somewhat difficult. The expression points back to πολλὰ παθεῖν, Mt. xvi. 21 (Mk. viii. 31; Lk. ix. 22), Mk. ix. 12 (cf. Mt. xvii. 12), Lk. xvii. 25; cf. xxiv. 26: ταῦτα παθεῖν. Without the object, as here, it appears also in Lk. xxiv. 46; Acts i. 3; iii. 18. The Pal. Evang. and the Peshito use here for πάσχειν the usual word for 'suffering': *ḥash*, which is also well known in Jewish-Galilaean. One suffers, *ḥāshēsh*, from pain in the bowels,[3] from toothache,[4] from the calculus.[5] 'He who suffers gets well eventually', *kōl deḥashēsh sōfēh mabrī*, says a proverb.[6] But in the Dominical words the reference is not to suffering, in contrast to being well, but to a suffering that includes in it His Death, the extent of which rests upon a special Divine decree, meant exclusively for Him, and which (according to Lk. xxiv. 44 f.) is written in the Law, in the Prophets, and in the Psalms. Isa. liii. 4, 7 could be considered to be the background for this expression, for it speaks there of the Servant of the Lord as being 'plagued', Hebrew *me'unne, na'ane*. In the Targum Isa. liii. 4; Ezek. xvi. 4, 7, the passive participle plural *me'annan*, which has the same root, is used for it. Were we to translate accordingly, it would be (in calling to mind the *ithpaal* of Onk. Lev. xxiii. 29): *'ad delā nit'annī*, 'before I shall be

[1] Cf. *Gram.* 265.
[2] p. Ter. 45 c; Lev. R. 37 (101 b).
[3] Lev. R. 37 (100 b).
[4] p. Kil. 32 b; Eccl. R. xi. 2 (127 a).
[5] Cant. R. ii. 16 (35 b).
[6] Lam. R. i. 1 (26 b).

plagued'. However, the word πάσχειν on our Lord's lips is not taken from any particular Scriptural passage, but is an expressive summary of what many passages contain. It is therefore rather bold to substitute παθεῖν by a word which is very close to it in meaning, but not entirely identical with it. Yet, as coming from our Lord, the word in its literal sense sounds rather strange (one feels it especially in Aramaic). It is scarcely probable that 'the suffering' has become to Him an already fixed expression, assumed to be understood by the Disciples without any further explanation. One expects an additional word, elucidating at least the thought that it was appointed by the Father, and expressed somewhat as follows: 'Until I suffer *according to all that is written concerning me*' (cf. Lk. xxii. 37); Aramaic '*ad delā nēḥōsh kekhōl mā dikhetīb 'alay*.

In the Greek-speaking Early Church the 'suffering' of the Χριστός must have become a fixed term, and from there ultimately it worked its way back into the words of our Lord. In Jewish terminology the idea of the 'chastisings' (*yissūrīm*) of the righteous, the propitiatory value of which is recognised on the basis of Isa. liii, and which is not absent from the conception of the Messiah, is closely related to it.[1] This expression is used of the punishment inflicted upon a son by his father (Deut. xxi. 18) and also of that inflicted by God (Lev. xxvi. 28), but the word can also refer to afflictions that are not punishments. When Ḥanina lamented: 'How heavy are the sufferings!' Joḥanan replied: 'But how great is their reward!'[2]; they bring to the sufferer valuable compensations in the age to come, and even now here. By means of suffering Israel received such precious gifts as the Law, the Land, and the future world.[3] But the suffering of the righteous has also a propitiatory value for others, as, for instance, in the case of the sufferings of Jehuda I[4] and Eleazar ben Shimon.[5] The latter even undertook to suffer voluntarily with this end in view, by saying: 'May all the

[1] Cf. *Der leidende und der sterbende Messias* and *Jesaja 53, das Prophetenwort vom Sühnleiden des Gottesknechtes*, 2nd ed. 1914; cf. also Levertoff, *Die religiöse Denkweise der Chasidim*, 154 f.

[2] Cant. R. ii. 16 (35 b).

[3] Mech. 73 a; Siphre Num. 73 b.

[4] p. Kil. 32 b; Ket. 35 a; b. Bab. m. 85 a.

[5] Eccl. R. xi. 2 (127 a); Pesikt. 94 b; cf. p. 58 f.

sufferings of Israel (*kōl yissūrēhōn deyisrāēl*) come upon me!' One might be tempted to base the expressions 'sufferings of Christ', παθήματα τοῦ Χριστοῦ (2 Cor. i. 5), θλίψεις τοῦ Χριστοῦ (Col. i. 24), on *yissūrē meshīḥā*, as Delitzsch does in the latter passage, while in the former one he uses *'innūyē ham-māshīaḥ*. In that case the corresponding verb in Lk. xxii. 15 would be *ityassar*, as it is said of Joḥanan: *ityassar wa'abad ḥāshēsh*, 'he was chastised and was made to suffer'.[1] Yet *'ad delā nityassar* would introduce a foreign element into the Words of our Lord, where παθεῖν places in the foreground the human feeling, not the Divine action. Here again it is quite impossible to concentrate fully into Jewish terminology all that the Words of Jesus mean.

The sentence following this (Lk. xxii. 16) gives the reason for the desire of our Lord: this Passover will be His last in this aeon. 'For I say unto you, I will not eat of it until it be fulfilled in the Kingdom of God'.

Aramaic: *deāmarnā lekhōn, delā nēkhōl tūb minnēh 'ad diyehē mitḳaiyam bemalkhūtā dishemaiyā.*

Nēkhōl minneh, 'we eat *of* it', seems to be smoother than the literal translation *nēkhelinnēh*, 'we eat it'. The Pal. Evang. also prefers the former. Our Lord probably used the expression 'Kingdom of heaven' instead of 'the Kingdom of God', *malkhūtā de'elāhā*.[2] Nestle originally explained the variant in D (καινὸν βρωθῇ for πληρωθῇ) by pointing out that the Hebrew *ākhal*, 'to eat', and *kālā*, 'to bring to an end', could easily be taken for one another. Later he considered πληρωθῇ as being a correction of the reading in D. This reading, however, has crept in through the similar expression in Mt. xxvi. 29; Mk. xiv. 25, and is at the same time a more comprehensible word than the not-easily understood 'fulfilment' of the Passover in the Kingdom of God. This 'being fulfilled' cannot mean merely 'being carried into effect' or 'being observed', as a commandment is fulfilled by being observed;[3] for the Passover stands here in the foreground of thought not as a commandment to be fulfilled but as a meal to be eaten. Neither is it permissible (because of

[1] Cant. R. ii. 16 (35 b). [2] Cf. *W.J.* 191 f.
[3] See above, p. 58.

2 Kings xxiii. 23; cf. Exod. xii. 48; Num. ix. 11, where *na'asā*, 'done,' is used of the Passover) to take the Dominical expression merely in the sense of 'done', which would have to be rendered into Aramaic by the Targumic *it'abēd*. If we are to stick to the expression in Luke, it can, in that case, hardly be taken as a parallel to the 'becoming full', συνπληροῦσθαι, of the day of Pentecost in Acts ii. 1; for, according to Lk. ix. 51, the latter is probably only a description of the final entrance of a day, which meant to the disciples of our Lord that one period had come to an end and a new one had begun, without referring to the counting of the seven weeks from the beginning of the harvest, commanded in Deut. xvi. 9; but this 'becoming full' (Aramaic *ishtelam* or *shelēm*) is not suitable here, where it has nothing to do with the conclusion of a period. Thus πληρωθῇ can only be understood as a rendering of *itḳaiyām*,[1] and the Passover is considered to be a prophecy to be fulfilled. The fulfilment in the domain of the Kingdom of God would, in this case, consist, not in a special Passover which will be revived, together with other festivals, in a more beautiful form, as, for instance, Rabbi Akiba prayed at the conclusion of the first part of the Hallel: 'Praised be He who redeemed us and redeemed our fathers from Egypt; so may the Lord our God and the God of our fathers let us reach in peace other festivals and pilgrimage-festivals in the future, to rejoice over the building of Thy city and have pleasure in Thy sacrificial service that we may eat there of Thy offerings and Passover-sacrifices'.[2] Our Lord, of course, did not think of the sacrificial service of the future and its joyous meals, but of the Meal of the Kingdom of God itself, concerning which He spoke also on another occasion (Lk. xiii. 29; xxii. 30). In that case, the fulfilment 'in' the Kingdom of God is not essentially different from the fulfilment 'through' it; for it is itself fundamentally the fulfilment of the Passover, as it brings into fruition, in the most perfect measure, and finally, the transition from bondage to freedom, and the consummation of the people of God.

[1] Cf. above, p. 58.   [2] Pes. x. 6.

4. THE CONCLUSION OF THE MEAL

Again we are reminded of the Paschal character of the Supper, when the Gospel narrators relate that a 'hymn' had been sung by our Lord and His disciples at the end of the Supper, before leaving the place where it was held (Mt. xxvi. 30; Mk. xiv. 26). Isa. xxx. 29 already shows that on a night in which a feast was inaugurated hymns were sung. Jewish tradition derives from this passage the duty of hymn-singing on a feast day.[1] Hence, the cycle of Psalms, called the *Hallel*, formed an integral part of every festival.[2] At the Passover this singing had to be performed by the people at the slaughtering of the Passover lambs in the Temple court,[3] and by every Paschal fellowship after the Passover meal.[4] According to Rabbinic tradition[5], such hymn-singing had taken place at the Egyptian Passover, as is also taken for granted in the Book of Jubilees (xlix. 6). The drinking of wine was indispensable on such occasions.[6] Of this joyous hymn-singing the proverb says: 'Even if the Pasch is only as big as an olive (i.e. for the individual participant),[7] the singing (*hallēlā*) cracks the roofs'.[8]

The first part of the singing had to begin before the actual meal. It ended with the conclusion of Psalm cxiii; according to some,[9] with Psalm cxiv; thus consisting at the most of Psalms cxiii and cxiv. After the meal and the consumption of the third cup of wine,[10] the second part, beginning with Psalm cxiv or cxv, followed; in which part it is certain that Psalm cxviii was included, for it was ordered that the end of this Psalm should, if possible, be chanted antiphonally with the children.[11] Possibly only one of the table-company sang all these Psalms and the others merely responded with the first verse as

[1] p. Pes. 36 d; b. Pes. 95 b; Araḥ. 10 b.
[2] Tos. Sukk. iii. 2; b. Taan. 28 b; Araḥ. 10 a.
[3] Pes. v. 7; ix. 3.
[4] Pes. ix. 3.
[5] Tos. Pes. viii. 22.
[6] b. Araḥ. 11 a; Jubil. xlix. 6.
[7] Cf. above, p. 110.
[8] p. Pes. 35 b; Cant. R. ii. 14 (33 b).
[9] Pes. x. 6; Tos. Pes. x. 9.
[10] See under XIV.
[11] Tos. Pes. x. 9; cf. b. Sukk. 38 b. According to Tos. Sot. vi. 3; p. Sot. 20 c, it sometimes happened that in the synagogue the precentor chanted the whole Hallel by himself and the congregation repeated after each verse the refrain of the beginning of the Psalm only. That could have been the case also at the Passover meal.

a refrain. The first part of the Hallel ended with an additional benediction—the praising of God, the Redeemer of Israel;[1] the second part was brought to an end by the 'benediction of song',[2] concerning the contents of which there was later a difference of opinion.[3] Psalm cxxxvi, the so-called Great Hallel, was also considered by some as a substitute for this.[4] On the other hand, an ordinary *epicomion*, i.e. the singing of secular drinking songs (which occasionally took place, together with the singing of Psalms, at circumcision celebrations),[5] was not permitted at the Passover.[6]

To our Lord Psalm cxviii (the conclusion of the Hallel) was very familiar. The verse concerning the stone rejected by the builders but becoming a corner-stone (Psalm cxviii. 22), He had applied to Himself when He uttered it against His adversaries at whose hands He expected death (Mt. xxi. 42; Mk. xii. 10; Lk. xx. 17); only a short time before, at His entry into the city and to the Temple, He was greeted with the Hosanna of this Psalm (*v.* 25) (Mt. xxi. 9, 15); its 'blessed be He who cometh in the name of the Lord' (*v.* 26) He considered (Mt. xxiii. 39) as the condition without which Israel should not see Him again: should it be fulfilled, then that which on the following morning He would proclaim to His judges as a verdict against them (Mt. xxvi. 64: 'From now ye shall see the Son of Man seated at the right hand of the power and coming with the clouds of heaven') would be turned into a blessing for His people. But at this moment the most important sentences in this Psalm must have been verses 17 f.: 'I shall not die, but live, and proclaim the works of the Lord. The Lord chastises me, but does not give me over to death'. With this watchword He stepped out from the Passover-chamber into the night of treachery.[7]

[1] Pes. x. 6; Tos. Pes. x. 9.

[2] Pes. x. 7.

[3] b. Pes. 118 a.

[4] p. Pes. 32 c; Taan. 67 a; b. Pes. 118 a, with uncertain tradition.

[5] Ruth R. 6 on iii. 13 (17 b); Eccl. R. vii. 8 (104 a).

[6] Pes. x. 8; Tos. Pes. x. 11; cf. p. Pes. 37 d, not understood by Beer, *Pesachim*, 199. Lietzmann, *Z.N.W.* 1926, 4 f., thinks of wanderings from one banquet to the other.

[7] Concerning the walk to Gethsemane and its relation to the Passover, cf. p. 93.

XIV. THE BENEDICTION AND THE WORDS CONCERNING THE BREAD AT THE INSTITUTION OF THE LORD'S SUPPER

The fact that our Lord, before the breaking and distributing of the Bread at the Paschal Supper, pronounced a 'blessing', makes it necessary to consider an important part of a pious Jewish custom.

The saying of grace before and (mostly) also after any kind of enjoyment,[1] especially that of food, became a fixed institution among the Jews long before Christ. At first it was probably performed only in connexion with sacrificial meals. According to 1 Sam. ix. 13, such a meal could not commence without being preceded by a 'blessing', which the Targum refers to the 'breaking of bread' with the blessing over food (*pārēs 'al mezōnā*). The saying of 'grace' at a sacrificial meal seems also to be assumed in Psalm xxii. 27; cxvi. 13; Isa. lxii. 9; and 'praise' after eating of Palestinian fruit, in Deut. viii. 10.[2] Subsequently it was held that 'the men of the great Synagogue', at the time of the last prophets, ordered that benedictions be said for every kind of enjoyment.[3] So the principle was laid down: 'He who enjoys any good things in this world without saying a blessing, is unfaithful (towards God's property), and is as though all commandments were not for him (i.e. he is, as it were, outside the Covenant, and can do what he likes)'.[4] Therefore Akiba enjoined: 'No pleasure should be partaken of without saying a blessing'.[5] Grace, especially before and after a proper meal, is absolutely obligatory.[6] Rabbi Meir (circa A.D. 130) said:[7] 'Thou findest not an Israelite who does not practise daily a hundred commandments'; and to prove it he pointed to the fact that no Israelite eats his bread without saying grace before and after.

This custom permeated the whole life of the Jewish people.

[1] Nid. vi. 10; Tos. Ber. iv. 10; b. Ber. 44 b; 37 a.

[2] On the latter passage traditional Jewish Law bases the duty of table-benedictions. Tos. Ber. vii. 1; p. Ber. 11 a; b. Ber. 48 b.

[3] b. Ber. 33 a; cf. M. Bloch, *Die Institutionen des Judentums*, I. 2. 202 f.

[4] Tos. Ber. iv. 1; p. Ber. 9 d.

[5] p. Ber. 10 a.

[6] Mech. 19 b; Tos. Ber. vii. 2; p. Ber. 11 a; Meg. 75 a; b. Ber. 48 b.

[7] p. Ber. 14 d.

St Paul had it in mind when he said (1 Tim. iv. 4): 'For every creature of God is good, and nothing is to be refused, if it be received with thanksgiving; for it is sanctified through the word of God and prayer' (cf. Rom. xiv. 6; 1 Cor. x. 30). Our Lord, who did not always conform to scribal ordinances, also followed Jewish tradition in this point. This is the meaning of *εὐλογεῖν*, often referred to in the Gospels in connexion with our Lord, i.e. the pronouncing of *εὐλογία* before the consumption of bread (Mt. xiv. 19; xxvi. 26; Mk. vi. 41; xiv. 22; Lk. xxiv. 30) and of wine (1 Cor. x. 16); also *εὐχαριστεῖν* (Mt. xv. 36; Mk. viii. 6; Lk. xxii. 19; John vi. 11, 23; 1 Cor. xi. 24) before the eating of bread, and (Mt. xxvi. 27; Mk. xiv. 23; Lk. xxii. 17) before the drinking of wine. It is true that these two terms can be differentiated in Hebrew and Aramaic: *εὐλογεῖν* would correspond to the Hebrew and the Aramaic *bārēkh*; *εὐχαριστεῖν* to the Hebrew *ōdé*, Aramaic *ōdī*. *Awdī* is also used in the Peshito; *ishtewaddī* of the same root—in the Pal. Evang. In the Jewish ritual the last but one benediction of the so-called 'eighteen benedictions' begins with *mōdīm anaḥnū*, which, therefore, is called *hōdāā*.[1] This word means 'thanksgiving', although it refers primarily to direct and public recognition of the reception of Divine benefits. Yet the application of this word to 'grace' before or after meals is quite foreign to the Jewish idiom. The only possible term is *bārēkh*. The different terms in the Gospels must thus be traced back to this single one. One can, however, understand the reason why Matthew and Mark use in the narratives dealing with the Last Supper 'bless' for the bread and 'thank' for the wine; because the latter took place at the conclusion of the meal. It is in any case to be borne in mind that it is not the elements of food and drink that were blest; these are not changed by the blessing into something new, to which the Divine now becomes somehow attached: the object of the benediction is God Himself, who is the Creator and Distributor of all good things. The relation between what is to be eaten or drunk and God consists in the fact that it comes from Him, and the significance of the blessing is just this, that

[1] Ber. v. 2, 3; Tos. Ber. iii. 14; p. Ber. 9 a; cf. W. J. (German edition), 300, 303.

before starting to eat and drink, the person recognises this fact. Only in so far are the food and the drink influenced by it as the blessing causes the consumption of them to become acts well-pleasing to God, the effect of which benefits the consumer. According to Jewish tradition, the blessing over wheaten bread was: 'Blessed art Thou who bringest forth food from the earth'.[1] Rab demanded that the name of God should be mentioned in the benediction, and Joḥanan that the sovereignty of God should be referred to.[2] Hence, the words *adōnāy elōhēnu, mēlekh hā'ōlām* ('Lord our God, King of the world') were added, and this became the fixed formula. But, nevertheless, the shepherd Benjamin was considered to have fulfilled his duty when he only prayed: 'Blessed be the Lord of this bread' (*berīkh mārēh dehāy pittā*).[3] Also the following were considered to be proper benedictions: when someone, for instance, on seeing white bread (*pittā neḳiyyā*) said: 'Blessed be He who created this wheat' (*berīkh diberā hādēn ḥiṭṭetā*);[4] or, seeing ordinary bread, said: 'Blessed be He who created this bread; how beautiful it is!'[5] One can take it for granted that our Lord referred to 'the Father in heaven' as the Giver of the bread. His blessing—if we assume that at the Paschal meal and at the blessing over the wine He used the more solemn liturgical form —would, in Aramaic, be as follows:

Berīkh att, abūnan debishemaiyā, demappēḳ laḥmā min ar'ā.

'Blessed art Thou, our Father in heaven, who bringeth forth bread from the earth'.

According to the fourth petition in the Lord's Prayer, and to His usual manner of speaking of God as the Dispenser of gifts to men and not (as in the Jewish formula) as Creator, His prayer might have taken another form, for instance:

Berīkh att, abūnan debishemaiyā, deyāhēb lan yōmā dēn laḥmā deṣorkhēnan (or *deḥusrānan*).[6]

'Blessed art Thou, our Father in heaven, who giveth us to-day the bread necessary for us'.

[1] Ber. vi. 1; Tos. Ber. iv. 5.
[2] b. Ber. 12 a; 40 b; cf. Siphre on Deut. 303 (128 b).
[3] b. Ber. 40 b. [4] p. Ned. 40 a. [5] Tos. Ber. iv. 5.
[6] Pesh. has the non-Palestinian *desunkānan*, 'our necessities'; the Pal. Evang.—the most improbable *de'utrīn*, 'of our riches' (i.e. 'our abundant bread').

The following Jewish prayer-formulae are parallels to this: 'I shall not leave this place until Thou hast satisfied me with the necessities of this day' (in reference to Deut. xxvi. 15);[1] and 'who prepareth the table according to the necessities of every individual and every body according to his needs'[2] (or 'sufficient for his needs').[3] This would specially explain how the Disciples recognised the Lord by His 'bread-breaking' (Lk. xxiv. 35), which need not have been a special way of breaking the bread, but referred rather to the whole ritual, including the eulogy. Jewish literature also speaks occasionally in this sense of the 'breaking of bread'.[4]

According to the peculiar opinion of Abba ben Ḥiyya, he who sits when eating should recline for the benediction, and he who reclines should cover his face for it.[5] It was more natural for him who reclined to sit up for the benediction, in order to have both hands free for the taking of the bread or the cup. This, in fact, is the official Rabbinic ordinance,[6] and we may assume that our Lord acted according to it.

He who pronounced the benediction had the bread in his hand at the time, which means that the 'taking' of the bread preceded the benediction. Our Lord 'took the bread' before saying the blessing (Mt. xxvi. 26; Mk. xiv. 22; Lk. xxii. 19; xxiv. 30; 1 Cor. xi. 23; cf. Mt. xiv. 19; xv. 36). This 'taking' of the bread is also mentioned in Rabbinic literature. It is related: *yehab lēh 'iggūlā deḳāsē* (read *deyiḳṣē*), *amar lēh sab bārēkh* (He gave him the bread in order that he might break [it, and] said to him: 'Take, speak the benediction');[7] *nāsēb 'iggūlā umebārēkh 'alōi* ('He takes the bread and speaks the blessing over it').[8] This 'taking', which is not to be confused with the laying of hands on one who is to be blessed (Gen. xlviii. 14; Mt. xix. 13, 15), purposes to show that it is the bread appointed for present use over which the blessing is to be spoken, in order that it should thereby be made fit for eating. This is the meaning

[1] Tanch. Ki tabo, 2; cf. p. Maas. sh. 56 c.
[2] Cant. R. vii. 2 (68 a).
[3] p. Ber. 8 b; Eccl. R. i. (65 b).
[4] b. Ber. 46 a; 47 a (where it also speaks of 'breaking' in the literal sense); p. Ber. 10 a; but cf. p. 138.
[5] p. Ber. 11 d.
[6] b, Ber. 51 b.
[7] p. Ber. 12 a; Lev. R. 9 (22 a).
[8] p. Ber. 10 a.

of *'aloi*, 'over it'. If it is a closed table fellowship, as at a Paschal meal, one of the company, at the commencement of the meal, says the blessing for all, which absolves all the other participants from their duty of saying it, but it has to be acknowledged by them with a loudly-pronounced 'amen'.[1] The father of the house is the most suitable person to say the benediction, 'because he knows the power of his bread'.[2] According to Rabbi Shim'on ben Yoḥai, the most suitable person to say the thanksgiving after the meal is the guest, as he can at the same time express gratitude to the host; it is essential that both the benediction before, and the thanksgiving after the meal should come from the heart.[3]

The one who says the benediction breaks the bread immediately after and distributes it among the participants, demonstrating thereby that all had been included in it.[4] Thus at the Last Supper our Lord 'broke it and gave it to the disciples (Mt. xxvi. 26; cf. Mk. xiv. 22; Lk. xxii. 19; xxiv. 30; in 1 Cor. xi. 24 only 'He broke it'). At the miraculous feedings also, the 'breaking' and 'distributing' (with the help of the Disciples) were the important factors, by which it was made clear that all the recipients of the bread were united before God into one table-fellowship (Mt. xiv. 19; xv. 36).[5]

For 'bread-breaking' *bāṣa'* is the usual Hebrew expression;[6] *ḳeṣā* is the Galilaean-Aramaic.[7] The Hebrew *pāras* for the distribution of bread already occurs in Isa. lviii. 7, and in later times *perūsā* meant a piece of bread in contrast to the whole loaf.[8] In both languages the expression merely means to separate, to tear off, not properly to break (which could only be used of a more or less firm or thick bread), and thus is applicable to every kind of bread, even to the soft loaves of pancake thickness which are often made in the East. It had,

[1] Ber. viii. 8; Tos. Ber. iii. 26; Meg. iv. 27; p. Ber. 12 c; Mo. k. 82 b; b. Ber. 47 a.

[2] p. Ber. 12 a.

[3] b. Ber. 46 a.

[4] The host has the opportunity on this occasion to show his 'beautiful eye', *'ayin yāphā*, i.e. his liberal and benevolent nature, b. Ber. 46 a.

[5] Cf. *O.W.* 188.

[6] b. Ber. 46 a.

[7] p. Ber. 10 a; 12 a; Sab. 8 d; Lev. R. vi. 3 (17 b); *ḳāṣayin 'iggūlā*, 'they distribute the bread'.

[8] p. Ber. 10 b; Tos. Ber. iv. 14, 15.

however, to be done by the hand. In the East, where there are no thick loaves, the use of the knife is superfluous; moreover, to the Orientals the application of a knife for the cutting of bread would have meant a violation of God's gift. In the Greek Church only is the Host 'slaughtered' (i.e. it is divided up with metal) for symbolic reasons.

The size of the piece apportioned to each person was variously fixed. It might be of the size of an olive only, or even smaller, in fact as small as a grain of coarse wheat flour (*sōletā*).[1] As the blessing over the bread has to be pronounced at every meal at which bread is used, there is no difference made between leavened and unleavened. The thin hard-baked *mazzoth* of the usual present-day Jewish Passover bread can, of course, only be *broken*. In Jerusalem and other places a more thick soft bread, in the form of a round cake, is used for the Passover supper.

The one who said the blessing did not put the pieces of bread directly into the hand of each participant (at a greater table fellowship it would not, in any case, have been easy to do so); often the pieces were probably passed on from one to the other, and, at any rate, put *before* each one (as we read of another article of food: *yehabat kummōy wa'akhal*, 'she put it *before him* and he ate').[2] The normal procedure in connexion with mourners (because of Lam. i. 17) was to put a piece of bread into the hand of each.[3]

After the distribution the one who had said the blessing (who, by the way, could transfer this honour to someone else) first took his piece and ate it, then the others followed suit.[4] Of Rab we hear that (probably in honour of the guests) after he broke the bread he took his piece with his left hand, ate it (*tā'ēm*), and distributed (*mephallēg*)[5] the rest with the right. The more natural procedure was for him to hold the bread in the left hand, break it with the right, pass on the pieces to the others, and then take a piece for himself, putting it into the mouth with the right hand.

[1] p. Ber. 10 a; b. Ber. 37 b.
[2] p. Abod. z. 41 a; cf. p. Ter. 45 c.
[3] *Halachoth gedoloth* (Warsaw 1875), 19; cf. Maimonides, *Hilch. Berachoth*, VII. 5; Shulchan Arukh, Orach Chayyim, 167, 18.
[4] p. Ber. 10 a; b. Ber. 47 a.
[5] p. Ber. 10 a.

All these formalities help us to visualise the scene of the Last Supper, and, as this Meal is perpetually renewed in Christendom, the celebration of the Eucharist in accordance with the original Institution depends upon knowledge of these externals; but, above all, they show how closely the details of the Last Supper are bound up with Jewish customs.

At a Jewish meal the distribution of the bread was not accompanied by any words of an interpreting character. Yet it is related that on the 9th of Ab, the memorial day of the destruction of Jerusalem, Rab used to take a damaged loaf at the end of the meal, and, after scattering ashes upon it, say: *zō hī seʿuddat tishāʿ beāb*, 'this is the meal of the ninth of Ab'.[1] Maimonides directs that at the Passover meal certain explanatory sentences should be said in connexion with the lamb, the bitter herbs, and the unleavened bread, beginning with *pesaḥ zē, merōr zē, maṣṣā zō*[2] (this Passover, these bitter herbs, etc.). He could give as an authority for this Gamaliel II, who (perhaps due to Exod. xii. 27) considered it a duty to attach to these three things special explanatory sayings.[3] It is also stated that the herbs and the bread were elevated.[4] The following Aramaic formula, which in its latest form originated probably in Babylon, was doubtless such an early explanatory word in connexion with the bread: *hā laḥmā ʿanyā da-akhalū abāhātanā dinephaḳū mē-arʿā demiṣraiyim, kōl di khephīn yētē weyēkhul wekhōl diṣerīkh lephesaḥ yētē wīphassaḥ*, 'Behold the bread of affliction[5] (lit. 'the afflicted bread', cf. Deut. xvi. 3)[6], which our fathers ate when they came out of the land of Egypt. Everyone who is hungry, let him come and eat (cf. Isa. lv. 1; John vii. 37; Rev. xxii. 17), and everyone who is obliged to keep the Passover, let him come and observe it!'. This formula, which might also have been used in the time of our Lord, belonged, moreover, to the special ritual of the Passover meal: it had nothing to do with the blessing over the bread (which must have been said at the beginning of the meal),

[1] p. Taan. end; Lam. R. iii. 16 (51 b).
[2] Hilch. Chamez umazza, viii.
[3] Pes. x. 5.
[4] b. Pes. 116 b.
[5] Cf. the Yemen vocalised prayer book, MS. Chamitzer.
[6] Maimonides as well as Onk. Yer. I. Deut. xvi. 3 uses the word 'afflicted' in an adjectival form, yet we also find the reading *deʿonyā*, 'of affliction'.

and yet it is of importance, as it shows that at the Passover meal the idea of investing the eating of the bread with a special significance suggested itself. This significance consisted in the remembrance of the liberation from Egypt, and in the thought of the observance of the duty of celebrating that remembrance by the eating of unleavened bread.

When at the Last Supper our Lord, after having said the blessing, distributed the bread with words of invitation and explanation, it was something unexpected and unusual. Could one visualise the action in such a fashion that, after the benediction, the bread held in the hand was first divided into many pieces and then distributed, then one would expect the interpretative words to have been said at the breaking, and the administrative, at the distribution. But in reality only one piece was always broken at a time and then distributed, so that the breaking ended only when the last of the company had received his portion. Then it is quite possible to think that the words of distribution were said before the words of interpretation. At other times our Lord certainly administered to His disciples the pieces of bread after the benediction, and in silence, and then He ate the bread with them. On this occasion, however, He could not Himself have eaten, because of the significance which He attached to the bread; and it is intelligible, therefore, why this time He had to express in words His invitation to the Disciples to eat, since now He could not give them the usual sign by starting to eat first, and they would not begin to eat before Him.[1]

In this sense we have to understand the words 'take, eat' (Mt. xxvi. 26; Mk. xiv. 22 has only 'eat'). In Aramaic *sabūn akhúlūn*.

The invitation to eat is not part of the ritual. As a natural phrase addressed to one to whom food is being offered, it can also be documented from Rabbinic literature. We read, for instance, of Bedouins giving to thirsty Jewish fugitives salty herbs and empty air-filled gourds, saying: 'Eat, and then drink', *akhúlūn weattūn shātay*.[2]

[1] Cf. p. Ber. 10 a; Orach Chayyim, 167, 15.
[2] p. Taan. 69 b (Venice edit. 1521).

According to all N.T. sources, our Lord said at the distribution of the bread: '*This is my body*' (Aramaic *dēn hū gūphī*). The Pal. Evang. renders the Greek text in Mt. xxvi. 26 word for word by *hādēn īt hū pugrī*.[1] But in Lk. xxii. 19, also 1 Cor. xi. 24,[2] this rendering of the Greek ἐστιν by '*īt*' is left out; it would only be justified when the predicate was meant to be specially emphasised, as if meaning: 'It is in truth'. But neither the Greek expression nor the context demand it; neither does the sense demand a special *hū* as a conjunction, which would have been necessary if, for instance, the administered bread were to be differentiated from other bread. Onkelos Targum follows the Hebrew in this, which usually does not have the *hū* in such a sentence. In Gen. xl. 12 it says: *dēn pushrāneh*, 'this—its interpretation'; Gen. ix. 12: *dā āt ḳeyām*, 'this—the covenant sign'; also in Biblical Aramaic (Dan. ii. 36): *denā ḥelmā*, 'this—the dream' (yet in iv. 27 emphatically: *dā hī bābél rabbetā*, '*this* is the great Babel'). In later literature the insertion of *hū* is more frequent. Exod. xv. 2 Onkelos translates: *dēn elāhī*, 'this—my God'; but the two Jerusalem Targums have: *dēn hū elāhī*. Similarly it says in the Palestinian Talmud: *dēn hū ḥassīdekhōn*, 'this (and no other) is your pious one';[3] *dēn hū malkā meshīḥā*, 'this is the King Messiah'.[3] Naturally, *hū* is unavoidable in the expression *dēn hū*, 'this is he';[4] and a connecting *hawā*, 'to be' in the retrospective: *lā hāwēnā anā*, 'it was not *I*'.[5] In the words of our Lord only *dēn*, or *dēn hū*, can be assumed. On the other hand, the Greek text does not suggest the solemn *hā*, 'behold', found in the above-mentioned *hā laḥmā* and in the sentence: *hā meshīḥakhōn dīdekhōn*, 'behold, your Messiah!'[6]

For 'My Body' the word *pugrī* of the Pal. Evang. is not appropriate, as in Jewish Aramaic this means a corpse. Neither could *hādēn garmī hū* be taken into consideration,[7] for that would mean 'This here is my bone', and not, as Meyer thinks, 'This am I myself', which would have to be in Aramaic: *dēn hū anā legarmī*. Moreover, it is incredible that the Early Church,

1 See A. S. Lewis, *A Palestinian-Syriac Lectionary*, Stud. Sin. VI. (1897).
2 p. Dem. 22 a; cf. *Gramm.*[2] 111 f.
3 p. Taan. 68 d.
4 Eccl. R. ix. 10 (115 b).
5 p. Ket. 35 a; cf. p. Kil. 32 b.
6 p. Kil. 32 c, with *dā* for *hā* p. Ket. 35 b.
7 Suggested by Meyer, *Jesu Muttersprache*, 90.

and, with her, St Paul, 'the Hebrew', should have so grossly misunderstood the words of our Lord, as to have taken what He meant to be 'Myself' as 'My Body'. Neither does the Hebrew expression *bāsār wādām* ('flesh and blood'),[1] frequently used in Jewish literature, belong here, as if the Flesh referred to the Bread and the Blood to the Wine; for this expression, which is also found in Mt. xvi. 17 and in John vi. 54 f. (in the latter passage it is used of the physical being of the Son of Man), characterises man in his physical aspect, in contrast to the realm of spirits, and for this thought there is not the slightest occasion here. The really applicable word for 'Body' here would be either *geshēm* (Dan. iii. 17), or *giwyā* (Gen. xlvii. 18, Onk.); or the word (unused in Onkelos Targum) *gūph* (Targum 1 Sam. xxxi. 12). The last-mentioned word is commonly used in later Jewish literature. *Hag-gūph haḳ-ḳādōsh*[2] or *gūphā ṣaddīḳā*[3] is the 'holy body' of a Rabbi which, just because it was holy, could not be exempted from suffering. *Gūph* in such cases stands in contrast to the soul. 'Is the soul not a guest in the body (*gūphā*)?'[4] it is asked. And again: 'One can love one's body (Hebrew *gūphō*) more than one's money (*māmōnō*).[5] 'My body (*gūphī*) trembled', said Zeira of himself, when he saw how ashes were scattered on the holy shrine.[6] A woman complained: 'Was it not better to suffer outside the body (*lebar min gūphā*) than inside the body (*legō gūphā*, i.e. in the soul)?'[7] Over the dead body (*gūphā*) the soul (*naphshā*) hovers for three days before finally leaving it.[8] While in the above passages the word stands for the animated human body, we also hear sometimes of the separation of body and soul in death.[9] Figuratively *gūphā* can stand for the 'essence', 'the chief thing'. *Gūphē 'abērā* means in Hebrew 'the chief kinds of sin';[10] *gūphē tōrā*—'the chief principles of the Law'.[11] Finally *gūph* can also express the idea of 'self'; *Begūphēh* means 'especially for him';[12] the

[1] p. Ber. 7 d; 13 b; Num. R. 14 (115 b) and frequently, but never in Aramaic.
[2] p. Taan. 64 d.
[3] p. Bikk. 65 c.
[4] Lev. R. 34 (91 b).
[5] b. Ber. 61 b.
[6] p. Taan. 65 a.
[7] p. Ket. 34 b.
[8] Lev. R. 18 (45 b).
[9] p. Mo. k. 82 b; Lev. R. 34 (91 b).
[10] Ab. v. 8.
[11] Ab. d. R. N. 27.
[12] Lev. R. 28 (76 a).

Hebrew *gūphō mekhubbād* means, 'he himself is honoured'.[1] Accordingly, in referring to the Paschal lamb we find the Hebrew phrase *gūphō shellap-pésaḥ*, 'the Passover lamb itself',[2] and it is rather remarkable how often, in consideration of the laws connected with the Passover lamb, *gūphō* is used in this sense; for instance, in Siphre on Numbers chap. 69 (18 a) nine times, in p. Pes. 36 d eight times. It was evidently usual to differentiate between the lamb as 'the body' of the Passover, and the Passover feast. Our Lord might have been influenced by this to point to His Body at the distribution of the bread, while not bringing it into direct conjunction with the Passover lamb. Thus, it would be possible to take *gūphī* in the sense of 'I myself'.[3] However, the fact that the Early Christians did not take it in this sense, as well as our Lord's reference to His Blood at the administration of the wine, necessitate the translation 'My Body'.

The words *dēn hū gūphī* by themselves could have meant to the disciples nothing other than: 'This bread, that I break into pieces and distribute, is My Body', to which, evidently, something similar would happen, and is thus destined to be broken and distributed. Whether it is to be concluded from this that our Lord referred to the manner of His Death, is very doubtful; for the distribution can only be a picturing of the purpose and effect of His Death, and the breaking is naturally a necessary presupposition of the distributing, in close connexion with the picture, and could mean nothing other than the violent dissolution of the present constitution of the Body, namely, His being put to Death. According to Mk. x. 33 f.; Lk. xviii. 32 f., He expected to be put to death by the Romans; according to Mt. xx. 19 (cf. John xii. 32 f.), by crucifixion, and the conditions of the time were such that there was the greatest probability that it would happen thus.

It has been asked, What was the outward occasion that caused our Lord to give a mystical interpretation to the bread about to be consumed, and, thus, make it food for the soul? As this

[1] Ab. iv. 6; Ab. d. R. N. 27. [2] Pes. x. 3; Tos. Pes. x. 9.

[3] Cf. Levertoff's note on this in his English edition of Siphre on Numbers, chap. 69.

idea is not found in Judaism, it has been said that it must have originated elsewhere. But there is no suggestion of a mystic food for the soul in the words of the Institution, and the connexion with Judaism is perfectly clear. The latter offered the usage which our Lord Himself, when He ate with His disciples, always observed. The new content which He gave to this custom emanated from the depth of His emotion. In this night He performed the breaking of bread, being certain of His approaching Death, His soul moved by what His Father had destined for Him. How natural then was it for Him to feel, when about to break the bread for distribution: 'This is just what will happen to Me at My death'. But the dying itself was not as important to Him as its purpose. The Disciples should know that it is good for them that He should go away, as it is expressed in John xvi. 7. His love for them opened His mouth. If the words were left without an explanation, then, in any case, they would be a fresh indication that He would be put to death, in harmony with the previous announcement, according to which, on this journey to Jerusalem for the feast He expected His Death (Mt. xx. 18 f.; Mk. x. 33 f.; Lk. xviii. 32 f.). But at the same time there was a further thought connected with it, namely, that this Death would be for their sake, a service rendered to them, according to the position which He took to Himself towards the Disciples (Mt. xx. 28; Mk. x. 45; Lk. xxii. 27; John xiii. 4 f.).[1] If so, His word about the Blood at the distribution of the wine fortified this thought, which was to accompany the Disciples as a legacy in the days that should follow, and force them to get a clear grasp of the meaning of the beneficence of this Death, and why the Blood has the power to confer these benefits. And so, Christian tradition has preserved the addition of explanatory words which, according to all witnesses, followed our Lord's words in connexion with the wine.

In 1 Cor. xi. 24 *τὸ ὑπὲρ ὑμῶν* is added to the interpreting words, the shortest form of which is in Matthew and Mark. Luke again adds to it *διδόμενον*. The Pauline form, which is rendered in the Pal. Evang. by *deṭibbekhōn*, 'for your sake', would in Jewish Aramaic be *da'alēkhōn*. But what is possible

[1] Cf. above, p. 118 f.

in Greek, appears in Aramaic as a very unusual heaviness. The Pauline formulation of the word must be considered as a hellenisation. The Lukan addition *διδόμενον* is unavoidable in Aramaic. On the other hand, the readings *θρυπτόμενον* D, *χλώμενον* D bc, present a difficulty, because in Aramaic *mitḳeṣē* in connexion with *gūphī* is scarcely possible. Thus, according to the Lukan form, the interpreting words in Aramaic were: *dēn hū gūphī demityehēb ʿalēkhōn.*

To 'give' the body for someone, naturally means to die; in Semitic idiom—to give one's soul; but because of the bread, in this case the yet unbroken loaf (*ʿiggūl*), our Lord spoke of the Body instead of the Soul. Is not He about to be destroyed by death as the loaf is even now being torn into bits? The Aramaic *mityehēb* corresponds exactly to the word 'given', and in the active sense it has also many parallels in Jewish literature. Of Jassa bar Ḥalputa, for instance, it is told that at his death blood poured down the roof-gutters of Laodicea, 'because he gave his soul for circumcision' (*dīhab naphshēh ʿal gezūretā*),[1] which probably means that he practised the rite of circumcision against the heathen government's prohibition. More frequent in this connexion is the verb *mesar*, 'to deliver up'. The community of Israel claims: 'I have delivered up my soul (*māserā naphshī*) to Thy Deity'.[2] Jacob, in view of the perilous situation of his children through his encounter with Esau, says: 'I have delivered up myself for them to death (Hebrew *māsarti ʿaṣmi lemītā ʿalēhem*)—I nursed them like the hen nurses her chickens'.[3] Of Abraham it says: 'He delivered up his soul (he risked his life), *mesar naphshēh*, in order to be circumcised'.[4] The question is asked: 'If thou hast delivered up thyself (Hebrew *māsarta ʿaṣmekhā*) for the commandments, what will be thy reward?'[5] It is the greatness of the accomplishment that stands in the foreground, when a person wishes to have his portion among those who die for the commandments (Hebrew *mētē bedérekh miṣwā*),[6] and also in the statement: 'The words of the Law are fulfilled (Hebrew *mitḳaiyemīn*) by him alone who lets himself

[1] p. Ab. z. 42 c.
[2] Tg. Cant. viii. 1.
[3] Lam. R. Peth (12 a).
[4] Tg. Yer. I. Gen. xxii. 1.
[5] Num. R. 14 (115 b).
[6] b. Sab. 118 b.

be killed (lit. 'who kills himself') for it' (Hebrew *mēmīt 'aṣmō 'aleha*).[1]

The accomplishment is also emphasised in Isa. liii. 12, where the Servant of God is promised a reward when he gives up his soul unto death; or, as the Targum has it, 'delivers his soul unto death' (*mesar lemōtā naphshēh*). The same expression is also found in the Jewish application of that word to Moses: 'who delivered himself up to death (for his people), was numbered among those who died in the desert, propitiated the sin of the golden calf, prayed for grace for repentant sinners in Israel'.[2] But this *mesar*, which lays the main emphasis on the activity of the person who gives himself, does not sound likely to have been that which came from the lips of Jesus. At this moment He thinks not of the reward which He can claim, still less of the absolutely unique accomplishment which He is to achieve; two matters only stand in the foreground of His consciousness: first and foremost, the Divine 'must' which requires His life, and endows His Death with its unique value; and, then, those whom this Death should benefit. He does not go to death for the sake of receiving something, but in obedience to the Father, and in love, primarily, towards those who surround Him now, to whom this Death is so necessary. In this St John rightly interpreted His emotion: 'As He had loved His own who were in the world, so He loved them to the end' (John xiii. 1). This feeling is fittingly expressed by the passive tense, *mityehēb 'alēkhōn*, 'given for you', which emphasises God as the Giver. The thought of the ransom[3] seems to lie here in the background, although it is not the giving but the *being given* that stands in the foreground.

Nothing is said concerning the reason why the Death of the Master was necessary to the Disciples. In this it can be seen that our Lord did not at the Last Supper wish to transmit to His Disciples a doctrine concerning the meaning of His Death; His words were rather a short and impulsive disclosure of the overflow of His heart. Such words of intense feeling one does

[1] b. Ber. 63 b.
[2] b. Sot. 14 a; cf. Dalman, *Jesaja* 53, 2nd ed. 20.
[3] Cf. p. 119.

at times express, but not enlarge upon; one does not expect, nor desire, an argument concerning them. Those who listen to them may either accept or reject them. This is the note which our Lord struck at His Last Supper with the Disciples, at the administration of the Bread; and so should His words be heard now.

XV. OUR LORD'S BENEDICTION OVER THE WINE AND HIS WORDS OF APPLICATION

In the East there is no meal without bread; but according to the Jewish conception no meal is complete without meat and wine.[1] At the Passover meal it was the Paschal lamb, and under certain conditions also the so-called 'festive sacrifice',[2] which supplied the former article of food; but wine, which the O.T. does not mention in connexion with the Passover, was also essential. Psalm xxiii. 5 already considers the 'full cup' as belonging to a proper meal. At the thank-offering meal the chalice was lifted up (Psalm cxvi. 13). Every festive meal was in later times simply termed a 'drinking-bout' (*mishtītā*),[3] to which the verb 'to eat' was applied: 'he who "eats" the preliminary wedding celebration, "eats" also the drinking-bout (the wedding banquet proper)'.[4] At a funeral meal it was considered to be normal to consume two cups before, five cups during, and three cups after the meal, altogether ten;[5] a considerable achievement which would have ended in impropriety, had it not been for the fact that certain pious duties were attached to these 'cups' before and after the meal. In Petra, where wine was not the native drink to the same extent as in Palestine, every participant of a drinking-bout was permitted to drink eleven cups.[6]

The drinking of wine at the Passover was even based on the O.T. Law. At a festival the Israelite had to eat and rejoice in the Presence of God (Deut. xxvii. 7; cf. xvi. 14); man is commanded to promote his wife's and his sons' joyousness at the great festivals: 'wherewith can one make them joyous?'—'with

1 p. Mo. k. 82 b; b. Taan. 30 a.
2 Cf. above, p. 87f.
3 p. Ber. 10 c; p. Shebi. 35 c; Lev. R. 11 (27 b).
4 p. Shebi. 35 c.
5 p. Ber. 6 a.
6 Strabo, xvi. 4, 26.

wine'.[1] And as to males, 'is it not appropriate for them to rejoice thus?'[2] 'Eating' in Deut. xxvii. 7 (according to the official scribal interpretation) refers to the consumption of meat;[3] but since the enjoyment derived from eating the meat of the festive sacrifice ceased with the destruction of the Temple,[4] wine supplies this enjoyment. Moreover, this duty to rejoice is specially bound up with the night of the first day of a feast (cf. Isa. xxx. 29),[5] and would thus be of particular significance for the Passover meal.

Beer,[6] by pointing to the Samaritan usage, attempts to prove that only after the time of the priestly legislature did wine begin to be considered as indispensable at a Passover meal. But the fact is that to the Samaritans the eating of the Paschal lamb is not a 'meal' at all, but, according to Exod. xii. 11, a hasty 'snack'.[7] To the Israelites, however, the Passover meant (as early as the time of Josiah, 2 Kings xxiii. 21; 2 Chron. xxxv. 11) a sacrifice; its consumption 'a sacrificial meal'; and hence wine was a constituent part of the meal. It is true that wine-oblations belonged neither to the 'Passover-offering' nor to the sacrifice of the first-born of animals,[8] but the private 'festive' sacrifices as well as the official offerings of the Mazzoth feast (Num. xxviii. 24) had their wine oblations. Why then should the domestic Passover celebration lack what was a duty in the Temple? That the drinking of wine at the Passover meal is mentioned in Jubil. xlix. 6, 9 for the first time is a mere accident; but it was natural that when, after the destruction of Jerusalem, the Passover sacrifices ceased, the greatest emphasis should have been put upon just this remnant of the ancient Passover ritual.

Four cups of wine were in later times the minimum for the Passover meal.[9] This was allegorically interpreted in different ways; e.g. four kinds of punishments to the heathen—to Israel

[1] p. Pes. 37 b; Tos. Pes. x. 4; b. Pes. 109 a.
[2] b. Pes. 109 a.
[3] Siphre on Deut. 64 (88 a); 69 (89 a); 138 (102 a); 141 (102 b); p. Ḥag. 76 b.
[4] b. Pes. 109 a.
[5] Siphre on Deut. 142 (102 b); b. Pes. 71 a; p. Ḥag. 76 a.
[6] *Pesachim*, 7, 48.
[7] Linder, *P.J.B.* 1912, 119; Dalman, *ibid.* 129 f.; Whiting, *Sam. Påskfest*, 42.
[8] Men. x. 6; p. Pes. 32 c.
[9] Pes. x. 1.

four kinds of consolations.[1] The fact is, however, that this amount was connected with a peculiar method of calculation. A 'cup of blessing' had to contain 'a quarter of a quarter of a log' of pure wine.[2] Thus, four such cups contained a quarter of a log, i.e. one-eighth litre of pure wine,[3] about the measure of a large modern wine-glass. The drinking of such a quarter of a log of wine was considered enough to make priests and judges temporarily unfit for their office.[4] A whole log (= one-half litre), it says, caused intoxication,[5] for, when Gamaliel II had drunk a quarter of a log of Italic wine he felt unable to undertake a case of dissolving a vow until he had ridden for three miles to let the intoxication pass off.[6] Thus, the amount of wine drunk at a Passover meal was just enough to promote high spirits; that it would not lead to actual intoxication was taken for granted, as experience taught that wine caused intoxication only when drunk after, but not when drunk during, a meal.[7] (Naturally, the effect of wine on those who were used to drink much was also known. One who was used to drink daily twelve xests (more than 6 litres) did not fall asleep if he only drank eleven.[8]) Moreover, the avoidance of intoxication was also due to the fact that it was drunk at intervals.[9] 'The drunkard drinks in one draught, the decent man in two, the proud man in three'.[10] And yet some Rabbis spoke of the physical after-effects of the four Passover cups upon them: Rabbi Jonah felt his until Pentecost had come round; Juda ben Ilay until the Feast of Tabernacles.[11]

It was taken for granted that the wine should be diluted with water. The strong Italic wine was mixed with three parts of water; so a cup containing one-sixteenth of a log of pure wine had to be large enough to contain three-sixteenths of a log of water and allow a space of one-sixteenth of a log free at the brim

[1] p. Pes. 37.
[2] b. Sab. 76 b; p. Sab. 11 a.
[3] Tos. Pes. x. 1; p. Pes. 37 c; Sab. 11 a; Shek. 47 b; b. Pes. 108 b.
[4] Num. R. 10 (68 b, 73 a); cf. Lev. x. 9 f.; Siphra, 46 b; 'as much as intoxicated', that is, a quarter of a log of forty-days-old wine.
[5] Num. R. 10 (72 b).
[6] Lev. R. 37 (101 b); Tos. Pes. i. 28; b. Erub. 64 b.
[7] p. Pes. 37 b.
[8] Lev. R. 12 (31 a).
[9] p. Pes. 37 c; Shek. 4 b; Ber. 11 a.
[10] b. Bez. 25 b.
[11] p. Pes. 37 c.

for drinking.[1] For the weaker Palestinian Saron wine, mixed only with twice its quantity of water,[2] smaller cups would suffice. According to Eliezer, the mixing was to be done before the benediction over the wine.[3] At the Passover meal this was not performed at one time in a great vessel for the purpose, but at each cup, in order that every cup should be an entity in itself. It is said: 'They mixed him the first cup'.[4] Moreover, the order according to rank was a subject for serious consideration; during the meal the preparation of each cup had to begin with the oldest participant—after the meal with the officiant, i.e. with the one who would say the benediction.[5]

As over the bread, so also over the wine, a benediction to the God who gave it had to be said, the usual formula of which was: 'Blessed art Thou who hast created the fruit of the vine' (Hebrew *bōrē pherī hag-géphen*).[6] The Aramaic translation would be: *berīkh att debārē pēraiyā deguphnā. Pēraiyā* (always in the plural) for 'the fruit of the vine' can be proven from Targum Joel i. 7; ii. 22; Jer. v. 17; Zech. iii. 10. *Ibbā* (Targum Zech. viii. 12), on the other hand, can scarcely be taken into consideration. When our Lord invoked the blessing over the wine (Mt. xxvi. 27; Mk. xiv. 23; Lk. xxii. 17), He probably expressed it in these traditional words, for later also He spoke not of wine generally, but, in an elevated style, of '*the produce* (γέννημα) *of the vine*' (Mt. xxvi. 29; Mk. xiv. 25; Lk. xxii. 18). Γέννημα leads back (according to Hab. iii. 17, LXX, where it stands for the 'produce' of the vine) to the Hebrew *jebūl*.[7] But it is probably only the Greek variant to καρπός which is used in Deut. xi. 17, LXX, for the Hebrew *yebūl*, whilst usually it corresponds to the Hebrew *perī*. Also Evang. Pal. considered *pēraiyā* sufficient for the rendering of the Greek.

Together with the blessing directly connected with the wine, and preceding every enjoyment of it, there were other benedictions attached to the wine cup. Psalm cxvi. 13 speaks of

[1] p. Pes. 37 c.
[2] Nidd. ii. 7; Num. R. 1 (2 b); Cant. R. vii. 3 (68 b); b. Sabb. 77 a.
[3] Ber. vii. 5.
[4] Pes. x. 2; Tos. Pes. x. 2; cf. Cant. R. i. 2 (7 b).
[5] Tos. Ber. v. 7.
[6] Ber. vi. 1; Tos. Ber. iv. 3.
[7] Targumic would be '*alaltā* (according to Lev. xxvi. 4; Deut. xxxii. 22).

'the cup of salvation' at which the name of God is proclaimed. This presupposes the custom of lifting up the cup at the sacrificial meal connected with the dissolution of a vow, amidst praises to God for His help. The latter Jewish custom, independent of sacrificial worship, knew as a particular cup 'the cup of sanctification' (*kāsā deḳiddūshā*),[1] over which God, who 'sanctified' (Hebrew *meḳaddēsh*) the Sabbath or Feast day, was praised. This usage must have had its origin in Jewish antiquity, and it also suggests an explanation of what is meant in Isa. xxx. 29 by the 'sanctification of a feast', namely, the drinking of wine to solemnise a festival. Different from this was 'the cup of blessing' proper, *kāsā debirkhetā*[2] (Hebrew *kōs shellab-berākhā*),[3] to which, after the meal, 'the blessing of food' (Hebrew *birkhat ham-māzōn*)[4] and also the 'blessing of invitation' (Hebrew *birkhat haz-zimmūn*)[5] were joined. This benediction could be said in any language[6] in order that everyone should know to Whom the blessing referred.[7] It was preceded by the invitation: 'Let us praise the Lord our God for the food which we enjoyed'.[8] Abraham demanded that his heathen guests should pray: 'Praised be the God of the world, because we have eaten of what belongs to him'.[9] When St Paul presumes the 'thanksgiving' for food as an established custom (Rom. xiv. 6; 1 Cor. x. 30; 1 Tim. iv. 4), the question is whether he refers to 'grace' *before* or *after* meals; but from the narrative concerning the 'thanksgiving' said by Shimon ben Shetaḥ at the table of King Jannai (103–70 B.C.),[10] one can conclude that this 'blessing' had become a Jewish custom long before the Christian era.

It was necessary to establish a fixed order for all the rites connected with festive meals. The school of Hillel advocated the following order: the mixing of the cup, the washing of hands, the benediction over the wine, the benediction of 'sanctification'.[11] If there was only one cup of wine, it was

[1] p. Ber. 11 c.
[2] b. Ber. 51 a.
[3] p. Ber. 11 c; b. Sot. 38 b.
[4] Sot. vii. 1; b. Bab. M. 87 a.
[5] Ber. vii. 1 f.; Tos. Ber. v. 14; vii. 1; p. Ber. 11 a.
[6] Sot. vii. 1.
[7] p. Sot. 21 b.
[8] Ber. vii. 3; p. Naz. 54 b; Gen. R. 91 (194 a).
[9] Gen. R. 49 (103 a).
[10] Gen. R. 91 (194 a).
[11] Ber. viii. 1, 2.

recommended that it should be kept for the conclusion of the meal and invoked upon it the 'blessing over the wine', the 'blessing of sanctification', and the 'blessing for the food'.[1] 'The wine after food'[2] was evidently considered to be the most essential part of the ritual, the one least likely to be foregone. At the Passover festival all these benedictions were naturally connected with 'the four cups of the "Passover night"' (*arba'tē kāsaiyā delēlē pisḥā*).[3] Over the first it was customary to say the 'blessing on the wine' and the 'blessing of sanctification'; the 'blessing for the food' was said over the third; the second cup belonged to the meal; the fourth was a part of the drinking-bout which followed the meal.

There were definite rules for the invocation of the benediction over the wine. At a festive meal it was said by one for all at the beginning and the end; but during the meal each participant had to say it for himself.[4] The procedure for corporate benediction was that he who was to officiate was asked: 'Take (the cup) and speak the blessing (*sab ubārēkh*)'.[5] To be thus asked was an honour, and to refuse it meant the deprivation of a blessing to oneself: 'he shortens his own life'. He would take the cup and say (if it be the 'blessing for the food'):[6] 'Let us say the blessing!' (*nesab kāsā wa'amar nebārēkh*).[7] The cup was to be 'undamaged', full, ornamented, and previously rinsed.[8] It was not uncommon for the officiant to cover his face;[9] the food and the bread[10] were also frequently covered, perhaps to keep away evil spirits. He would uplift the cup during the benediction with his right hand 'a hand's breadth' over the table,[11] and his eyes would be directed towards the cup[12] (prayers were generally said with downcast eyes).[13] We read of our Lord,

1 p. Ber. 7 d; b. Ber. 52 a.
2 Ber. viii. 8.
3 p. Sab. 11 a; Pes. 47 c; Shek. 47 c.
4 Ber. vi. 5, 6; cf. p. Ber. 10 c.
5 Lev. R. 9 (22 a); p. Ber. 11 c.
6 b. Ber. 55 a.
7 p. Ber. 11 c; b. Ber. 51 b.
8 p. Ber. 11 d; b. Ber. 51 a.
9 b. Ber. 51 a.
10 p. Pes. 37 b; b. Pes. 100 a f.
11 p. Ber. 11 d; cf. Psalm cxvi. 13. According to b. Ber. 51 a it had to be done with both hands. When a blessing was to be invoked upon oil and wine at the same time, each of these was taken in a separate hand; there is a discussion on whether the wine was to be taken in the right or in the left hand. b. Ber. 43 b; Tos. Ber. vi. 5.
12 p. Ber. 11 c f.
13 b. Yeb. 105 b.

however, that both when saying the blessing and when praying He lifted up His eyes towards heaven (Mt. xiv. 19; Mk. vi. 41; vii. 34; John xi. 41; xvii. 1). The wine was no more blessed than the bread—but God, *over* the wine, for creating the fruit from which it is produced. When the blessing had been confirmed by the 'amen' of all who sat at table, the wine was released for use. If each had his own cup, they could begin to drink before him who said the blessing;[1] but as a rule the officiant, by starting to drink, would have given the sign for the others to follow his example.[2]

Either from aesthetic[3] or hygienic[4] scruples it was not generally the custom to have one cup for all, but each had his own.[5] One can however deduce from certain passages that this was not the case with the 'cup of blessing'. According to one rubric, the latter was to be 'given' with the right hand,[6] which means that it was passed on to others; as it says, for instance, in one place concerning 'the children of the house', i.e. the wife.[7] When the angels enquired after Sarah (Gen. xviii. 9), they wished to send her the 'cup of blessing'.[8] Later it was described as a general custom that the 'cup of sanctification' on Sabbaths and festivals was passed on by the officiating person to the rest of the company, after he himself had drunk from it.[9] At marriage festivals in Jerusalem this is the custom to this day in connexion with the 'cup of sanctification', which cup is repeatedly refilled.[10] Every one present would in this way participate in the merit of the eulogy. The one who officiated could also pour out from his 'perfect' cup into the 'imperfect' ones of the company, and by this act transfer to all present the merit of having kept the obligation of drinking from a 'perfect' cup.[11] It is very probable that originally the custom was to deal with the wine as with the bread, to pass round the cup of him who officiated, even when each participant had his own cup.

[1] p. Ber. 10 a.
[2] Cf. p. 139.
[3] Tos. Ber. v. 10.
[4] Derech Erez 9 (Akiba).
[5] p. Ber. 10 a.
[6] b. Ber. 51 a.
[7] b. Ber. 57 a.
[8] b. Bab. m. 87 a.
[9] Maimonides, *Hilch. Shabb.* 29, 7; Orach Chayyim, 271, 12 f.
[10] According to Baer's *Siddur*, 363, two cups are put in readiness from the start, and he who says the blessing takes a sip from each.
[11] Rabbenu Asher on Ber. 7; Orach Chayyim, 271, 16.

This wine-drinking was not of a 'covenant' significance, but meant a participation in the benediction. As after partaking of the 'bread of the blessing' each one could then eat of other bread, so after the drinking from the 'cup of blessing' could he drink of his own cup. It is at the same time conceivable that in poorer households there was not always a sufficient number of cups and not enough wine, so the company had to be satisfied with one cup. Islam did away with the old drinking customs of Palestine, and affected even Christians. Yet among peasants and Bedouins it can be observed that coffee is served in one small cup, which is refilled for each of the company. As to the 'wine of benediction', it was naturally not the enjoyment of the wine as such that mattered, but the participation in the benediction.

It is certainly improbable that in connexion with the wine-blessing and the thanksgiving prayer our Lord should have felt Himself bound by the details of Rabbinic ordinances. The N.T. records of the Last Supper, however, show that the custom which those Rabbinic ordinances purposed to regulate was His also. The records differ among themselves in this only, that they describe the administration of the bread and wine in a different order: Matthew and Mark mention first the bread and then the wine; St Paul says expressly that the blessing of the wine took place 'after the meal'; according to Luke, however (xxii. 17), the wine was administered at the beginning of the meal and (in the original text) he does not mention it again. Following the wine-ritual of the Passover meal, it can be assumed that this referred to the first two of the 'four cups', i.e. to those of the 'blessing of the wine' and the 'blessing of sanctification'. In the Jewish ritual the latter was followed by the benediction over the bread, and according to the Lukan account our Lord (since He Himself did not partake of the wine) must have spoken directly after this benediction His words in connexion with the bread. According to Matthew, Mark and St Paul, on the other hand, it was most probably the third cup—the one which is connected with the blessing of the food, or with the thanksgiving prayer. This fits in with the fact that, according to Matthew and Mark, He gave 'thanks' in connexion with the wine, and that St Paul calls the cup which the Lord took after the meal (1 Cor. xi. 25) the 'cup of blessing' (1 Cor. x. 16), i.e. exactly as this cup is named among the Jews.[1] There is no need to consider the *fourth* cup, that of the drinking-bout, especially as the 'hymn of praise' is mentioned at the end also in the Gospel record.[2] Our Lord's declaration (Mt. xxvi. 27; Mk. xiv. 25) that He would not drink in this aeon of the product of the vine, can be well conceived to have occurred at the conclusion of the meal proper. It means, above all, that He would not partake again at a festive meal; but it does not exclude the possibility of thinking that He had drunk some wine at this meal, now drawing to a close. Should there have been more drinking after this, our Lord would by this saying have excluded Himself from taking part in it. At the same time it is conceivable that the effect of His words was to make the Disciples cease from drinking any more and that the meal was brought to an end without the fourth cup and without the customary after-meal drinking.

St Luke (xxii. 18) lets the concluding words come at the beginning of the meal, so that, according to him, our Lord, while desiring to *eat* of the Passover for the last time, refused altogether to drink the wine. Accordingly, it might be suggested that these words had a certain connexion with the so-called 'avowals of renunciation' (*issārīm*) which the Law (Num. xxx. 3) presumes as an old custom. Traditional law does, in fact, deal with cases of renunciation from wine, and one of the casuistic deductions is that the avowal not to eat grapes does not include wine, and that the mentioning of wine does not include *apple* wine.[3] The solemn declaration not to drink wine is closely related to the Nazaraean vow (Num. vi. 3 f.), which vow certainly included abstinence from wine. The Mishna declares: 'If the cup is being mixed for someone and he says, "I am a Nazaraean in relation to it", he is a Nazaraean (in the full sense of the word)'.[4] Is it possible to ascribe this kind of avowal to our Lord? It would seem to be more in accordance with His spirit that in

[1] Cf. above, p. 149.
[2] Cf. above, p. 131 f.
[3] Ned. vi. 6, 9.
[4] Naz. ii. 3; cf. Num. R. 10 (73 a): 'Even if one only says: "I am a Nazaraean in relation to the wine", he is a perfect Nazaraean'.

His words (in conjunction with what follows immediately after) He only emphasised the fact that with this meal all wine-drinking had, for Him, come to an end, until a new aeon would bring forth a new occasion for it.

As St Luke is a later witness than St Paul, it is not probable that his account presents an earlier source. This leads to the question of the origin of the form of the Lukan narrative. What is to be emphasised is that, also according to the third Gospel, the words of our Lord in connexion with the wine pointed particularly to His approaching Death; in this it is akin to the interpreting words contained in the other sources. Yet every reference to the value of this Death for the Disciples is left out, and our Lord's refusal to partake of the wine stands out, which might have occasioned the tradition represented by Luke which sets the words concerning the wine at the beginning of the meal; in that case it was natural for our Lord not to have waited to the end of the meal to express His refusal in words corresponding to His emotion. It is, however, not incredible that the words in connexion with the wine were *suppressed*, since they might be misunderstood, and lead to accusations against Christ's followers, as what, in fact, did happen soon enough (accusations which would indeed have been justified, if Beer[1] were right in seeing beyond the wine administered by our Lord 'a sublimated form of the ancient blood-covenant', and behind the bread 'a refined form of the ancient human sacrifice'). To the Jews, who were strictly prohibited from the consummation of blood (Gen. ix. 4; Lev. xvii. 12; Deut. xii. 23), so much so that they even removed the blood from the meat of a slaughtered animal, the drinking of wine which should signify blood would naturally be an abomination. Among the pagans, one thought of mystery meals with actual consumption of blood, a reproach which underlies the researches of Plinius as early as A.D. 112,[2] and

[1] *Pesachim*, 101. According to D. Nielsen, *Der dreieinige Gott in religions-historischer Beleuchtung*, I. 145 (1922), the Christian Eucharist is accordingly 'a piece of gross paganism'. But the question is not what lay historically behind the sacrificial system of Israel, but what ideas were connected with it in the time of our Lord; besides, our Lord never viewed His work from the point of view of the sacrificial ritual.

[2] Lietzmann in *Geschichtliche Studien, Albert Hauck dargebracht*, 38.

something similar was suspected to have taken place among Christians; an accusation which Christians themselves transferred later to the Jewish Paschal meal. It is possible that in the Lukan tradition the conviction predominated that our Lord's mind concerning the value of His Death was sufficiently expressed in the interpreting words concerning the bread, and that there was no further need therefore to repeat it in connexion with the wine. What was done here to the tradition, the Fourth Gospel dared to do to an even greater extent, by separating the words of our Lord concerning His flesh and His blood (John vi. 53–56) entirely from the bread and wine and from His Last Supper. Yet, even in this, the offence which our Lord's words caused is to be felt: 'Many of His disciples, when they heard this, said: "this speech is hard, who can hear it?"' (John vi. 60). The direct claim to see in the wine His blood would have had the same, or even a worse, effect. One has to look for the historical reality in the accounts of St Paul, St Matthew, and St Mark, and not in those of St Luke and St John. Just what seemed to the latter a probable stumbling-block is, after all, what actually did take place; for the 'cup of blessing' which, according to 1 Cor. x. 16, was already a fixed institution even among Gentile Christians about twenty years after the Crucifixion, must be considered a sufficient proof of it.

Thus, it was certainly at the conclusion of the meal, probably at the 'cup of blessing' for food, that our Lord, as at the beginning in connexion with the bread, reminded the Disciples of His Death. He knew that this Passover would be His last, and that He had His Disciples with Him for the last time. On such an intimate occasion He could not have begun and ended the fellowship-meal without having presented to them the approaching important event of His Death, for which He was preparing Himself, in the right light. He did not use any lyrical parting words, transferring to them His own sorrowfulness, but gave His last orders in manly and heroic fashion, as a genuine warrior about to start on a dangerous adventure.

All accounts presume that Jesus, having said the Prayer of Thanksgiving, offered the cup to the Disciples. Mark records (xiv. 23):

'And He took the cup, thanked, gave it to them, and they all drank of it'.

Aramaic: ***unesab kāsā ubārēkh wīhab lehōn ushetōn minnah kullehōn.***

Matthew xxvi. 27 has the direct bidding:

'Drink ye all of it'.

Aramaic: ***ishtōn minnah kullekhōn.***

As the cup was mentioned before, 'of it' refers to it, and in Aramaic the feminine suffix must therefore be used. The masculine suffix would refer to the wine, which, however, had not previously been mentioned. In Luke xxii. 17 it speaks more expressly of the cup:

'Take it and distribute (share) it among yourselves'.

Aramaic: ***sabbūnah uphallegūnah bēnēkhōn.***

The Pal. Evang. rendering of τοῦτο by a special *hādēn* as the object of the taking, is due to its slavishly-literal adherence to the Greek text and cannot be expected to have been used by our Lord, as His cup could not have been different from the other cups. For 'distribute' the following sentences can serve as parallels: 'he distributed it (the money) among others' (*hawā mephallēg leḥōrānīn*);[1] 'she distributed to the sick' (*mephallegā lebīshaiyā*).[2] The fuller form of the sentence in Luke intends to emphasise the fact that He did not desire to drink the wine, and is thus due entirely to Luke's own individual presentation of the event. Yet it is rather strange that our Lord should have considered it of such importance that the others *should* partake of it; it sounds as if the drinking from this cup had a significance which Luke does not disclose. One also expects that our Lord would have spoken in a general way, at the commencement of the meal, concerning the partaking of the wine during the meal. Why this solemn treatment of just this cup, if Jesus merely wished to tell them that He would not drink of it? It is all perfectly clear, however, if we assume that when our Lord offered

[1] p. Pea, 21 b.
[2] Eccl. R. iv. 6 (89 b); Pesikt. 95 b.

'the cup of blessing' to them He attached a special interpretation to it (repressed by Luke), which explained why He Himself did not drink of it but wished *them* to do so.

In Matthew (xxvi. 28) and Mark (xiv. 24) the words of interpretation in connexion with the wine are:

'This is my blood'.

Aramaic: *dēn* (*hādēn*) *hū idmī.*

Τοῦτο naturally refers not to the cup but to its contents; the Aramaic expression, however, permits both meanings. For the use of *hādēn* and *hū* compare above, p. 141. *Idmī*, as the Galilaean form of *demī*, is documented in my *Jüd. Aram. Grammatik*, 2nd edit. p. 202.[1] One expects a similar interpretive sentence in connexion with the wine to that connected with the bread. 'This is my blood' would then mean, 'this wine which I proffer you is like unto My blood which shall flow for your benefit'. The blood, which is thus conceived of as being apart from the body, stands for the outpoured life; for, according to Israelitish psychology, when the life-blood flows, the soul, with the blood as its seat, leaves the body with it (Gen. ix. 4; Lev. xvii. 14; Deut. xii. 23). As in connexion with the bread, so with the wine: nothing can be deduced from the words as to the manner of death which our Lord expected; just as it could not be deduced from Gen. ix. 5 f., where God declares punishment for the shedding of blood, that any other kind of murder is not punishable. 'Save the blood of the one by the blood of the other',[2] it says in a Talmudic interpretation of Gen. ix. 5 f., which passage is applied to the saving of a person who is being pursued; but even in that rabbinical sentence it is not the actual shedding of blood that matters, but the purpose to be attained, namely the taking and saving of life. Wine, according to the Israelitish conception, is 'the blood of grapes' (Gen. xlix. 11; Deut. xxxii. 14; 1 Macc. vi. 34; Sir. xxxix. 26; l. 15); *red* wine was preferred for the Passover meal.[3] How natural then was it for Him, who was about to die a violent death, to have it brought to mind at the sight of the blood-red

[1] See also p. Maas. Sh. 56 d. [2] b. Sanh. 72 b.

[3] p. Pes. 37 c; Shek. 47 b; Sab. 11 a; b. Pes. 108 b; Men. 87 a; founded on Prov. xxiii. 31, where red wine is assumed.

contents of the cup! Another thing would probably also have suggested it; the cup, as pictured in the Prophets (Isa. li. 17; Jer. xxv. 15; Ezec. xxiii. 23) and the Psalms (e.g. xi. 6; lx. 5; lxxv. 9), is a symbol of a bitter destiny: that of one forced to empty the cup to the dregs with all its bitter contents.[1] Our Lord often used this simile in His last days, applying it to the end which He was approaching (Mt. xx. 22; xxvi. 39, 42; John xviii. 11). Is not the cup which He now holds like unto the lot which His Father has apportioned to Him? And is not the wine in the cup like unto the blood which is to be demanded of Him? On the way to Jerusalem He asked the Disciples, who were looking forward to thrones of honour (Mt. xx. 22; Mk. x. 38): 'Can ye drink the cup that I shall drink?' and now He holds this cup in His Hand. But He suppresses the agony which this cup will shortly bring Him, and turns His thoughts resolutely to the refreshment which His Death will bring to others. The wine is to Him now, as it were, the accomplished fact of His Death. This He proffers to His disciples.

That our Lord distinctly pointed out the reason why His blood will have a special significance for others, Matthew, Mark, and St Paul agree. It has a relation to a covenant ('settlement', διαθήκη). According to Matthew and Mark it is 'my blood of the covenant'; according to St Paul it is the cup itself which is 'the new covenant in my blood'. We will take first the extended interpreting words according to the first expression:

'This is my blood of the covenant'.

Aramaic: *dēn (hādēn) hū idmī deliḳeyāmā.*

The rather hard *idmī diḳeyāmā* is avoided by the insertion of *del* (= *di le*), which, in the Hebrew *shelle*, is already found in Cant. iii. 7, and occurs in Onkelos, e.g. Gen. xl. 5, *naḥtōmā dī lemalkā*, 'the baker of the king'. The sentence would then be an abbreviated expression for *dēn hū idmī dehū idmā diḳeyāmā* ('this is my blood which is the blood of the covenant'). But the Aramaic idiom also permits the pronoun in *idmī* to be applied to the whole predicative; compare *bēt ṣelōtī*, 'my house of

[1] Also the Jewish liturgical language uses this imagery, 'May he keep far from you the cup of bitterness' (Aramaic *ya'dē minnekhōn kāsā demārīrā*), it says in Yekum Purkan, Siddur Yemen.

prayer' (Targum Isa. lvi. 7); *bēt ḳodshanā*, 'our holy house' (Targum Isa. lxiv. 10). This leads to the translation 'This is my covenant-blood'. The interpreting words would in this case mean: 'The wine of the cup which I offer to you, signifies to you a covenant-blood, which, moreover, will soon be contained in my blood'. But if this sense was intended, one would expect in the Semitic original a more concise form than the literal rendering of the Greek text attempted above. Thus we would come to the following structure:

dēn hū adam ḳeyāmī,

where, in the translation, the pronoun added to the *ḳeyām* would relate to the whole predicative, and the same meaning would be reached: 'This is my covenant-blood'. It is natural that in Greek the pronoun was connected with the first part of the predicative, and the result was that the second part could only be dragged in, as is the case in the Greek formulation: *τοῦτό ἐστιν τὸ αἷμά μου τῆς διαθήκης*. Of course, it is also possible that the original sentence did not contain the words *τῆς διαθήκης*, but that they were added subsequently to the words 'the blood shed for many', and, just for this reason, they do *not* quite fit into this sentence. Yet the task remains to examine whether any sense can be got out of the existing text to which, by the way, St Paul also testifies with his (though somewhat different) reading.

In the Pauline structure ('This cup is a new covenant in my blood') the cup is substituted for the indefinite 'this' of Matthew and Mark. Its content is the covenant itself, which is at the same time described as a *new* one, and only subsequently this is explained by the fact that the content of the cup corresponds to the Blood of Jesus. The peculiar equation, not of the wine and the blood, but of the cup and the covenant, may be due to the avoidance of the offence which the other formulation might have given to Hellenic sensibility.[1] Besides, the characterisation of the covenant as a 'new' one would have put even more heaviness into the formulation in Matthew and Mark, and thus a rearrangement of the sentence seemed advisable, so that

[1] Cf. above, p. 157.

'the new covenant' should stand at the head, and the 'blood' be put back to the end. If that be so, then the Pauline formulation presupposes that of the Synoptic, and we need not enquire after an Aramaic original in the former. The literal translation would be:

hādā kāsā hī ḳeyāmā ḥadattā be' idmī.

This does not sound better in Aramaic than in Greek. A part of the awkwardness could be smoothed down if one were to put *debe' idmī*, and thus bring this word into closer contact with *ḳeyāmā*. That would have to be translated: 'This cup is the new covenant connected with my blood'. The rendering of διαθήκη by *ḳeyām* needs to be explained. As a matter of fact, the Greek word could be used as it stands even in an Aramaic environment; the Palestinian and Syriac translations of the N.T. actually leave this Greek word untranslated. In post-Biblical Jewish literature *diatēḳē* means a will and testament;[1] and, as 'the transference of property in case of death', it is differentiated from the Hebrew *mattānā*, 'the granting of something as a gift', which becomes valid immediately, even before the death of the giver.[2] It was an axiom that a later will and testament abrogates a former.[3] A partial suspension meant an entire invalidation.[4] *Diatēḳē* and *mattānā* are applied to the apportioning of the dew to Abraham (Psalm cx. 3), in order to characterise it as irrevocable.[5] But nowhere is the O.T. *berīt* translated with *diatēḳē*. Only when our Lord had wished to designate His blood as a 'will and testament' would He have used *diatēḳē*. In itself this would not have been an impossibility, He could have bequeathed His blood testamentarily to the Disciples; but then His interpreting words would have had to have been: *dēn hū idmī dehū diatēḳē dīlī 'al yedēkhōn*, 'This is my blood, which is my testament for you'. Furthermore, the 'new testament' of the Pauline formulation could be brought into harmony with this idea, only if one should turn (with St Paul and the author of the Epistle to the Hebrews) every

[1] Bab. m. i. 7; Bab. b. viii. 7; Mo. k. iii. 3; Tos. Sab. viii. 13; Bab. b. viii. 8; ix. 14; xi. 6; Gen. R. 59 (125 a).

[2] p. Pea 17 d; cf. Heb. ix. 16.

[3] p. Bab. b. 16 b; cf. Tos. Bab. b. viii. 10 and Heb. viii. 13.

[4] p. Sanh. 20 c; Lev. R. 19 (48 a); Cant. R. v. 11 (58 b).

[5] p. Ber. 9 b; Taan. 63 b.

O.T. *berīt* into the legal form of a will and testament (Gal. iii. 15; Heb. ix. 16 f.), which could not possibly have been meant by our Lord, especially not in connexion with an 'agreement' which is evidently not His but God's. Even St Paul did not understand it differently; for 'the new agreement' of his formulation can only be the one which God promised (Jer. xxxi. 31 f.), to which the Apostle also points in Rom. xi. 27. And so διαθήκη goes back to the Hebrew *berīt* and this, or its Aramaic equivalent, we must presume in the words of Institution. It is rather surprising, however, that in Jewish literature (apart from the Targums) there is no Aramaic substitute for *berīt*; the Hebrew word only is used. One might conclude from this that the words of Institution (for the wine, and hence also for the bread, as well as the 'blessings' over both) were spoken by our Lord in Hebrew; and it would be somewhat daring to consider it impossible that He, under the circumstances, should have used the holy language.

In Hebrew the words in connexion with the wine would be *ze dāmī shellab-berīt*, or, according to the shorter form, *ze dam berītī*;[1] but just this shows that the choice of the kindred language does not in this case mean any real difference. The Aramaic form has the same sense, granted that *ḳeyām* was understood to mean the same thing as *berīt*, which is probable, as (though the word was not used in the language of daily life) from the Synagogual translation of the Law and the Prophets it must have been well known as the Aramaic word for *berīt*.

This equation of *berīt* and *ḳeyām* is the reason for rendering the conception designated by it not by 'covenant'[2] but by 'agreement'. 'Covenant' always suggests the joining together of several parties; the 'agreement' is the establishment of this union. *Ḳeyām* is something that is being erected, established, settled, and can therefore also mean an oath (Hebrew *shebū'ā*),[3] a vow (Hebrew *néder*),[4] an ordinance (Hebrew *ḥōḳ* or *ḥuḳḳā*),[5] a commandment (Dan. vi. 8, 16). In Hebrew, *berīt ḳōdesh*

[1] Franz Delitzsch in his Hebrew New Testament (in order to avoid the late-Hebrew *shel*) renders it: *ze dāmī dam hab-berīt*.

[2] In the translation, however, we found it more appropriate to use 'covenant'. Tr.

[3] Onk. Num. xxx. 3.

[4] Onk. Gen. xxviii. 20.

[5] Onk. Exod. xii. 14; xviii. 16.

(Dan. xi. 28–30, cf. 32) means thus the religion of God's Law. In a derivative sense the word is used of the special 'law' which is apportioned to the 'atmosphere' of every place.[1] It is stated as a principle of interpretation that 'there is no *berīt* apart from the Law'.[2] Also the terms *ben berīt, benē berīt*, often applied to Israelites when referring to their special legal position,[3] do not express the fact of their being 'covenanters', but that of being members of the 'settlement' founded by God, the contents of which 'settlement' is His Law. Of a human agreement only the word is used in the phrase *anshē berītekhā*, 'the men of thy *berīt*',[4] and *ēshet berītekhā*, 'the wife of thy *berīt*'.[5] Yet it need not therefore be denied that this 'agreement' or 'settlement', decisive as the Divine factor in it is, can only be realised when the people for whom it is meant actually accept it. As it speaks in Ezec. (xvi. 8) of God's entry into a *berīt*, so can the members of the 'community of the new *berīt* in the land of Damascus'[6] enter (*bā'u*)[7] into an 'agreement', which is God's. The binding of oneself to the proper keeping of the Law is the essence of the whole action.

Thus the underlying thought connected with *berīt* is the obligation to live a life well-pleasing to God; but only in so far as the obligation is, as far as possible, actually carried out at present; while Jeremiah (xxxi. 31 f.) beholds a more perfect realisation of it in the future. Mal. iii. 1 also brings the 'agreement' of God with Israel into relationship with the future, when he speaks of 'the messenger of the *berīt*', in whom God Himself, as the guardian of this '*berīt*', appears in the midst of His people, and where (in the probably later-inserted verses 22–24) it speaks of the returning Elijah, whose figure was probably connected with the eschatologically interpreted 'prophet like unto Moses' (Deut. xviii. 15). The Jews, when thinking of the

[1] Gen. R. 34 (70 b). [2] Mech. 5 a.
[3] Bab. K. i. 2, 3; Tos. Sanh. xi. 4; p. Sanh. 22 d; b. Sanh. 72 b.
[4] Ob. 7. [5] Mal. ii. 14.
[6] Cf. S. Schechter, *Documents of Jewish Sectaries*, 1; Meyer, *Die Gemeinde des Neuen Bundes im Lande Damaskus*, *Abh. P.A.W.* 1919, 9, chaps. 2. 2; 5. 12; 6. 19; 7. 6 f.; 8. 21; 19. 5.
[7] The entrance into the community of God is described also in Deut. xxiii. 2 by the word *bō*. The contrast to this is the 'forsaking' of the *berīt* (Hebrew '*āzab*), Dan. xi. 30.

messenger whose coming they desired (Mal. iii. 1), expected God's help in accordance with the nature of this agreement, while the prophet pointed out that this 'messenger' will, at first, even turn against them, in order that God's people may be made worthy to become an organ of salvation. That this realisation of the Divine 'agreement' in the life of Israel, which Malachi as well as Jeremiah expected in the future, was of great consequence to the contemporaries of Christ and even to Himself, can be seen from the relationship to the Elijah-expectation of Malachi into which the Baptist as well as our Lord were put (Mt. xi. 14; xvi. 14; xvii. 10 f.; Mk. viii. 28; Lk. i. 17; ix. 19; John i. 21; cf. vi. 14; vii. 40). This significance of the 'agreement' could not have been lost sight of at a Passover meal, where Elijah, as we have seen, stood in the foreground as the 'Messenger of the *berīt*' of the future expectation which the feast and its meal awakened.

In this direction we shall also have to look for the conception connected with *berīt* or *ḳeyām* in the words of the Institution. The underlying thought is God's '*agreement*' with His people, in so far as it concerns their inward life. And as this 'agreement' is connected with blood, it must be asked, which key for the understanding of this relationship does the O.T. supply, so that this short saying of our Lord could be apprehended intelligently?

The first thing to be noticed is that the Dominical expression reminds one of the solemn act on Sinai by which the people of Israel entered into an obligation to keep the Law (Exod. xxiv. 4 f.). The one half of the blood of the sacrifices, offered in the name of the people, Moses poured out towards the altar; the other half towards the people. And at the latter action he spoke the explanatory words (xxiv. 8): 'This is the blood of the *berīt* (Onk. *dēn dam ḳeyāmā*) which the Lord has made with you on the foundation of all these words'. A Jewish interpretation says that God's portion of the blood had to be poured towards the people, and the people's portion towards the altar (for God).[1] The essence of the whole act was the apportioning of the blood to both parties under the consideration of the

[1] Lev. R. 6 (18 a).

engagement into which they were entering. In the interpreting words of our Lord His blood would stand as a parallel to the sacrificial blood which was poured towards the people, and His administration of the wine would signify the presentment of the *berīt* as it was understood by Him. How His blood can have this value is suggested (but not explained in detail) by His putting it on a level with the sacrificial blood. In any case, the remark of Rabbi Isaac in connexion with Exod. xxiv is inapplicable here. That act reminded the Rabbi of a king who administered the oath to his legions on the sign of a sword, in order to demonstrate to them that they would be beheaded if they did not fulfil their duties.[1] Onkelos and Targum Yer. I remark also that the second half of the blood was poured out towards the altar, 'in order to propitiate the people'. They think thus of a propitiation of the blood; which would quite fit in with our Lord's application.

Much as the Dominical expression and its application at the administration of the wine may be reminiscent of Exod. xxiv, it is still rather remarkable that He should have taken for granted that His allusion to that narrative, which seems to have but little occupied the Jewish mind at that period, would be grasped at once by the Disciples. The conception of the 'covenant'-blood might have originated from this, but something else must have caused it to become a central thought just then. The expression used by our Lord suggests Zech. ix. 11, concerning 'the blood of the covenant' with Zion, for which sake her prisoners will be made free. An inelegant Jewish interpretation refers this to the law of menstruation (Lev. xv. 19 f.), the observance of which will bring forth Israel's redemption.[2] Nearer the point would be the allusion to the custom (on which probably Exod. iv. 25 is based) of sacrificing and blood-smearing at a marriage, as it is among the *ḥellīye*-sacrifices of the Bedouins of to-day. The marriage relationship between God and Zion (Isa. liv. 5) is at the background, but farther back stand the occurrences in connexion with the Exodus from Egypt. The Targum on this passage actually connects it with these: 'Also ye, for whom an "agreement" over the blood was appointed, I have redeemed

[1] Lev. R. 6 (17 b). [2] Lev. R. 19 (50 b).

from the slavery of Egypt'. At the same time, the direct reference is to the blood of the Passover lambs, which brings into fruition God's 'covenant' at the redemption from Egypt. According to Exod. vi. 4 f., this was the *berīt* with the Patriarchs, but Jer. xxxi. 31 and Ezek. xvi. 59 f. (cf. xx. 5) speak of God's *berīt* at the coming out from Egypt as the decisive factor, without thinking specially of Exod. xxiv. All the occurrences at the Exodus meant an 'agreement' of God with Israel, and it was not a far-fetched thought to consider the Paschal blood as the blood of this 'agreement'. Our Lord certainly did not, when administering the wine, think of Zech. ix. 11; but the Jewish ideas attached to that passage are valuable, since they show what was understood by 'covenant-blood'.

In later Judaism the *berīt* of God with Israel began to be connected with the sign of circumcision (Gen. xvii. 10). 'The blood of the *berīt*' meant the blood of the circumcision, which rite had to be performed even on him who was 'born circumcised'.[1] The notion thus arose that Israel was redeemed from Egypt by the merit of two kinds of blood: the Paschal blood, and the blood of circumcision.[2] Israel enters into a 'blood-relationship' with God on the basis of these double 'bloods'.[3] It gives loveliness to Israel.[4] God says: 'I am occupied with decrees of capital punishments, but I declare unto you, how I mercifully take pity on you by means of the Paschal blood and the blood of circumcision, and I propitiate your souls';[5] or: 'I see the Paschal blood and propitiate you, that your joy may be complete'.[6] In order to avoid a magic conception of the value of the Passover blood, it is emphasised:[7] 'It is not the *blood* that God saw, but He manifested Himself in order to save them as a reward for observing the commandments'. According to Tg. Yer. I. Exod. xii. 13 (cf. Tg. Cant. ii. 9), the execution of the command to smear the door-posts with the Paschal blood is, in union with the circumcision, the foundation of the reward upon which the effect of the blood rests.

1 Tos. Sab. xv. 9; p. Yeb. 9 a; Gen. R. 46 (97 b).
2 Exod. R. 17 (45 a). 3 Ruth R. vi. on iii. 8 (16 b).
4 Cant. R. i. 5 (14 a). 5 Exod. R. 15 (36 a).
6 Exod. R. 15 (35 b); cf. for the last words John xv. 11.
7 Mech. on Exod. xxiii. 12 (12 a).

Setting aside, as outside the range of our Lord's thoughts, the connexion with the blood of circumcision, there remains the Passover blood as that of the 'agreement', for which He would now substitute His own blood. Although the blood of the Paschal lamb, the meat of which He had eaten, was now ordinary offering-blood, without any propitiatory effect,[1] yet the dutiful remembrance (expressed in words) of the Egyptian Passover in itself awakened the attention to the application of blood which once had prevented a threatening destruction, and had been the necessary condition for the redemption from Egypt. This thought was near to the mind of our Lord, as it was to that of the Disciples, and the help which it gives to the understanding of His short sentence shows that we are on the right track. The red wine in the cup turned the mind of Jesus to the past, when the blood on the door-posts of Egypt once wrought redemption, as well as to the near future, when His blood, i.e. His own life, would be poured out. The Jews, when going over the ten plagues of Egypt, at the second cup of the Passover supper, dip a finger into the wine and then scatter the drops into another cup, counting, as the finger is shaken, up to ten, to symbolise that these plagues will come upon Israel's enemies but not upon Israel;[2] and at the fourth cup they pray (in the words of Psalm lxxvi) that God may pour out His anger upon the nations who know Him not.[3]

Our Lord, in bidding His disciples drink of the wine, thought, in direct opposition to this sentiment, of the benefits which His blood will procure for men, which evidently must consist in the 'agreement' of which He spoke.

It is clear, first of all, that Jesus' blood of 'agreement' would not have been necessary if the *berīt* of God with the fathers, well known to all Israelites, had still been in force, to such an

[1] Cf. above, p. 87.

[2] I have witnessed this in Constantinople on the 27th March, 1899; but see also Landshuth, *Haggada*, 20; Japhet, *Haggada*, 1884, 34; *Siddur Kolbo*, 1878, 500; *Siddur ha-Shelah*, 1884, 522; and especially Levisohn, *Mekore Minhagim*, 1846, 73 f.; *Sepher Maharil*, 1874, 15 b.

[3] Kimcha da-Abishona says in *Machzor Romi* (1540) in reference to this verse and custom: 'With this cup we accomplish the command (of the four Passover cups); and now do Thou also what Thou hast promised (us): pour out the four cups of punishment over the Gentiles'.

extent, as to convey to them all the blessings contained in it; and if the former 'blood of the *berīt*' had fulfilled its purpose permanently. In that case, God's 'agreement' for which He now was laying the foundation would transcend the former one even as to its content. As He speaks of the Temple which will be built by Him (Mt. xxvi. 61; John ii. 19; cf. Acts vi. 14), and puts His new 'Law' in apposition to that which was 'said to the ancients' (Mt. v. 21 f.), so does He speak of His blood of the 'covenant'. What He said at the distribution of the wine was indeed bold, removing the ground with one swoop from under the Passover feast and the rite of circumcision; which, in fact, did away with the whole Old Testament dispensation, and put something new in its place—from the point of view of Judaism a most destructive and 'blasphemous' saying. This utterance, however, brought up the question for the Disciples as to whether they wished to build their future life on the foundation of His Death. To die with Jesus, as Peter desired (Mt. xxvi. 35), were easy in comparison with this. It can be understood that among the Disciples there was one who, on hearing such words, resolved to accomplish his long-spun plan, and to do what he could even on this very night in order that the death that Jesus spoke of should become a reality; then one would see what efficacy this supposed blood of the 'covenant' really possessed; whether it was a dream or—what seemed impossible—the means of entrance into the Kingdom of God.

As there can be no doubt that it was Israel's sin that hindered God's 'covenant' from becoming effective, the Death of Jesus would mean the removal of this hindrance. The statements in Isa. liii concerning the death of the Servant of the Lord who mediates propitiation to many, could alone supply the lacking explanation here.[1] It is self-understood that the achievement of this Death, as well as the 'covenant' which it effects, must have a far-reaching significance, a significance which, according to Mt. xxi. 33 f.; Mk. xii. 1 f.; Lk. xx. 9 f., cannot be limited to the sphere of Israel. At the moment, however, the emphasis fell upon the application of this fact to the small circle of the Disciples, who, in so far as they were and remained this, were

[1] See below.

also the only real recipients of the gift and of the service dedicated to them.

The supplements to the Dominical words in connexion with the wine, in their traditional form, make clear what could also be derived from their shorter form. St Paul (1 Cor. xi. 25) describes the 'covenant' of God, in relation to which the blood of Jesus stands, as 'new'. He must have thought (in harmony with Heb. viii. 8 f.) of the 'new *berīt*' (Hebrew *berīt ḥadāshā*; Targum *ḳeyāmā ḥadattā*) of Jer. xxxi. 31 f., which God will establish in the future, and which will have its firm foundation in forgiveness of sin. One might think that 'the community of the new *berīt* in the land of Damascus' also based its self-characterisation on this prophetic word, but there is no direct reference to it, although it also says that God forgives the sins of those who turn from lawlessness to the ordinances of the Mosaic Law (iii. 12). To our Lord, in any case, other prophetic words must have been of greater significance. According to Isa. xlii. 6 and xlix. 8, God makes His Servant 'a *berīt* for the people' (Hebrew *berīt'ām*; Tg. *ḳeyām'am*), and of this Servant it is stated in Isa. liii. 10, 12, that in order to be this he will have to pass through death, and by it become the Mediator to many for the forgiveness of sin, and so reach the position due to the Servant of God. In the whole of the O.T. here alone is it to be found that there is a relationship between the *berīt* of God and the death of its Mediator. Therefore, our Lord could only have made clear to the Disciples the divinely-appointed necessity of His Death from this scripture, when He (according to Mt. xvi. 21; xx. 18 f.; xxvi. 2; Mk. viii. 31; ix. 12; x. 33 f.; Lk. ix. 22; xviii. 31 f.) instructed them concerning it. That He desired to be a Servant and, as such, pay the ransom 'for many' (Mt. xx. 28; Mk. x. 45)[1] must also be understood in connexion with Isa. liii. 12, where the Servant of God pours out his life 'for many'. In Lk. xxii. 37 we find that our Lord directly referred to this passage, and this proves that He occupied Himself with that important chapter in Deutero-Isaiah. It also means that whatever turned His thoughts at the Passover meal to the blood of the 'covenant', it was not any rite after that

[1] Cf. above, p. 117 f.

fashion which He wished to inaugurate that was to Him the content of His Death, but rather the personal accomplishment of an act of obedience towards the Divine Will, for the benefit of those to whom this Will offered the highest good.

The other additions point in the same direction. In Matthew and Mark the blood of the 'covenant' is more definitely described as

'shed for many'.

Aramaic: *demishtephēkh 'al saggī'īn.*

The Pal. Evang. has in Matthew *dileṭēb saggī'ē mishtephēkh*; in Luke *deḥallūphēkhōn mishtephēkh*. Syr. Sin. has in Mark *deḥalāph saggī'ē mit'ashēd. Leṭēb* is for Jewish Aramaic out of the question. *Ḥallūphē* and *ḥalāph* would mean 'instead of', and thus suggest vicarious suffering, which is not hinted at in the Greek ὑπέρ. Therefore it is best to use *'al*. 'To pray for someone' is in Jewish Aramaic *ṣallī 'al*;[1] 'to stand surety for one' is *'ārēb 'al*;[2] 'to reconcile someone' is *paiyēs 'al*.[3] The Hebrew *be'ad*, 'for', is almost constantly, and in connexion with the effect of propitiation of the sacrifice on persons *always*, translated with *'al* (see Lev. xvi. 6, 11, 24); and also in later Hebrew 'to effect propitiation for' is always *kipper 'al*.[4] For the 'shedding' of blood Onkelos and Yer. Targum have (Gen. ix. 6) *ashad*, but it is possible that *shephakh*, 'to pour out', would express better what is meant here; for a murderer *sheds* blood, while a priest *pours* the blood of the sin-offering out on to the base of the altar; Jesus, as the Possessor of life, pours out His precious Blood as though it were of little value. In this sense it is also said of the Jewish martyrs that they 'pour out their blood for the sanctification of the name of God', Hebrew *shōphekhīn dāmān 'al ḳedūshat shemī*.[5] Rabbi Meir said of criminals who had been executed that God grieved over the blood of the wicked which was 'shed' (Hebrew *nishpākh*).[6]

The 'many', to whom the blood of Jesus will be of service, point to the 'many' who, in Isa. liii. 11 f., are mentioned as those whom the suffering of the Servant of God will benefit,

[1] p. Pea 21 a; Sanh. 25 d, 29 a.
[2] p. Er. 22 a.
[3] p. Ber. 13 d.
[4] p. Yom. 38 b; b. Ber. 55 a; Sukk. 55 b; Bab. B. 10 b.
[5] Cant. R. ii. 7 (29 b).
[6] Sanh. vi. 5.

and on whom, therefore, He has a claim. In the prophecy the 'many' is meant to give an impression of the greatness of the future achievement of the Servant of God, who at present is alone,[1] and our Lord's reference to that word expressed appropriately what was in His mind; He also stood alone and seemed to perish and entirely fail to accomplish His task, but it was just this perishing that wrought the good of the 'many' who looked at Him without understanding.[2] The Disciples should know this, because they also belonged to the 'many'. If it were not for Isa. liii. 12, our Lord would scarcely have used this expression.

The reference to the purpose ('for the forgiveness of sins'), peculiar to Matthew, must also be based upon Isa. liii. The Pal. Evang. renders it by *lishebūḳīn desikhlān*. In Jewish Aramaic it would be *limeḥīlat ḥōbaiyā*. But it is still more commendable to dissolve the abstract form (a form which, with the exception of Lk. xxiv. 47, was quite unusual to our Lord) into the purposive sentence: *begēn deyishtabeḳūn ḥōbēhōn*, 'in order that their sins may be forgiven'. Although in Jer. xxxi. 34 forgiveness of sin is connected with God's new 'covenant', it is only from Isa. liii that we gather that it is the suffering of the Servant of God which leads to it, because it means a carrying of the sins of the 'many' (verses 4 and 12). The Targum turns it into 'their sins being forgiven (*ishtebēḳ*) for his sake', and expresses it in verse 6 in the sentence: 'it was pleasing to the Lord to forgive the sins of us all for his sake' (*lemishbaḳ ḥōbē kullánā bedīlēh*). The Targum (against the sense of the word, and probably from a polemical motive against the Christian interpretation of this word) changes the suffering of death of the Servant of God into a mere intercession, when it says of him in verse 12: 'for the sins of many[3] he prays'. The sin-offering becomes a 'paraclete', when it precedes the 'doron' (the present) of the burnt-offering.[4] Thus the Targum also could see the value of the suffering in the intercession of the sufferer; but the fact that it never actually mentions suffering must be taken as a conscious suppression. To Jesus, the suffering, as it is portrayed in the

[1] Cf. Dalman, *Jesaja* 53, 2nd ed. 57.
[2] Cf. S. E. Aurelius, *Jesu tanke om sitt lidande och sin död*, 1919, 11.
[3] The right reading is *ḥōbē saggī'īn*, instead of *ḥōbīn saggī'īn*.
[4] b. Zeb. 7 b.

Hebrew text of Isa. liii, is a fact; but the supplementary addition to His own interpreting words expresses the benefit resulting from this suffering, in the same way as the Targum expresses the result of the intercession of the Servant. Forgiveness of sin is evidently the indispensable presupposition for the participation in the Divine order of things which Jesus was about to establish.

All the additions may belong to a later record of the interpreting words of our Lord, if (notwithstanding the Pauline account) one were to shorten His saying to 'This is my blood which is shed for you'.[1] But, in any case, these additions just express what our Lord meant by His words concerning the wine; for, when in the synagogue of Nazareth He designated Himself rightly as the One in whom the proclaimer of salvation of Isa. lxi had appeared, He was convinced at the same time that He would die not only *like* unto, but *as*, the Servant of God of Isa. liii.

The Dominical words in connexion with the wine give no hint why His Death has the quality of ministering towards God's 'covenant'. That God had preordained His Death, our Lord silently takes for granted. Judaism has always opposed this idea. Ḥilkia called 'foolish liars' those who say of God that 'He has a Son and allows him to be killed'. Could God, who was unable to look upon the slaughtering of Isaac, 'have allowed His own Son to be killed, without destroying the whole world and turning it into chaos?'[2] Judaism thus considers that the mercy and love of God would be upset, if He had let His Son die. The legal principle, according to which 'one should not sacrifice one life for the sake of another' (Hebrew *ēn dōḥīn néphesh mippenē néphesh*)[3], could also be used by the Rabbis as a strong argument against it. King Joachim was said to have complained that the 'great Sanhedrin' transgressed against this principle in delivering him to Nebuchadnezzar.[4] Concerning one who was unjustly punished, the proverb says ironically: 'Shila is guilty and Johanna is brought to judgment'.[5]

[1] See above, p. 159.
[2] Ag. Ber. 69; cf. Bacher, *Agada der Pal. Amoräer*, III. 690.
[3] Ohol. vii. 6; p. Sab. 14 d; San. 26 c; b. San. 72 b.
[4] Lev. R. 19 (49 b); Gen. R. 94 (204 b).
[5] Gen. R. 25 (52 b); 40 (81 b); 64 (135 a); Ruth R. i. 1 (4 b).

Yet even Judaism knows that strict justice cannot always be applied. What it does not of itself demand, the consideration of the common weal may make categorically imperative. Rabbi Jehoshua ben Levi once said to a runaway who was being sought by the Roman government: 'It is better that this man (= thou) should be killed than that the community should be punished for his (= thy) sake',[1] thus persuading him to give himself up.[2] Also, God could be moved to consider the welfare of the community and not let justice run its full course. When Abraham interceded for Sodom, he is supposed to have said to God: 'If Thou dost desire to let the world be sustained, there can be no justice (Hebrew *dīn*); and when Thou dost demand justice, there can be no world. Why holdest Thou both ends of the rope? Thou wouldst have both, the world and justice (which is impossible)! Have one of them! If Thou dost not let off a little (of the justice), then the world cannot exist'.[3] Thus, consideration of the common weal can lead to acts which have nothing to do with strict justice, and yet appear to be morally just.

Moreover, the consideration of justice itself and its claims leads occasionally to actions which the principle of right does not as such demand. It is, for instance, a duty in certain circumstances to kill a would-be murderer before he has actually been able to commit the crime, and thus save (according to Gen. ix. 5) one life by means of another.[4] With admiration it is narrated of the son of Shim'on ben Shetaḥ, whom his own father condemned to death on being accused of a criminal act, that when he 'went out in order to be executed', and the witnesses shouted, 'We are liars', he said to his father, who wished to lead him back: 'Father (*abbā*), if thou wishest that salvation should come through thee, make me the threshold (i.e. do not consider me)!'[5] The legally pronounced punishment should be allowed to take effect, in order that the course of justice should remain undisturbed. A transference of punishment is considered possible when one who was unjustly con-

[1] An argument which Caiaphas applied in another form, John xi. 50.
[2] Gen. R. 94 (204 b); cf. p. Ter. 46 b.
[3] Gen. R. 39 (78 b); Lev. R. 10 (24 b); Pesikt. 125 b f.
[4] b. Sanh. 72.
[5] p. Sanh. 23 b.

demned to death should ask God that his death may propitiate all his sins, with the exception of the one for which he was thus wrongly condemned, so that the court of justice may in that way be absolved from guilt.[1] A person may, for the sake of the preservation of justice, take upon himself the punishment which belongs to another. The widow of Eleazar ben Shim'on told of him: 'When he sat studying the Law, he would go on with it as long as he wished and then say: "May all the chastisements of Israel come upon me!" and as he said—so it came to pass. And when the time of study came [again], he would say: "May every single one [of the chastisements] go back to its own place!"'[2] Then the pain which had come upon him would leave him. Jehuda, who desired to marry this widow, declared that he could do likewise. He called for the sufferings, and they came; but when he wished them to depart, they would not obey. So he suffered for thirteen years from toothache, and during that time no woman with child died in Palestine, no miscarriage took place, and rain always fell in the right season, all because of his vicarious suffering.[3] The greater value of Eleazar's suffering is explained as having been due to the fact that its motive was love to the people of Israel and to the Law, while Jehuda's suffering came upon him because of an inglorious act of his.[4] Rabbi Shim'on ben Yoḥai said: 'Every drop which dripped from that pious man (who had allowed himself to be bitten in order to say something to Ahab, 1 Kings xx. 37) propitiated the whole of Israel', because by it he protected them from being destroyed in the war with the Syrians.[5]

On the same basis rests Isa. liii. 4–6, where the Servant of God carries in His sufferings the punishment for the sins of others, evidently because there is no other way by which to free them from retribution; and the Divine order of justice demands that sin should not remain unpunished. Segal[6] considers it inconceivable to Jewish thought that God's justice should find satisfaction in the propitiatory death of His Son. Yet it is not

[1] p. Sanh. 23 b and Tos. Sanh. ix. 5.
[2] Eccl. R. xi. 2 (127 a); Pesikt. 94 b.
[3] Gen. R. 33 (66 a); 97 (207 b); b. Ket. 35 a; b. Bab. m. 85 a.
[4] b. Bab. m. 85 a.
[5] p. Sanh. 30 c.
[6] *Morija und Golgotha*, 1915, 13 f.

quite so unreasonable to believe that God, out of love to humanity, should have shown His righteousness, 'that He might Himself be (known) as just, and the justifier of him that hath faith in Jesus', i.e. who accepts for himself the effect of the Death of Jesus, as it is expressed by St Paul (Rom. iii. 26). This Pauline interpretation of the significance of the Cross must be considered also as the background for the thoughts of our Lord Himself, although He never directly spoke thus of His Death. When He, who was appointed to be the Head of the Kingdom (sovereignty) of God among men, died, in order that they might take part in God's 'covenant' by which this Kingdom could be fully established, it is clear that men could not enter this Kingdom unless they recognised that it was their sin that caused His Death, and thereby admit that the righteousness of God has to be satisfied. All the sufferings of the Rabbis, supposed to have vicariously spared their compatriots earthly punishments, were based upon Isa. liii,[1] but none of them with the same justification as the voluntary Death of Jesus, the result of which Death He offered to His disciples in the cup, at the end of His last Passover meal. Significant as the fact of this Death is, the disposition in which it was accomplished is no less significant. His words at the distribution of the bread and the wine inform us concerning it; but also His conduct to the last, a subject which will be studied in Part v, is an illustration of it.

XVI. THE WORDS OF INSTITUTION AND THE MEAL OF CONSUMMATION

St Luke and St Paul add to the interpreting words for the bread *τοῦτο ποιεῖτε εἰς τὴν ἐμὴν ἀνάμνησιν*. Syr. Hier. has for this in 1 Cor. xi. 24 *hādā hawō 'ābedīn ledukhrānā dīlī*; in Lk. xxii. 19 *hādā* is substituted by *hādēn*; *dukhrānā* by *dukhrānī*. Meyer[2] refers *τοῦτο* to *σῶμα*: the body of the Master should be made a sign of remembrance by the Disciples.

The usual interpretation of it as referring to the action just performed by our Lord, is the more natural. Perhaps *kedēn*, *hākhēn*, or *hākhedēn*, 'so', at the head of the sentence, would be

[1] Dalman, *Jesaja* 53, 2 f. [2] *Jesu Muttersprache*, 91.

better than *hādā*, although the latter corresponds more literally to the Greek. Thus the bidding would run in Aramaic as follows:

hākhedēn ʻabīdūn (hawōn ʻābedīn) ledukhrānī.

To emphasise the *dukhrān* (remembrance) by *dīlī* (my), would only be necessary if the remembering of Jesus were to be put in apposition to the remembering of someone else; but the accentuation lies undoubtedly on the *remembrance*. The Jews break the bread at every meal and distribute it; the Disciples, however, from henceforth should do it each time in remembrance of Him. The custom of bread-breaking was an established thing, and there was no need for our Lord to have instituted it; what was new was that His followers should at this rite think not only of the heavenly Giver of the bread,[1] but also of Him who is about to die for them. To Gentiles, not acquainted with this Jewish usage, it had to be introduced, and here was the danger that the breaking of bread as such might be turned into a ritual carrying significance in itself, as actually seems to have taken place among the Corinthians (cf. 1 Cor. xi. 26 f.). The thought of the institution of a remembrance was not outside the sphere of the Passover meal, for, apart from the wine, most of what was done at this meal was in remembrance of something, and had almost the character of a symbol. At the eating of the unleavened bread the coming out of Egypt was to be remembered (Exod. xiii. 3, 9; Deut. xvi. 3); the Paschal offering itself was meant to be a 'remembrance' (Exod. xii. 14). It corresponded with these ordinances that when the Passover lamb was eaten it was remembered that God had 'passed over (*pāsaḥ*) the houses of our fathers in Egypt'; at the eating of the unleavened bread it was remembered that 'our fathers were redeemed from Egypt'; at the bitter herbs (*mārōr*) that 'the Egyptians embittered (*mārerū*) the life of our fathers in Egypt' (cf. Exod. i. 14).[2] A Samaritan would add also that the blood at the door-posts should (according to Exod. xii. 14) be a remembrance (*dikhrān*) for all time.[3] The ancient admonition to express also in words the remembrance of the occurrences at the Exodus from Egypt (Exod. xii. 27; xiii. 8), and the

[1] Cf. above, p. 135 f. [2] Pes. x. 5.
[3] Heidenheim, *Bibl. Sam.* III. 33 b.

traditional legal ordinances concerning it,[1] prevented the meaning of the custom from being forgotten. Hillel at one time (in keeping to the literal wording of Num. ix. 11) put together a piece of meat from the Passover lamb, a piece of unleavened bread, and the bitter herbs, and ate them as one mouthful. Later it was (and still is) done likewise (naturally without the Passover meat) 'in remembrance of the Temple' (Hebrew *zēkher lam-miḳdāsh*).[2] By itself, Num. ix. 11, like Exod. xii. 8, was understood only as an enjoining of the triple duty, not as referring to the way in which it was to be observed.[3] Thus a formalistic observance of the Law resulted in a lasting custom, 'in remembrance of the Temple'. Even in exile the festive palms of the Feast of Tabernacles were carried in procession on all the seven days,[4] 'in remembrance of the Temple'. Moses is supposed, according to the Samaritan tradition, to have instituted a remembrance of the fast which he once kept with the community, a remembrance which will never cease.[5] Remembrance customs of different kinds, to which belong also the tabernacle of the Feast of Tabernacles according to Lev. xxiii. 43, and the lights of the Feast of Dedication of the Temple according to the later interpretation of its origin,[6] are widely spread in Judaism. To our Lord it did not, as we have seen, mean the institution of a new custom, but only the giving of a new significance to the old, which should from henceforth continually envisage Him in the midst of the Meal-fellowship of the Disciples. His purpose was certainly not to displace by this remembrance of Himself the prayer of praise to God, the Giver of the bread; nor does He give direct orders as to the way in which this remembrance of Him should find its expression, whether, for instance, it should be something apart from the usual benediction, or inserted into it, as (according to *The Teaching of the Apostles*, ix. 2 f.) was done later. St Paul admonishes that the Death of the Lord should, at any rate, be proclaimed in connexion with it (1 Cor. xi. 26), and this certainly was the purpose of our Lord Himself.

[1] Pes. x. 4, 5; Tos. Pes. x. 9. [2] b. Pes. 115 a.

[3] Siphre on Num. 69 (18 a); Mech. Bo. 6 (6 b). But see Machzor Vitry, 282; Landshuth, *Hagada*, 34 f.

[4] Sukk. iii. 12. [5] Bibl. Sam. iii. 157 a. [6] b. Sab. 21 b.

It is possible that originally it was only St Paul (1 Cor. xi. 24) who recorded that Christ instituted the breaking of bread in remembrance of Him. The purpose of the Apostle, however, was not to bring the usage itself into remembrance, this having been already established as the 'Meal of the Lord' (1 Cor. xi. 20), and celebrated everywhere in the churches (cf. Acts ii. 42; xx. 7); but the significance of the Institution not having always been kept in mind, he considered it necessary to enjoin it. The Evangelists could well leave out the Lord's ordinance, as their intention was not to describe the origin of the Eucharist but the occurrences of the last night in the Master's Life on earth. That the Early Church already considered it of importance to be united with her invisible Lord in the breaking of the bread, cannot be doubted (cf. Acts ii. 42). If our Lord did not institute it Himself, it was something which arose among His disciples in connexion with that unforgettable Last Supper with the Master, as every new 'breaking of bread' reminded them of His bread-breaking. But even if this were the historic truth, a truth, it would have to be assumed, which St Paul was already unaware of (which seems incredible), yet it is an experienced fact that one cannot come into closer contact with the Person of Jesus unless one breaks the bread not in spirit only but in actual bodily reality, as though one reclines with the Disciples round His table in Jerusalem, in the chamber of the Passover meal, on the night when one of His own delivered Him unto Death.

Only in St Paul's account are the interpreting words in connexion with the wine (1 Cor. xi. 25) followed by a command that the Disciples should repeat among themselves that which Jesus had done at the Last Supper. These words are the very same as those connected with the bread, but are extended here by the mention of the occasion on which it should take place: 'as oft as ye shall drink it'. In the Christian Palestinian Aramaic it is rendered: *kol imati de'attūn shātayin*. This *kol emat de* is used also in Targum Yer. I. Lev. xxiii. 42 in the same sense and is also sufficiently documented for the Galilaean Aramaic by *ēmat de* 'then when'.[1] The Aramaic *kol ēmat de'attun shātayin*

[1] p. Taan. 64 a; 'then when (*ēmat de*) ye wish, he also wishes'.

sounds as general as does the Greek original. Accordingly, one might refer the sentence to every consumption of wine, if the custom itself did not presuppose a plurality of persons, and thereby made it clear that it referred to a *communal* drinking of wine, and hence to a solemn meal which, as was shown above,[1] was called a drinking-bout. As used by our Lord it could only mean: 'As oft as ye, as My disciples, are gathered (as ye are now) to a common meal and conclude it with the drinking of wine'. The last words are of importance; no *festive* meal would be without wine; the *domestic* meal would often be without. Our Lord does not insist that wine should be drunk at a meal in order to commemorate Him, but that when it is done, He must not be forgotten. The remembrance at the wine and at the bread are independent of one another, but it is self-understood that a complete meal offers the opportunity for both.

In our Lord's Institution, however, the central thought is not the purely human petition: 'Do not forget me!' and the mere wish to keep intact the hitherto personal relationship to the Disciples. Behind it is the conviction that they, on their side, will need to have Him as their Master in the future also. In the interregnum, until His return, those who wait for Him must not fall asleep (Mt. xxiv. 42; xxv. 13; Mk. xiii. 33, 37; Lk. xxi. 36).[2] It is imperative for them to confess Him as their absent Lord, and not to deny Him (Mt. x. 32 f.; Lk. ix. 26), in order that He may recognise them as His own when He returns. Moreover, they must also confess Him, who is about to die, because others reject Him, who is God's Messenger, and because His Death opens to them God's 'covenant', the content of which is the 'sovereignty of heaven'. The remembering of Jesus (expressed in words) at every meal as Him who died for their benefit, is an incomparable means towards this, since nothing else exists to express the bodily communion with the Master, a communion interrupted only for a time, and which is the normal relationship between Him and them. What the Passover meal signified to the Israel of the old covenant, the Supper,

[1] Cf. above, p. 147.

[2] Cf. John xv. 1 f., which is perhaps meant to be a conscious parallel to the Institution of the Eucharist in Luke and 1 Corinthians.

endowed by Jesus with a new content, proffers, in a perfect fashion, to the community of His blood-covenant.

According to what has been said before, the remembrance of the Meal of the consummated Kingdom of God would have formed a part of the words of Christ at the administration of the wine. In the Jewish Passover also there is a reference to the Kingdom,[1] but it stands there principally for the political freedom and undisturbed life of the people of God in Palestine, following on the Divine punishment of Israel's oppressors; but to our Lord it meant the realisation of perfect communion with God, which included a communion of a new kind between His disciples and Himself. In Matthew and Mark the reference to the future meal is meant to strengthen the allusion to His Death contained in the interpreting words, by making it clear that very soon communion with the Disciples, as it had hitherto existed, is coming to an end, but will be taken up again after an interruption of an unknown duration, and in a more perfect form. Thoughts expressed in a different form in John xvi. 16–22 have their Synoptic counterpart here. In Luke, the words of our Lord concerning the meal of consummation explain chiefly the reason why only the Disciples should drink of this cup; but there also it serves the purpose of emphasising the earnestness of the moment, and at the same time it directs their eyes to the forthcoming glorious future.

In Mt. xxvi. 29 and Mk. xiv. 25 it says:

'Verily I say unto you, I will not drink henceforth [Mark "any more"] of this [Mark "the"] product of the vine until that day when I drink it new with you [not in Mark] in my Father's [Mark "God's"] Kingdom'.

Aramaic: *āmēn āmar anā lekhōn delā nishtē min kaddūn* (*tūbān*) *min* (*hālēn*) *pēraiyā deguphnā 'ad yōmā denishtē minnehōn* (*'immekhōn*) *we'innūn ḥadetīn bemalkhūtā de'abbā* (*de'elāhā*).

For the Hebrew *āmēn*, compare above, p. 30 f. For the elevated phrase concerning the wine, compare p. 150. The use of the first person plural in the imperfect for the first person singular was general in Galilaean Aramaic.[2] The following can also be mentioned as an example: *habēh lī nishteyēh*, 'Give it (the

[1] See above, p. 124. [2] Cf. Dalman, *Gram.* 2nd ed. 265.

wine) to me, I (we) want to drink it'.[1] According to the Aramaic idiom the interpreting words before 'the product of the vine' in Matthew need not refer to the wine which is just now in the cup, but to wine generally.[2] The immediate connexion between *nishtē* and the 'products' in the apodosis seems to be rather doubtful, hence the insertion of *min* in the protasis is repeated here. The predicate 'new' can scarcely be imitated in Aramaic, and must probably be considered as a Greek construction, although the Pal. Evang. puts *ḥadtā*. The Pes. has it also in Matthew, but in Mark it characteristically uses the adverb *ḥadtāit*, which is linguistically probably more correct, but such an adverb is not found at our disposal here. Thus we can only insert *we'innūn*, which invests the newness of the future with a special significance. The Matthean 'Father' instead of the Markan 'God' is quite appropriate, since it deals with the new world which God has appointed to His Son. According to Luke (xxii. 18), who before this (verse 16) has a parallel reference to the eating of the Passover,[3] it would have to be rendered in Aramaic: *de'āmar anā lekhōn delā nishtē min kaddūn min pērōhi deguphnā 'ad detētē malkhūtā de' elāhā*. Linguistically this is as possible as the formulation in Matthew and Mark. For the 'coming' of the Kingdom (reign) of God, compare Mt. vi. 10; Lk. xi. 2; xvii. 20.[4]

Our Lord (like the scribes) often compared the 'Kingdom' of heaven with a meal to which God invites mankind. In this case the meal of the 'Kingdom' is, to our Lord, not merely a parable but as real as the Passover meal which just then was coming to an end. He rejoiced in the fact that He will participate in it and that His disciples will sit with Him at the table (cf. Lk. xiii. 29; xiv. 15). The wine of which they will partake will be new, in contrast to the wine they were drinking; as also the Jerusalem of the future will be new, and as God will have made all things new (Rev. iii. 12; xxi. 2, 5), since there will be also a new heaven and a new earth (Isa. lxv. 17; lxvi. 22; Rev. xxi. 1). In all this is the meal of the future differentiated from that of the present; as also in Esther R. 2 (9 b), the banquet is described at which

[1] p. Ter. 45 c.

[2] Cf. above, p. 162.

[3] Cf. above, p. 127 f.

[4] See also *W.J.* 88, Germ. ed.

King Ahasuerus was supposed to have asked the Jews: 'Can your God do for you more than this?', and, in view of Isa. lxiv. 3, the answer he received was: 'Were He (God) to put before us such a banquet, we would say, "We have already eaten this at the table of Ahasuerus"'. But otherwise material colourings are prevalent in the picture of the future meal in Jewish literature. The Targum to Cant. (viii. 2) describes the meal of the Leviathan[1] at which 'we will drink old wine which was preserved in the grapes since the time when the world was created'.[2] Again, we read of the cup which will be placed before David and which, according to the numeric value of the word *rewāyā* in Psalm xxiii. 5, will contain 221 logs of wine.[3] Of this cup the following is told: 'When the eating and drinking is ended, the cup of blessing will be offered to our father Abraham; but when he shall declare himself unworthy to say the benediction, it will be given to Isaac, who will pass it on to Jacob, and from Jacob it will pass to Moses, from him to Joshua, and at last reach David, and he, although content according to Psalm xvi. 1 to sit on the threshold of the house of God,[4] says: "I will say the benediction, it suits me"; for it says (Psalm cxvi. 13) "I lift up the cup of salvation[5] and call on the name of the Lord"'.[6]

An essential constituent of the Jewish Passover liturgy (also in Jerusalem) has been since early times the exclamation: 'This year here, in the coming year in the land of Israel; this year as slaves, next year as free-men!'[7] The removal of the Divine judgment of the Exile from the Land is the most important presupposition for the hope of the perfect Passover celebration

[1] Concerning the banquet of the Leviathan, cf. b. Bab. b. 74 b.

[2] Cf. with this Creation- or Paradise-wine, b. Sanh. 99 a; Tg. Eccl. ix. 7; Tg. Yer. I. Gen. xxvii. 25.

[3] Midr. on Psalms, xxiii. 5; b. Yom. 76 a.

[4] Midr. on Psalms, xvi. 1.

[5] That this will take place in the future world is also mentioned in Tg. Psalm cxvi. 13, according to Gen. R. 88 (189 a); p. Pes. 37 c.

[6] b. Pes. 119 b.

[7] *Seder Rab Amram Gaon* (1865), I. 38; Landshuth, *Hagada*, 7; Japhet, *Haggadah*, 8 (a mixture of Hebrew and Aramaic); purely Aramaic in *Machzor Romi* (Bologna 1540): *hā-shattā hākhā leshattā deātyā be'ar'ā deyisrāēl, hā-shattā 'abdē leshattā deātyā be'ar'ā deyisrāēl benē ḥōrīn*. The reason for the use of Aramaic is given in the commentary: 'In Jerusalem joyous tidings were told in Aramaic'.

of a freed people. At the Last Supper the redemption of the past, of which the Passover celebration was a memorial, also turned the thoughts to the future Redemption, but to our Lord the imperfection of the present was infinitely greater than it was to the most pious of His people. He missed in the whole celebration, because of the obstacles of sin and death, the perfectly experienced fatherly love of God. In His expectation, therefore, everything racially-narrow and legally-formal, and everything of this earth earthy, is set aside before the great reality of the sovereignty of God, which will then determine resolutely that which is inward and that which is outward. No 'Lord's Supper' can be complete and according to the intention of our Lord's Institution, that does not direct the mind to this and put Him in the centre, whom His disciples will again have in their midst. The Communion Liturgy of the Moravians ends with the invitation taken from 1 Cor. xi. 26: 'As often as ye eat this bread and drink this cup, ye should proclaim the Lord's Death till He come'; at which the congregation responds: 'Till He come—to the great Supper, at which, in the banqueting-hall of the consummation, His bride will behold Him closely. Come, Lord Jesus! the Bride calls'.

PART FIVE

AT THE CROSS

XVII. THE CROSS IN JEWISH LITERATURE AND JESUS' WAY TO THE CROSS

CRUCIFIXION was not a Jewish mode of execution. When Jesus reproached the scribes and Pharisees, affirming that they would kill and crucify those whom He would send unto them (Mt. xxiii. 34), and when He said of Himself that the Son of Man would be delivered up to be crucified (Mt. xxvi. 2), He referred to a heathen method of execution, brought about, as He had expressly pointed out (Mt. xx. 19; Mk. x. 34; Lk. xviii. 32), by the Jews. Being condemned to death for blasphemy (which the Jewish Law defined later as 'cursing God with the express mention of His name'),[1] He would first have been stoned (according to Lev. xxiv. 14), then hanged. Hanging was conceived to be an exposure of the condemned criminal (Deut. xxi. 22 f.; Joshua x. 26).[2] From the point of view of traditional Law (according to the opinion of the majority of the scribes) only blasphemers and Jews condemned for idolatry were thus to be 'exposed'; as in the Deuteronomic expression (Deut. xxi. 23) *ḳilelat elōhīm*, 'the curse of God' (interpreted to mean 'cursing God'), relating to one hanged, was found a suggestion of the crime.[3] Furthermore, all those 'who stretch out their hands against an essential article (Hebrew *'ikkār*) of the Law' (i.e. deny one of its fundamentals) should be treated in a like manner.[4] Only from the point of view of these judicial conceptions can the Crucifixion of our Lord be brought into relationship with the Jewish criminal Law.

The criminal was even undressed before the stoning took

[1] Sanh. vii. 5. Thus, the condemnation of our Lord was not in accordance with the traditional Law.

[2] Cf. Siphre Deut. 221 (114 b); Siphra, 105 b; Sanh. vi. 4; Tos. Sanh. ix. 6; Jos. *Ant.* VI. 8. 6.

[3] Siphre Deut. 221 (114 b); Sanh. vi. 4; according to Meir, the expression suggests God's sorrow for the blood of the wicked having to be shed; Sanh. vi. 5.

[4] p. Sanh. 23 c.

place, the covering necessary for decency alone was left.[1] This was also done in cases of women criminals by turning the face to the gallows while the hands were bound upwards on to it.[2] Thus, the hanging was meant to be a sign of dishonour. It was considered unseemly that the near relations of the crucified should remain in the same town, 'until the whole flesh has disappeared and the deceased unrecognisable from the remains of his body'.[3] This would also be applied to one hanged in accordance with Jewish regulations. Moreover, 'the hanged one' is (cf. Deut. xxi. 23) above all, a 'curse of God', i.e. is accursed by Him, excluded from the sphere of His protection and His beneficence; as it was rightly understood by St Paul according to the Greek translation (Gal. iii. 13). Rabbinic tradition[4] interprets it in the sense of 'cursing', i.e. 'insulting, blaspheming, God'; the Onkelos Targum, therefore, sees in *kilelat elohim* the guilt only of man; while Targum Yer. I also thinks of the insult to the image of God which such a spectacle must be, and thus seems to have in mind Rabbi Meir's interpretation of this phrase.[5] Because it had this character, hanging had to be put off until the evening, so that the exposure should last but a short time, and burial, which, according to the Law (Deut. xxi. 23; cf. Joshua viii. 29; x. 26), had to take place before night, should follow immediately.[6] In this way justice was satisfied, the criminal treated with consideration, and the land spared a further defilement by the corpse. The removal from the Cross of the body of Jesus and those of them who were crucified with Him on the Sabbath eve, is in John xix. 31 considered from the point of view of the sanctity of the Sabbath. This has no basis either in the Mosaic Law or in Jewish tradition; nor did it require any such motive. If the reason given is not due to the Evangelist's imperfect knowledge of the actual law, nothing remains but to assume that he considered it legitimate to connect it with the special circumstances of the time.[7]

[1] Siphre Deut. 221; Sanh. vi. 3; Tos. Sanh. ix. 6.
[2] Sanh. vi. 4.
[3] Sem. ii. 13.
[4] Cf. above.
[5] Tos. Sanh. ix. 7; b. Sanh. 46 b; cf. also below, p. 194, in connexion with the story of the twins.
[6] Siphre, *ibid.*; Tos. Sanh. ix. 6.
[7] Cf. also above, p. 105 f.

The Rabbis point out that only those condemned by the representatives of the foreign power (Hebrew *harūgē malkhiiyōt*) were hanged alive.[1] In the O.T. however the term used for hanging is the same, whether it is applied to the hanging *after* the execution, or to hanging as the actual mode of execution, which latter is found in Gen. xl. 22; Esther vii. 9 f.; Ezra vi. 11; they are both called *tālā* in Hebrew, and hence the same word for both is used also in later Hebrew, without differentiating between the various kinds of hanging.[2] The expression for this in the Targum is invariably *ṣelab*, and the gibbet used for this purpose is called *ṣelīb* there (Deut. xxi. 22; Josh. x. 26; Esther Tg. ii. 7, 9 f.). This root is also found in Galilaean Aramaic,[3] and in the Pal. Evang. and Syrus Harclensis it is exclusively used for 'to crucify', but it has also entered into later Hebrew.[4] The Babylonian Aramaic equivalent is *zeḳaph*,[5] which is also preferred by the Peshito, and is used in Biblical Aramaic (Esther vi. 11). Because of this it is not always certain which sort of hanging is meant, but it also shows that all sorts came under the same category. Although crucifixion was not the legally Jewish manner of hanging, it would yet have been quite possible for a Jew to think that, if Jesus of Nazareth was a blasphemer, full justice was done to Him by this mode of execution. Eleazar ben Shimon stood weeping *under the cross* (*ḳām tōtē zeḳīphā*) on which a washerman, against whom he had witnessed, was hanged; but he was comforted when he found that the man and his son had, on the Day of Atonement, committed rape upon a betrothed virgin—since stoning, followed by hanging, was the punishment for the crime.[6]

The Roman government in Palestine often employed crucifixion as a mode of punishment, and naturally Jews also, whether guilty or innocent, could be thus executed. Even a Jewish King, Alexander Jannaeus, crucified on one occasion not less than 800 persons in Jerusalem itself;[7] and no juridical

[1] Siphre Deut. 221; b. Sanh. 46 b.
[2] Sanh. vi. 4; b. Sanh. 46 b.
[3] p. Ḥag. 78 a; Sanh. 23 c; Eccl. R. vii. 26 (129 b); Gen. R. 65 (141 a).
[4] Yeb. xvi. 3; Sab. vi. 10; p. Gitt. 48 c; Tos. Ohal. iv. 11.
[5] b. Bab. m. 59 b; 83 b; Ab. z. 18 b.
[6] b. Bab. m. 83 b.
[7] Jos. *Ant.* XIII. 14. 2; Klausner, *Historia isreēlit*, II. 130, rejects the testimony of Josephus without sufficient proof.

problems arose in connexion with this mode of execution. The blood of a dead person is, according to the Law, both impure and a source of defilement; but what about the blood running from one on the cross (Hebrew *ṣālūb*)? When a quarter of a log of blood was found *under* him, it was considered 'pure', i.e. 'undefiling'; while the same measure of blood dripping down from him when already dead, was 'impure'. Yet Rabbi Jehuda argued that even the latter was 'pure', because 'the last blood-drop of death' drips down onto the wood, and thus does not reach the ground, where the blood of a living person only could gather.[1] The principle applied was that defilement from touching a dying person begins only after the soul has left the body.[2]

That one crucified could continue to live for a considerable time, was important from the point of view of the Law; since his wife could re-marry only when his death was attested to with certainty. Hence no proof of this could be given concerning one who was nailed (Hebrew *ṣālūb* and *niṣlāb*) to the cross (Hebrew *ṣelūb*), 'before his soul has left him' (Hebrew *'ad shettēṣē naphshō*). Even if the body had been seen drawn and quartered, or hanging on the cross, so that wild beasts devoured the flesh, witnesses of the death would only be accepted after three days had passed;[3] the reason evidently being that under such conditions it would be impossible that life could remain longer in the body. It was always, however, the general opinion that the separation of the soul from the body only took place after three days had elapsed.[4] One who had been crucified was once actually saved again by the intercession of a noble woman; or heaven (i.e. God) had pity on him.[5] Haman demanded that Mordecai should be hanged on the gallows (*ṣelībā*), because not one of his compatriots had ever yet been saved.[6] He was of course mistaken in this case, for it was said of Mordecai: 'Yesterday he was to be hanged, to-day he hangs those who wanted to hang him' (Hebrew *ṣōlēb et ṣōlebāw*).[7] Haman,

[1] Tos. Ohal. iv. 11.

[2] Ohal. i. 6; b. Yeb. 120 b; Naz. 43 b.

[3] Yeb. xvi. 3; Tos. Yeb. xiv. 4; b. Yeb. 120 b.

[4] p. Yeb. 15 c; Lev. R. 18 (45 b).

[5] p. Yeb. 15 c; b. Yeb. 120 b.

[6] Esther R. 9 on v. 10 (25 b).

[7] Gen. R. 30 (59 b); cf. Exod. R. 20 (53 b).

moreover, prepared a rope and nails for him.[1] The nails used for a crucifixion (which, according to John xx. 25, cf. verses 20, 27, were used for the hands of our Lord, and, according to Lk. xxiv. 39, also for His feet) played a certain rôle in Jewish superstition. Such a nail was carried about as a protection and a remedy, a 'burden' which was also permitted on a Sabbath.[2]

'Jesus carried His Cross and went out', according to John xix. 17; while the Synoptists emphasise that 'when they went out' (Mt. xxvii. 32) they put the Cross upon another (Mt. xxvii. 32; Mk. xv. 21; Lk. xxiii. 26), so that they might continue to mock Him, maybe, as King (Mt. xxvii. 27 f.; Mk. xv. 16 f.; John xix. 2 f.), and perhaps also to supply 'the King of the Jews' with a servant. Mk. xv. 20 also speaks of 'His being led out', and, moreover, this being 'led out' had a legal significance, in so far as a blasphemer had to be stoned 'outside the camp' (cf. Lev. xxiv. 14), i.e. according to tradition, outside the three camps (that of the Shekhina, of the Levites, and of Israel).[3] Now, in regard to 'holiness', 'the camp of Israel' in Jerusalem was confined to the city within the walls,[4] and legally, therefore, the stoning and the hanging had to take place outside Jerusalem. The place of the execution of our Lord might have been chosen to be outside the city in any case, even apart from any consideration by the Romans for the Jewish Law. And yet, to the author of the Epistle to the Hebrews (xiii. 12) it seemed significant that this should have corresponded to the demands of the Jewish Law, and that this action meant therefore exclusion from the community of the people of God.[5]

To such 'goings out' there are also parallels in Jewish sources. There is a differentiation made between the 'going out' in order to be judged and the 'going out' in order to be executed.[6] Together with Jesus 'two robbers' (λῃσταί) were led to the place of execution (Mt. xxvii. 38; Mk. xv. 27; cf. Lk. xxiii. 32). For robbers to be hanged would seem natural. There is a

[1] Esther R. 9 on vi. 11 (27 a). [2] Sab. vi. 10.
[3] Siphra 105 b; b. Sanh. 42 b f.
[4] Tos. Kel. Bab. b. i. 12; Num. R. 7; cf. *P.J.B.* 1909, 33.
[5] Concerning Golgotha see *O.W.* 365 f., Dalman, *Jerusalem und seine Umgebung* (1929), A. 4. [6] Gitt. iii. 4.

proverb concerning one who joined a robber-band only once and was caught: 'The latest among the robbers is the first among the crucified'.[1] Of a *lēsṭēs* and one whom this robber falsely designated as his accomplice in a murder, it says: 'Both of them went out (*nāpheḳīn*) carrying two beams' (*ṭe'īnīn tartē shāryān*).[2] When, in a parable, a king sees how the thicker end of the beam is put upon his son and exclaims: 'Put on me as much as you will, I will carry it!'[3] it probably refers to a voluntary carrying of the cross. It must have been the executioner's mates who 'carried the beam', when Jose ben Joezer 'stepped before it in order to be crucified' (*azal ḳummē*[4] *shārītā lemisṭelāba*). His wicked nephew Jakum, who, although it was Sabbath, was riding a horse at that time, shouted to him mockingly: 'Behold my horse which *my* master lets me ride, and thy horse upon which thy Master (God) makes thee sit!'[5] Jose ben Joezer belonged probably to the eight hundred whom King Jannaeus caused to be crucified in the year 88 B.C.[6] and was no doubt put to death as a Pharisaic adversary of a cruel king. At a later date, Rabbi Nathan had occasion to lament: 'What has happened that thou goest out to be crucified?' and the community of Israel makes answer: 'It is because I ate unleavened bread (of the Passover feast)'—'Why have they lashed thee?'—'Because I carried palm-branches (of the Feast of Tabernacles); these chastisements have won me favour from my Father in heaven'.[7] In this sense Rabbi Ammi said:[8] 'Think not [lit. thou thinkest] [that the phrase] "either a Jew or a crucified" is offensive; it is not offensive, but on the contrary, laudatory (i.e. a Jew is ready to be crucified for his religion)'.

Isaac, himself carrying the wood for the sacrifice (Gen. xxii. 6), reminded the Rabbis of 'one who carries the cross on his

[1] Eccl. R. vii. 26 (109 b).
[2] p. Ber. 5 c.
[3] Midr. on Psalms, xxii. 9 (22).
[4] This must be read instead of *ḳummēh*. Schlatter, *Der Märtyrer*, 54, inserts *ṭe'īn* behind *ḳummēh*, and translates: 'He walked in front of him (i.e. his nephew) carrying the beam'.
[5] Gen. R. 65 (141 a); Midr. on Psalms xi. 7.
[6] *Ant.* XIII. 14. 2; *Bell. Jud.* I. 4. 6.
[7] Lev. R. 32 (86 b); Mech. 68 b; cf. Zech. xiii. 6.
[8] Exod. R. 42 (100 b).

shoulders' (Hebrew *shehū ṭō'ēn ṣelūbō bikhetēphō*).[1] Jesus said (Mt. xvi. 24; cf. x. 38; Mk. viii. 34; Lk. ix. 23):

'If any man will come after me, let him deny himself and take his cross and follow me'.

Aramaic: *bar nāshā debā'ē mehallākhā bāteray, yehē khāphar begarmēh weyiṭ'an ṣelībēh weyētē bāteray.*

Instead of *begarmēh*, *benaphshēh* ('his soul') would also be possible, as, in fact, the Peshito has, and which could refer to life. The Greek text, however, does not suggest it. In Aramaic and Hebrew, 'to follow' can only be expressed with 'to go', 'to come behind someone'. 'Follow us!' (Hebrew *ṭaiyēl aḥarēnu*) said Gamaliel to one who came to him with a petition, and who then actually followed him and his associates (Hebrew *hitḥīl meṭaiyēl aḥarēhem*).[2] 'A place whereto my teacher cannot follow me' is in Hebrew *māḳōm she'ēn rabbī yākhōl lābō aḥaray*.[3] 'A serpent followed him' (Aramaic *azal bāterēh*).[4] 'He ran after him' (Hebrew *rāṣ aḥarāw*).[5] 'He ran after them' (Aramaic *nephaḳ pārē bāterēhōn*).[6] The figurative application of this expression is in Rabbinic literature without example. On the lips of our Lord the phrase must be connected with the picture of the carrying of the Cross; Jesus Himself is portrayed as a cross-bearer and His disciples must join Him on His way to execution. An appropriate illustration of the sense in which this is meant is found in a Rabbinic interpretation of Deut. xxviii. 66, where the Midrash (in connexion with the words 'thy life shall hang in doubt before thee') points to 'him who goes out in order to be crucified' (Hebrew *ze shehū yōṣē lehiṣṣālēb*).[7] Our Lord does not think of the bearing of any suffering, but, as He explains it (Mt. xvi. 25; Lk. xiv. 26 f.), of a voluntary and (according to Lk. ix. 23) daily renunciation of life, which is so whole-hearted as to be like that of one who goes with perfect willingness to his appointed death. This is the meaning also of the denial of self which He demands, and which also was not a current expression, for there is no parallel to it in Jewish literature, and

[1] Gen. R. 56 (118 b).
[2] Lev. R. 37 (101 b).
[3] Mech. 2 a.
[4] p. Sab. 8 c.
[5] Ab. d. R. N. 41; cf. Der. Er. 4 (*hālakh*); b. Taan. 40 b (*hāyā meṭaiyēl*).
[6] p. Mo. k. 81 d.
[7] Esther R. i. 1 (1 a).

it must therefore be taken in its full austerity, in the sense of entire separation from one's own self, acknowledging it no longer, and, therefore, delivering it willingly to death. In this spirit our Lord actually carried His Cross.

Judaism praises one who, for the sake of the Law, makes himself insignificant (Hebrew *meḳaṭṭēn*);[1] becomes a fool (Hebrew *menabbēl*);[2] makes himself as a slave (Hebrew *mesīm 'aṣmō khe'ébed*);[3] plagues himself (Hebrew *mekhattēt*);[4] yea, kills himself (Hebrew *mēmīt*).[5] But Judaism has never demanded self-denial, especially in the following of a Person who denies Himself not in the service of the Law but of God who wishes to establish His reign on earth in a new way. If our Lord had thought here of Isaac going towards Moriah, the difference between Him and the latter must also have been clear to Him. Isaac carried the wood for the sacrifice without knowing what Abraham was going to do with it, and Abraham's knife was stopped before it could pierce Isaac's heart; Jesus knew the will of God, who could not spare His Son this way and its end: therefore He had to drink of the cup of self-denial to the dregs. The willingness of Isaac to let himself be bound as a sacrifice (upon which the Biblical narrative does not enlarge) is described by the Rabbis as having been so perfect that he even asked his father to bind him firmly, so that he might not tremble and thus make the sacrifice invalid;[6] and to this voluntarily endured 'binding of Isaac' (Hebrew *'aḳēdat yiṣḥāḳ*) on the altar, great consequences were attached: until this day it affects God's pity towards Israel when He remembers it.[7] In the Passover blood God saw the blood of Isaac[8] (which, however, had not actually been shed!) and because of it spared the first-born of His people. Thus the carrying of the cross became a symbol for the most great and difficult human accomplishment. It is self-understood that the way of the Cross which our Lord walked can claim a greater significance and a more far-reaching effect than Isaac's offering.

[1] p. Sot. 24 b; b. Bab. m. 85 b.
[2] b. Ber. 63 b.
[3] b. Bab. m. 85 b.
[4] b. Ber. 63 b.
[5] *Ibid.*; b. Sab. 83 b; Git. 57 b.
[6] Gen. R. 56 (119 b); Pirke R. Eliezer, 31.
[7] p. Taan. 65 d.
[8] Mech. 8 a.

It was human sympathy with sorrow that made the Jerusalemite women start a death lamentation over Jesus on His way to the Cross, by beating themselves and weeping (κόπτεσθαι, Lk. xxiii. 27). 'When one goes out in order to be crucified (Hebrew *yāṣā liṣṣālēb*) his father weeps over him, and his mother weeps over him and beats her breast (Hebrew *mitḥabbéṭet*), and they say: "Woe unto me!" But the woe is his who goes out to be crucified'.[1] Rabbi Ḥanina ben Teradyon, being condemned to be burnt, reprimanded his daughter, who wept and wailed and beat her breast (Hebrew *mitḥabbéṭet*), with the words: 'When thou bewailest and lamentest and beatest thyself, were it not better surely that (earthly) fire should consume me (a fire which has to be kindled) than the fire (of hell) which needs no kindling?'[2] Of greater earnestness is our Lord's reprimand of womanly sympathy (Lk. xxiii. 28):

'Ye daughters of Jerusalem! Weep not over me, but weep for yourselves and for your children!'

Aramaic: *benāt yerūshlēm, lā tihweyān bākhyān ʻalay, ellā bekhan ʻal garmēkhēn weʻal benēkhēn.*

Sympathy for Himself our Lord requites by sympathy for the lamenters, which should make them reflect how little they had grasped the meaning and importance of His having been condemned to die upon the Cross—that it was caused through Jerusalem's rejection of her Saviour, and must, therefore, result in the greatest calamity for them.

Arriving at the place with the Aramaic name of Golgoltā,[3] which rightly reminded the Evangelists of a 'skull' (Mt. xxvii. 33; Mk. xv. 22; Lk. xxiii. 33; John xix. 17), Jesus was given to drink wine mingled with myrrh (Mk. xv. 23), but refused it. According to Lk. xxiii. 36, the drink which was offered mockingly by the soldiers instead of wine was vinegar; according to Mt. xxvii. 34 (probably because of Psalm lxix. 22)—vinegar mingled with gall. But Mark is most probably right in stating that it was a narcotic drink. It used to be the custom for women of rank in Jerusalem to offer on their own initiative to the condemned, incense in a cup of wine (according to the advice in

[1] Siphre on Deut. 308 (133 b). [2] Sem. 8.
[3] This form in Pal. Evang., see also *P.J.B.* 1913, 98 f.; *O.W.* 365.

Prov. xxxi. 6 f.), in order that the consciousness should be numbed and the pain alleviated.[1] Naturally, the wine was undiluted.[2] Incense and myrrh were probably meant also to strengthen the narcotic effect by their scent. Our Lord did not accept even this expression of sympathy; He wished to drink the Father's cup unmixed and without abatement (cf. Mt. xx. 20; John xviii. 11).

In a trilingual inscription the soldiers, by the order of Pilate (John xix. 18 f.), designated the Crucified One as the 'King of the Jews' (Mt. xxvii. 37) (in Aramaic *malkā dīhūdāē*).[3] This designation, the mocking character of which would be felt more than anything by the Jews, recalls a parable of Rabbi Meir. Of a king's twin sons who looked exactly alike, one became king while the other joined a robber-band (*lēsṭaiyā*). The latter was caught and nailed to a cross (Hebrew *ṣelūb*). Every passer-by (Hebrew *'ōbēr wāshāb*) said: 'it looks just as though the king himself were crucified'. He was therefore taken down.[4] At the Cross passers-by (Mt. xxvii. 39; Mk. xv. 29) felt only the contrast between Jesus' present position and what He previously was and had claimed to be. He who had behaved as the Lord of the Temple was now mocked (Mk. xv. 29; cf. Mt. xxvii. 40): 'woe unto him who destroys the Temple and builds it in three days!' (Aramaic *way dephākhar hēkhlā ubānōhi bitelātā yōmīn*)—as it is expressed in an Aramaic proverb: 'Hunter, how they hunt for thee! Breaker of doors (*pākhōr tar'aiyā*), how broken and destroyed is thy door!'[5] He who worked miracles was mocked (Mt. xxvii. 42; Mk. xv. 31): 'others He helped, Himself He cannot help!' In this was repeated the proverb which Jesus had read in the minds of His countrymen in Nazareth.[6] Rabbinic literature has it in the following form: 'Physician, heal thy lameness!'[7] and applied it figuratively. Here it was meant literally.

Jesus was silent at this. He could have drawn attention, as He did when He was captured (Mt. xxvi. 53 f.), to the lot destined for Him by God, which excluded self-help as well as

[1] p. Sanh. 43 a; Sem. ii. 9.
[2] Num. R. 10 (68 b).
[3] Cf. above, pp. 7, 15.
[4] Tos. Sanh. ix. 7; b. Sanh. 46 b.
[5] Gen. R. 67 (142 b).
[6] Cf. above, p. 50.
[7] Gen. R. 23 (49 b).

Divine intervention. But He was silent, confirming what is written in Isa. liii concerning the silent patience of the Servant of God. To this passage Rabbi Jose ben Chanina might have referred in his remarkable allegorical interpretation of the narrative concerning the arrival of Jacob in Haran (Gen. xxix. 4 f.). It runs:[1] 'The shepherds say: "We are from Haran"—(it means:) We flee from the wrath (*ḥārōn*) of God. Jacob says: "Do you know Laban?" (i.e.) Do you know him who will make your sins white (*labbēn*) as snow (Isa. i. 18)? "Is it well with him (*shālōm*)?"—The shepherds answer: "It is well". "By whose merit?"—The shepherds say: "Behold, Rachel comes with the sheep"'. The Rabbi evidently regarded Rachel as a successful propitiator,[2] as it is written (Jer. xxxi. 14): 'thus the Lord has said; Rachel weeps for her children, etc.' It would have been more to the point if he had referred to Isa. liii. 7: 'behold He comes, who is like a lamb led to the slaughter and like a sheep (*rāḥēl*) dumb before her shearers, and openeth not his mouth'. Such a silently-suffering, sin-destroying, and wrath-appeasing Saviour, stands before us in the silent Man on the Cross.

XVIII. THE FIRST THREE WORDS FROM THE CROSS

For Himself our Lord did not plead, but for others. His first word referred to the soldiers who nailed Him to the Cross (Lk. xxiii. 34):

> 'My Father, forgive them, for they know not what they do'.
> Aramaic: *abbā shebōḳ lehōn lētēhōn ḥākhemīn mā 'ābedīn.*

Abbā means '*my* Father'.[3] *Shebaḳ*, 'to let', can also mean 'to let off', 'to release'. The disciple of Jose the Galilaean once said to him: 'Rabbi, release this woman from thee (let her go)' (Aramaic *rabbī shebōḳ hādā ittetā minnākh*).[4] A similar expression the Disciples probably used (Mt. xv. 23): 'Let her (the Canaanite woman) from thee!' (send her away) (Aramaic *shubḳah minnākh*). *Shebak* in the sense of 'let' is found in the sentence: *shebakū*

[1] Gen. R. 70 (151 b).
[2] So she is represented in Lam. R. Peth (73 a).
[3] See *Gram.* 198.
[4] Lev. R. 35 (95 a).

demārē ḥōbā deyigbē ḥōbēh ('let the creditor draw in his claim').[1] But it is also used for 'letting off' (cancelling) a debt. *Yehē sherī lākh yehē shebīḳ lākh*, 'let it be soluble to thee, let it be cancelled to thee!' it says of a debt which has not been called in;[2] of a wrong done to one's fellow it says: *sherī lan wanan shāray lākh*, 'absolve us and we will absolve thee';[3] of wrong done to God: *yāē le'ēl rab deshābēḳ leḥōbīn rabrebīn*, 'it suits a great God to absolve great debts!'[4] The Aramaic expression used by our Lord when addressing the lame man (Mk. ii. 5) must accordingly have been: *berī ḥōbākh shebīḳīn lākh*, 'My son, thy debts are cancelled to thee!' Similarly, a woman in Askelon expressed her desire to forgive her neighbour, who abused her, all but one of her offences: *'al kullā sherī ushebīḳ lākh*.[5] Asking God to forgive on grounds of the ignorance of the guilty reminds one of a phrase used concerning the venerable Shemuel bar Isaac, who felt it his duty to dance in a wedding procession before the bride: 'Let be, that ancient knows not what he does!' (Aramaic *arpūn lēh lēt āhān sābā yāda' mā 'ābēd*).[6] So it was an expression frequently used in daily life that our Lord applied to the action of the non-Jewish soldiers. The greater guilt of those Jews who delivered Him up to the heathen authorities was probably also in the background (John xix. 11), but was not expressed and was not urged before God.

When Ḥanina ben Teradyon was about to be burnt to death, he convinced his reluctant executioner that God Himself had ordained it, and would therefore demand Ḥanina's blood from him, the executioner, if he did not fulfil his duty. Thereupon the latter also threw himself into the flames to join Ḥanina in death; and a Divine voice assured him of eternal life.[7] Acquittal from punishment is proclaimed here to one, who in the service of a Divine decree executes an unjust human judgment; and the voluntary carrying out of the same sentence on himself brings to him also eternal life. Our Lord does not appeal for forgive-

[1] Eccl. R. xi. 2 (127 a).
[2] Pesikt. 137 b.
[3] p. Mo. k. 81 d; cf. Shebi. 35 b. To 'let' for forgive reminds one of Mt. xvi. 19; xviii. 18; cf. John xx. 23.
[4] Lev. R. 5 (16 a).
[5] Lam. R. i. 11 (32 b).
[6] p. Ab. z. 42 a; Gen. R. 59 (124 a) says on the contrary: 'For he knows what he does'; cf. b. Ket. 17 a.
[7] Mass. Kalla, end.

ness on such artificial grounds. The cause for excuse is to Him the ignorance concerning the injustice of a certain action. But it is of importance that He not only finds a reason for excuse in this, but that He rests His plea to God on it. For herein also He shows Himself to be the Servant of God who (according to Isa. liii. 12) pleads for the wicked.

Jesus was mocked not only by those who passed by the Cross, but also by one who was crucified with Him. Mockery of this kind once resulted in a person being punished for an action which he had not committed. He mocked a robber who was standing before the judge (*ḳām lēh gāḥēkh ḳol ḳebālēh*, literally: 'he stood mocking'; cf. Lk. xxiii. 10: 'they stood accusing'; verse 35: 'He stood beholding'),[1] and when the robber was asked: 'Who was with thee?' he pointed in revenge to the mocker as his fellow in the crime: 'that mocker was with me' (*āhān degāhēkh hū 'immī*).[2] How different is the fellowship which our Lord promised to the robber who did not join the others in their mockery.

This robber said:

'My Lord, remember me when thou comest into thy reign!' (Lk. xxiii. 42).

Aramaic: *mārī, anhar lī kidētētē bemalkhūtākh.*

It is impossible to address a person in Aramaic with *mār* ('Lord') alone.[3] Κύριε without a pronoun is a Grecism as is πάτερ without a pronoun (Lk. xviii. 12, 18; ὁ πατήρ Mt. xi. 26; τέκνον (for υἱέ) Mt. ix. 2; Mk. ii. 5; Lk. ii. 48; xv. 31; θύγατερ (θυγάτηρ) Mt. ix. 22; Mk. v. 34; Lk. viii. 48; ἀδελφέ Acts ix. 17; φίλε Lk. xi. 5; xiv. 10; ἑταῖρε Mt. xx. 13; xxii. 12; xxvi. 50). In Aramaic the only possible equivalents (which are also used in the Peshito) are *abbā, berī, berattī, aḥī, ḥabrī*, while the Pal. Evang. often translates literally. For 'remember' the Galilaean expression is *anhar*; cf. *anā manhar lēh*: 'I think of him', 'I remember him'.[4] But neither is the root *dekhar* impossible. Onkelos and Targum Yer. I have in Gen. xl. 14 *tidkerinnani* (the

[1] Cf. *W.J.* 23.
[2] p. Ber. 5 c; for this expression cf. 'this was also with him' (Lk. xxii. 56; cf. Mt. xxvi. 71 and Mk. xiv. 65).
[3] *W.J.* 325 f., 327 f.
[4] Gen. R. 33 (65 b).

better reading is probably, according to verse 23, the Itpeel *tiddakherinnani*). The imperative would then be *iddakherinnani*, 'remember thou me'. ὅταν can be rendered merely by *kide* or *ēmat de*.[1]

Concerning *bemalkhūtākh*, the Aramaic form makes it probable that here, as in Mt. xvi. 28, it refers not to the domain into which Jesus will return but rather to the royal power which at present He does not possess and which will later make it possible for Him to plead for others. *Bemalkhūtākh* would in that case mean the same as 'being King'.[2] Moreover, he took it for granted that Jesus will not be just a King of the Jews, as others were before Him, for in that case He would not be able to help a criminal once he had been executed. What he meant was that Jesus would 'come' as the God-Anointed One in the full sense of the word, i.e. appear from the invisible sphere. The often-heard question, 'When cometh the Messiah?' (*ēmat ātē meshīaḥ*),[3] will then be answered, and that future for which a dying Rabbi wished to be in readiness, when he said *in ātē meshīḥā wa'anā me'attad* ('when the Messiah cometh, in order that I may be prepared'),[4] become an actuality. But His kingship must, like God's, extend to the living and the dead, and He must be able to show forth mercy. For the 'robber' asks for an act of grace, which cannot be fulfilled in this life; he does not base this on the Jewish conception that the experience of an earthly punishment gives one a claim to be absolved from the state of punishment in the world beyond. When a criminal prays on the way to the place of execution, 'May my death be a propitiation for all my transgressions', his confession is supposed to bring him forgiveness,[5] as it did to Achor, to whom Joshua (according to Joshua vii. 25) said before the stoning 'To-day thou art *'ākhōr* (turbid), but thou art not *'ākhōr* in the future world'.[6] The 'robber' wishes to see with his own eyes the kingship of Jesus, as it is promised (Isa. liii. 9, Targum) to the wicked whose souls God has purified, that they shall behold 'the kingship of their Messiah' (*malkhūt meshīḥahōn*). It was only his companionship

[1] *Gram.* 234.
[2] *W.J.* 133.
[3] b. Sanh. 98 a.
[4] p. Ket. 35 a.
[5] Sanh. vi. 2; cf. above, p. 81.
[6] *Ibid.*; p. Sanh. 23 b; b. Sanh. 44 b.

on the Cross that gave him the temerity to put forward this bold petition; as Joseph's companionship with Pharaoh's butler in prison gave him like courage (Gen. xl. 14). Consequently, it was not works, but faith in the future glory of the One who was being crucified with him, that underlaid his petition.

Our Lord's answer was (Lk. xxiii. 43):

'Amen, I say unto thee, to-day thou wilt be with me in paradise'.
Aramaic: *āmēn āmarnā lākh, yōmā dēn att ʿimmī beginnetā deʿēden.*

The accentuation of 'to-day' probably permits the suppression of the future-form ἔσῃ. Otherwise it would have to be expressed with *tehē*, or, more exactly, with *att ʿatīd lemihwē.*[1]

Paradise (Hebrew *gan ʿēden*, Aramaic *ginnetā deʿēden*)[2] is the place of the pious after death, in contrast to 'hell' (Hebrew *gēhinnōm*, Aramaic *gēhinnām*),[3] the place of the wicked. According to tradition, both are only a hand's breadth distance from, and visible to, each other.[4] Every one wishes with Rabbi Zeʿera: 'May I inherit paradise' (*īrat gan ʿēden*).[5] On leaving the house-of-study the scholar prays: 'I work to inherit paradise'.[6] Shimʿon ben Lakish knew a gate-keeper who often refreshed him with a drink of water. This gate-keeper seated himself once beside the famous scholar, and said: 'Rabbi, rememberest thou (*nehīr att*) how I and you used to go to the synagogue? Thou hast gained merit (*zekhēt*) (by being a student of the Law), but this man (I) has gained no merit (*zākhē*). Pray for me that my portion may be with thee in the future world (*ṣallī ʿalay deyihwē ḥulāḳī ʿimmākh leʿālemā deātē*)'. Shimʿon answered: 'What should we obtain for thee by praying? That thou shouldst (some day) come to join the people belonging to thy trade: for every one is directed (by God) to a place specially prepared for his own class'.[7] The 'with thee' of the gate-keeper is by Rabbi Shimʿon thus refused, while our Lord promises the robber His 'with me'. For Rabbi Shimʿon the

[1] For this expression cf. *Gram.* 268 f.
[2] Tg. Joel ii. 3; but Hebrew *gan ʿēden* in an Aramaic context, Tg. Eccl. ix. 7; p. Kidd. 61 b.
[3] Tg. Isa. liii. 9; cf. *Gram.* 183.
[4] Eccl. R. vii. 14 (117 a); cf. Lk. xvi. 23.
[5] p. Kidd. 61 b.
[6] p. Ber. 7 a.
[7] Eccl. R. iii. 9 (82 b).

gulf between the learned and unlearned remained unbridged even in the world beyond; for, 'although all have to taste death, yet everyone has his own world'.[1]

The words which Samuel said to Saul, when appearing from the grave (1 Sam. xxviii. 19), 'to-morrow thou and thy sons will be with me', sounds differently when we add Rabbi Joḥanan's interpretation: 'with me, that is, in my division' (Hebrew *bimeḥīṣātī*),[2] that is, the rejected Saul will be where the man and seer of God is. This was used as a proof that Saul's sins were forgiven because he was now ashamed of them. How quickly can one gain Paradise! Jose ben Joezer, when on the way to crucifixion, pointed out to his godless nephew[3] how the reward of the pious can be measured from God's long-suffering towards the wicked; and, from the heavy lot which God destines for the pious—the greatness of the punishment to them. Thereupon, the nephew, by an artificial device, it is said, underwent all the four kinds of execution referred to in the Law, and by this means propitiated his sins even before his uncle gave up the ghost on the cross. The latter admiringly remarked that his nephew had, after all, preceded him on the way to paradise.[4] When, during the Hadrianic persecutions, Ḥanina ben Teradyon was to be burnt—together with his scroll of the Law—a 'philosopher' was so impressed by him that he publicly took his part. When the Eparch exclaimed to the 'philosopher': 'to-morrow thy punishment will be the same as his', he answered: 'thou hast brought me a good message! To-morrow my portion will be with him in the Age to come'.[5]

Such narratives may, in a sense, be considered as parallels to the Saviour's word to the penitent thief. But it is significant that our Lord did not say anything concerning repentance or the punishment of sin; nor did He suggest that there was any claim for forgiveness because of merit. He gave more than He was asked for; already a King, He opened to the criminal who believed in Him the door to the place towards which He Himself was hastening. According to the free decision of the Lord of

[1] Eccl. R. 12 (129 a f.).
[2] Lev. R. 26 (71 a); b. Er. 53 b; Ber. 12 b.
[3] See above, p. 190.
[4] Gen. R. 65 (141 a f.).
[5] Siphre Deut. 307 (133 a).

the vineyard (Mt. xx. 14 f.) the last labourer receives the same reward as the first, while in the Jewish parable,[1] often quoted as a parallel to this, the last is considered equal to the first for the reason that he has accomplished more in two hours than all the rest in a whole day.

While hanging on the cross the condemned had time in his last anxious hours to think of his relatives. Jewish marital legislation insisted that everything should be definitely settled[2] before it was too late. It happened, for instance, that one who was crucified gave his wife, shortly before expiring, freedom to marry again, and so a bill of divorcement could be written out, which enabled her to marry another man before the actual death of her present husband. The law concerning such cases was as follows: 'Even when he merely points out by signs from the cross that he wishes that a bill of divorcement should be written, it is to be done, and handed to the wife, provided that his soul still cleaves to him'.[3] We also read of a Persian Jew, who, when dying, said: 'Give to the wife of this man (i.e. to my wife) the bill of divorcement!'[4]

According to St John our Lord gave definite directions to His Mother and to the Disciple 'whom He loved', which were His last will and testament, and which made the latter a special legatee, meaning that He appointed this Disciple to represent Him now as a son to His Mother, hereby conferring upon him the duty of protecting and supporting her. This shows that He considered this Disciple to have been the one of whom He approved most, and also that He did not in any way think lightly of His earthly duties.

To His Mother He said (John xix. 26):

'Woman, behold thy son!'

Aramaic: *ittā hā berīkh.*

The Disciple 'whom He loved' received the corresponding injunction:

'Behold thy mother!'

Aramaic: *hā immākh.*

[1] Eccl. R. v. 11 (97 a); Cant. R. vi. 2 (63 a); p. Ber. 5 c.

[2] Cf. above, p. 188.

[3] p. Gitt. 48 c; Tos. Git. vii. 1, where *le'ishtī* must be read instead of *le'ishtō*; b. Yeb. 120 b.

[4] p. Kid. 64 b.

The Mother of Jesus was entitled to be addressed with *immā*, 'my mother'. Even Shi'mon ben Yoḥai, whose mother annoyed him by chattering on the Sabbath, said to her: *immā, shabbetā hī*, 'Mother, it is Sabbath'.[1] When one's mother is addressed as 'woman', it means a relinquishment of physical relationship. Thus it is undoubtedly to be understood both here and in John ii. 4.

The question is, however, whether the Aramaic word used by our Lord was *ittā*, as it is in the Syriac translations, or whether γύναι must be considered a Grecism, since in Greek it is the usual form of addressing a woman, while Rabbinic literature contains no parallel to it (although there is no lack of occasion for it). A woman or a girl, if she is a stranger, is occasionally addressed as 'my daughter' (Hebrew *bittī*),[2] as also our Lord addressed the woman with an issue (Mt. ix. 22; Mk. v. 34; Lk. viii. 48). Similarly, a young man, even a stranger, can be called 'my son' (Hebrew *benī*),[3] as Jesus addressed (Mt. ix. 2; Mk. ii. 5) the lame one who was no longer a child. But usually when a woman who is a stranger is spoken to, she is not addressed by any such word. Perhaps our Lord merely said: 'Behold, thy son', and what was left out in Aramaic was expressed in Greek by the addition of the usual γύναι. To formulate the whole sentence in idiomatic Aramaic, one would have to use the third person.[4] It would then run: *hā berah dehādā ittetā*, 'behold the son of that woman' (i.e. thy son). But this phrasing was chiefly used in connexion with something bad. Even in Mt. xv. 28 (the Canaanite woman); in Lk. xiii. 12 (the lame woman); in Lk. xxii. 57 (the maid-servant); in John iv. 21 (the Samaritan woman); or in John xx. 13, 15 (Mary Magdalene), γύναι could not well be rendered thus. In all these passages no emphasis is laid on the word by which the person is addressed. Only in John xx. 13, 15 the word has a certain significance, in so far as it stands in contrast to 'Mary' in verse 16, wherewith our Lord pointed to the old personal relationship, but it is not necessarily so even there. In all these

[1] p. Sab. 15 b.
[2] Siphre 130 a; Lam. R. i. 1 (24 b).
[3] Lam. R. i. 1 (24 b); p. Ber. 13 b; cf. above, p. 197.
[4] *Gram.* 108; *W.J.* 249 f.

cases the assumption of the Grecism would be the easiest solution of the problem. The same applies to Lk. v. 20, where Jesus addressed the lame man as *ἄνθρωπε*, 'man' (Mt. ix. 2; Mk. ii. 5 have *τέκνον* instead); to Lk. xii. 14 when addressing a man of the people; to xxii. 58, 60, when Peter addresses the man in the high-priest's court. In the first and the last passages, at any rate, it is certain that the word could not signify disparagement, as if the person thus addressed were 'merely' a man. Peshito softens it by translating with *gabrā*; the Pal. Evang. also renders it here literally with *barnāsh*, which, in Hebrew literature, is found as a form of address only in Micah vi. 8 and Ezek. ii. 1 f. In short, it looks as if the word was not in the original sentence, but is a Grecism.[1]

At the same time it is not impossible that for a certain purpose an otherwise unusual form of address was used. A bad son called his father *sābā, sābā*, 'old man, old man'.[2] A physician would naturally be addressed as *āsyā*, 'healer'.[3] Thus *ittā* in John ii. 4 and xix. 26 might well have been used purposely. The same is the case with *ṭelītā*, 'girl' (Mk. v. 41 in Aramaic—Lk. viii. 54 *ἡ παῖς*) and with *νεανίσκε* (Lk. vii. 14), which probably is a rendering of *ṭalyā*. In both cases dead were raised, and hence, instead of the personal 'my son', 'my daughter', the solemn address took the place of the proper name. That the father of John the Baptist addressed his child solemnly with *παιδίον* (Lk. i. 76) is a similar case.

'Behold' (Aramaic *hā*) was used when a thing was being delivered, and so can be justified here. A bill of divorcement is delivered with the words *hā gittēkh* ('behold, here is thy divorcement bill!').[4] Someone answered a person who asked for a hen: *hā lākh ṭimītah* ('behold, here hast thou its value').[5] 'He who says: behold, here thou hast (*hā lākh*) five! is a fool'.[6] A woman is told of her husband's return from a far country: 'Behold, thy husband' (Hebrew *harē ba'alēkh*).[7] The testamentary sentence of our Lord was not merely the statement of a fact, but a presentation first of a friend—as a compensation for the Son; then of a mother—as a compensation for a friend.

[1] See also *W.J.* 40.
[2] p. Pea 15 c.
[3] Gen. R. 23 (49 b).
[4] p. Git. 49 b.
[5] p. Shek. 49 b.
[6] p. Sanh. 26 b, 30 a.
[7] Pesikt. 147 a.

XIX. THE THREE WORDS OF THE EXPIRING SAVIOUR

Jesus, after having prayed for His crucifiers, spoken to the penitent thief, and given directions about His Mother, was silent. Darkness covered the land from noon until three in the afternoon (Mt. xxvii. 45; Mk. xv. 33; Lk. xxiii. 44). As at the time of the full moon an eclipse of the sun is out of the question, and as only Luke speaks of the sun, it must have been a sirocco vapour which became so thick that it blotted out the sunlight, even hid the sun altogether, as I myself experienced on the 9th of April 1913 (i.e. at Easter time) at the Sea of Tiberias.[1] Then an east wind or a calm can be presumed; the heightened temperature and an increased dryness of the air is nerve-racking, but the absence of the sun-rays has a certain soothing effect. Mediaeval presentations of the Crucifixion showed, above the Cross, sun and moon covering their faces, lamenting the while. According to Amos viii. 9, the setting of the sun at noon was considered a Divine judgment. The darkening of the light, according to Jewish conceptions, is an evil omen for the whole world; an eclipse of the sun—especially for the Gentiles; an eclipse of the moon—for the 'enemies of Israel' (i.e. for Israel).[2] At the death of Rabbi Joḥanan the funeral-orator said: 'It is a bad day for Israel, like unto that on which the sun sets at mid-day'.[3] The eclipse of the moon at the time when the brave men, who removed the eagle of Herod from the Temple, were burnt, was considered to be a sign of God's displeasure.[4] To the Gospel narrators the darkness must have meant a terrible sign of something unusual, at which God seemed to have turned away from the world. Into this darkness the anxious call of our Lord resounded (Mt. xxvii. 46; Mk. xv. 34):

'My God, my God, why hast Thou forsaken me?'

In Hebrew: *ēlī, ēlī lāmmā 'azabtáni.*

Both Evangelists have this in the original. At first it seems that their motive was to transmit this (according to their account)

[1] *P.J.B.* 1913, 49.
[2] Mech. 3 a; Tos. Sukk. ii. 3; b. Sukk. 29 a.
[3] b. Mo. k. 25 b.
[4] Jos. *Ant.* XVII. 6. 4.

last Word from the Cross exactly as it was uttered. But it was probably merely in order to explain how the bystanders could have thought that Jesus called for Elias (Mt. xxvii. 47; Mk. xv. 35). The texts are uncertain concerning the actual language in which our Lord uttered these words. Apart from the Hebrew form[1] in Cod. D we find in the manuscripts ℵAB the purely Aramaic: *elāhī elāhī lemā shebaḳtani*. The Targum has Psalm xxii. 2 partly in Hebrew and partly in Aramaic, as also Onk. often retains the Hebrew *ēl*.[2] The fact that it sounded like calling for Elias, makes it certain that the words in Hebrew were: *ēlī, ēlī*. In that case, it would be most natural (and in connexion with a Biblical phrase also most appropriate) to assume that the whole sentence was uttered in Hebrew, i.e. Psalm xxii. 2 expressed in the original form. Jesus was now not speaking for others, but bursting out of the trance of silence, He gave vent to His gathered emotions, and this, not in a word of prayer formed by Himself, but in a Psalm-verse which forced itself to His lips. This proves His familiarity with Scripture, and reveals, above all, what was going on in His mind; but it is also in keeping with the need of the Dying who cannot any longer find words of His own.

Some Jews, who perhaps were not quite familiar with the holy language, and thought that Jesus called for Elias, attempted to prevent one who wished to assist the Sufferer from doing so. They shouted (Mt. xxvii. 49; cf. Mk. xv. 36): 'Let be! Let us see whether Elias will come to save him' (Aramaic *shubḳēh deniḥmē in yētē ēliyyā weyiphrōḳinnēh*). It must have been customary among the Jews to expect help from Elias. As he had ascended alive to heaven (2 Kings ii. 11), he was considered to be equal with the angels. He flies in the air like an eagle;[3] Gabriel and Michael, however, could fly faster than he: Gabriel comes in one flight, Michael in two, Elias in four, the angel of death in eight, but in the time of plague in one.[4] Definite special acts of help were recorded of Elias. He came, for instance, to Rabbi Jehuda and healed his toothache by laying a finger upon him.[5] When Eleazer ben Perata was to have been

[1] Cf. for this *Gram.* 156, 221, 365; *W.J.* 53.
[2] Brederek, *Konkordanz zum Targum Onkelos*, 3.
[3] Midr. on Psalms, viii. 9; Targum Eccl. x. 20.
[4] b. Ber. 4 b. [5] p. Ket. 35 a.

judged by the Roman authorities, Elias removed him to a place four hundred miles outside their domain.[1] A similar manifestation of Elias' help might have been expected here by those who spoke. On the other hand, one is not to think here of Elijah as the herald of the Messiah,[2] for as such he could not be the saviour of Him who is greater than himself. Elijah, who does not appear on the eve of the Sabbaths or holy days,[3] but is eager to reward faithful Sabbath observance, is expected to appear at the beginning of a new week and fortify those who wait for the redemption of Israel.[4] Many songs and hymns referring to him are recited before and after the Habdalah ceremony.[5] Later Elijah was expected to come on a Passover,[6] and at the rite of circumcision a chair is placed for him as the 'messenger of circumcision' (Hebrew *mal'akh hab-berit*, Mal. iii. 1).[7] Our Lord's thoughts of Elijah, however, were far removed from those of many Jews. Another Jewish thought was much nearer to His mind: 'When one is in need let him call neither upon Gabriel nor upon Michael, but upon Me, and I will answer him immediately'.[8]

The way Esther behaved, according to a certain Midrash, on the three fast-days instituted by herself (Esther iv. 16), can be brought as an illustration of the use our Lord made of Psalm xxii. 2. On the first day she prayed: 'My God!' On the second day again: 'My God'. On the third day: 'Why hast Thou forsaken me?' But when at last she prayed with a loud voice 'My God, my God, why hast Thou forsaken me?' her prayer was at once answered.[9] When Esther, however, in connexion with this prayer, is said to have put the following claim before God: 'Three ordinances hast Thou given me; one concerning menstruation, another concerning the heave-offering from

[1] b. Ned. 50 a.

[2] Mal. iii. 23; Mt. xvii. 10; cf. Dalman, *Der leidende und der sterbende Messias*, 8 f.; Levertoff, *Die religiöse Denkweise*, appendix.

[3] Er. 43 b.

[4] Abudraham, *Hilkhot Mezoe Shabbat*.

[5] The Rabbinical term for the benedictions and prayers by means of which a division is made between times of varying degrees of holiness, e.g. between Sabbath and week days, festival and work-day, or Sabbath and festival.

[6] See above, p. 125.

[7] Levisohn, *Sepher Mekore Minhagim*, 93 f.; Finkenstein, *Sepher Mekore Minhagim*, 34; Landshuth, *Siddur hegyon leb*, 207 f.

[8] p. Ber. 13 a.

[9] Midr. on Psalms, xxii. 2.

dough, and the third concerning Sabbath-lights; and although I am in the house of a wicked person I have not transgressed any of these',[1] one realises how foreign such a Judaism must have been to our Lord. There was nothing in the tone of His cry to suggest that He appealed to God's assistance as a reward for certain accomplishments, but neither was it an expression of despair. The Psalmist himself did not intend it to be that, nor did Jewish interpretation so explain it. It was also far from the mind of the Evangelists; to them, on the contrary, it exhibited the state of mind of one who even in the travail of death was conscious that He belonged to God, and now reminded His Father that He could not well leave Him in the lurch.

It is not difficult to understand the reason why our Lord quoted from this Psalm. Was not He mocked like the one who speaks in verses 7–9? His body and soul are in a state of dissolution (verses 15–16). His hands and feet are pierced (verse 17), His garments divided (verse 19). (Matthew suggests this relationship in xxvii. 35–43; cf. Lk. xxiii. 34; while John xix. 24 points directly to this Psalm.) Should not then God also hasten to help Him and occasion the praise which is to resound when the reign of God will extend over the whole world (verses 20, 26, 29)? To Jesus Psalm xxii was a song of David. If it is David who speaks in Psalm cx of the Messiah sitting at the right hand of God (Mt. xxii. 42 f.), then Psalm xxii must have meant to Him a portrayal of the Servant of God who, according to Isa. liii, marches towards death; and so this Psalm was a scripture which it was His aim to realise. The cry of anxiety which He adopts from it is, at the same time, an act of obedience. *Patri inserviendo consumor.*

According to Mt. xxvii. 48; Mk. xv. 36, the bystanders, hearing Jesus' cry of anguish, desired to give Him refreshment. It seems that a cane, a sponge, and vinegar were kept in readiness for that purpose. Reeds, which grow not only at the Jordan but also in the surroundings of Jerusalem in damp places, were used in the latter place for different purposes. The hyssop, which is probably identical with the wild Marjoram (*Origanum*

[1] Midr. on Psalms, xxii. 2.

Maru),[1] could not be applied in this case, and in John xix. 29 it probably entered into the text by a scribal error (ὑσσώπῳ for ὑσσῷ, 'javelin'). A javelin could naturally take the place of the reed. Vinegar was prepared in Palestine from wine, the which, fermented with barley, was known as 'southern' or 'Edomite' vinegar.[2] The reapers, because of the heat, dipped their bread in vinegar,[3] and food made with vinegar was brought to the threshing floor.[4] For the soothing of toothache vinegar was kept in the mouth, as 'it is good for what is bad, but bad for what is good'.[5] It also served as an embrocation for sciatica.[6] The saying was: 'vinegar calms and refreshes the soul'.[7] It is good in hot weather.[8] It is rather remarkable that Boas' words to Ruth[9] are in the Midrash on that book (15 a) referred to the Messiah. 'Approach to this place', i.e. approach to the Kingdom; 'and eat from the bread', i.e. from the bread of the Kingdom; 'and dip thy bread in vinegar', i.e. the sufferings, as it is said (Isa. liii. 5): 'and he was pierced for our sins'.

St John's Gospel substitutes for the cry of anguish in Matthew and Mark a word which expresses Jesus' thirst (John xix. 28):

'I thirst'.

Aramaic: *ṣāḥēnā*.

This word was uttered by the sick Rabbi Ḥaggai when Rabbi Manna visited him on a fast-day; but as soon as the latter permitted him to drink, his thirst vanished (even before drinking). A more serious case was the following: A man was walking in Jerusalem with his little daughter. She said: 'Father, I am thirsty' (*abbā ṣāḥyā anā*). He answered: 'Wait a little'. She repeated: 'Father, I am thirsty', and received the same answer. At the third time she died.[10] Another story again tells of the despair arising from thirst. In the besieged Jerusalem a distinguished person sent out his little boy to fetch water. He looked out for him from the roof. When the boy returned

[1] Dalman, *Arbeit und Sitte in Palästina*, I. 371, 543 f.
[2] Pes. vii. 1; p. Pes. 29 d; b. Pes. 42 b.
[3] Ruth ii. 14; Lev. R. 34 (93 a).
[4] Ruth R. ii. 14 (15 a).
[5] p. Sab. 14 c.
[6] Sab. xiv. 4; p. Sab. 14 c f.; Shebi, 38 a; b. Sab. 111 a; Bez. 18 b.
[7] p. Sab. 14 d; Yom. 45 a.
[8] b. Sab. 113 b.
[9] Ruth ii. 14.
[10] Both narratives in p. Yoma 43 d.

without the water, the father called to him: 'Throw the jug to the ground before me!' And the man threw himself down from the roof and died, and the broken members of his body mingled with the fragments of the broken jug.[1] How intensely Palestinians feel the pangs of thirst, I saw on the 23rd of April 1900 in the Judaean desert. A Bedouin girl carrying brushwood threw her bundle to the ground, crying loudly. When asked what the matter was she said ''*atshāne*', 'thirsty'. The thirst of Jesus was due especially to the inner and outer heat, as, from the evening before, when He had refrained from partaking of the wine, He had had nothing.[2] However, it is not certain whether this was meant to be a request for something to drink, like the request of the desert wanderers: *habū lan nishtē da'anan ṣāhay* ('Give us to drink, for we thirst').[3] The Fourth Gospel points out that our Lord fulfilled the Scripture by this word (and also in the very fact itself of having been thirsty). The Evangelist could have thought only of Psalm lxix. 22, that is, of the words: 'In my thirst they gave me vinegar to drink', and he thus puts into the mind of our Lord a Psalm, which, like Psalm xxii, begins with the cry of anguish: 'God, help me, for the waters are come in unto my soul'. Moreover, by contrast with this thirst of Jesus the Evangelist views the fact that He had been the One who had had that living water to offer which alone can quench thirst for ever (John iv. 14; vi. 35; vii. 37). The woman of Samaria had once said to Him (John iv. 15): 'Give me to drink', and now He Himself calls: 'I thirst'. To St John this is the extremest depth to which the only begotten Son of God had descended.

The refreshing effect of the vinegar did not cause a return of vitality; according to Mt. xxvii. 50; Mk. xv. 37; John xix. 30, (with a loud cry) immediately after this came the end. In Luke (xxiii. 46), corresponding to this call and the preceding cry of anguish, the last word was:

'Father, into Thy hands I commend my spirit'.

Aramaic: *abbā bīdākh aphḳēd rūḥī.*

[1] Lam. R. iv. 2 (57 b). Other stories of thirst, *ibid.* iv. 4 (57 b); p. Pes. 37 b; Taan. 69 b.
[2] Cf. above, p. 140 f.
[3] p. Taan. 69 b.

Abbā was the usual word by which our Lord addressed God. The sentence itself is taken from Psalm xxxi. 6; the order of the words in Aramaic are formed accordingly. It might, therefore, have been spoken in Hebrew: *beyādekhā aphḳīd rūḥi*. Here, again, the prayer of Jesus was expressed by a Psalm phrase. Instead, however, of being a request to be saved from great distress, it is an expression of trust. The verb *aphḳēd*[1] (Hebrew *hiphḳīd*[2]) is a term taken from legal phraseology, which means, giving a person a thing to keep in trust; naturally, the keeper's trust consists in this, that he should in due course return it.[3] The soul of man is entrusted to him by God (Hebrew *piḳḳādōn*), and man therefore cannot dispose of it as he will· which was the argument used by Hadrian's wife when he claimed Divine prerogatives.[4] On the other hand, every night during sleep, man delivers his soul into God's keeping. Pinḥas ben Hama said (alluding to Psalm xxxi. 6):[5] 'Every evening we deliver our souls into Thy keeping and Thou givest them back (to us every morning), by which we recognise that Thou art a righteous God (*elōhīm ṣaddīḳ*; based on *ēl emét* in Psalm xxxi. 6). Therefore we say every morning (in the morning prayer): "Who returnest the souls to the dead corpses"'. In the Psalm it is one who, on being threatened by enemies with death, gives his life to God in trust, not in order that it should cease to be, but that He may keep it during the time of danger. Jesus, although uttering the same words, meant something different. On His lips the words implied real renunciation of life, in the hope of finding it again in God, Who is here thought of not as the Creator to whom expiring life goes back (Eccl. xii. 7), but (in accordance with the same verse in the Psalm) as the trustworthy Keeper of the life of His saints, who recovers possession of that which had fallen into the power of strangers. To His Father Jesus commended His precious possession in order that it might be well guarded in Paradise, and that He might receive it again when God should re-install Him in this world.

[1] p. Ber. 4 c; Bab. m. 9 a f.; Taan. 64 b.
[2] Bab. m. iii. 1.
[3] *Ibid.*; Shebu. v. 1; Tos. Bab. m. iii. 5; Shebu. ii. 7 f.
[4] Tanch. Shoph. on Deut. xix. 14; cf. 2 Tim. i. 12, 14.
[5] Midr. on Psalms 7 (8).

XX. THE CONCLUDING WORD ACCORDING TO ST JOHN, AND THE DEATH OF CHRIST

In the Gospel of St John the last Word from the Cross had a different content from that in Luke (John xix. 30):

'It is finished'.

Aramaic: *mushlam.*

For the rendering into Aramaic there are several possibilities. Franz Delitzsch translated it into Hebrew with *kullā*, probably in view of the *finishing* of the works of the six days of creation, expressed in Gen. ii. 1 by this word; although one might also think of the Hebrew *kālā* in Ezra i. 1; Dan. xii. 7, used of fulfilment of prophecy. In new Hebrew the Niph'al *nigmar* (the Targumic *gemar*, Ezek. xxiii. 24, goes back to *gāmar*) corresponds to the Biblical *kālā* and has the same meaning. Of a part of the work of creation it says: *nigmerā melakhtān*, 'their production was finished';[1] of the decided verdict in a judicial case: *nigmar had-dīn*, 'the judgment was settled once and for all'.[2] In the active sense it is said: *gāmar melakhtō*, 'he accomplished his work';[3] *gāmar pisḥō*, 'he finished his Passover' (i.e. all the duties connected with it).[4]

Onkelos (Gen. ii. 1; Exod. ix. 18) has *ishtakhlálū* for 'they were finished', a word which also entered into new Hebrew,[5] but is not found in Galilaean Aramaic. In Gen. ii. 1 it is therefore substituted in Targum Jer. I by the equivalent word *shelīmū*. One could also mention as an instance *shelēmat*, 'it (the work) was finished',[6] and *shelīm ḳiṣṣā*, 'the time-period came to an end'.[7] In fact, the singular *shelēm* or *shelīm* is used in Pal. Evang. John xix. 30. When, however, not only the fact that it had come to an end, but also that the task was accomplished, should be expressed, one has to use the causative stem of the same root. *Ashlēm* means 'to accomplish a task' in Onk. Yer. I. Exod. v. 13, 14; 'to make full' the sins of the fathers, in Onk.

[1] Gen. R. 12 (24 b).
[2] Sanh. vi. 1; p. Sanh. 22 b; in the active sense: *gōmerīn had-dīn*, 'one settles the judgment', Sanh. iv. 1; Tos. Sanh. vi. 4.
[3] p. Sab. 10 a.
[4] Mech. Exod. xii. 27 (13 a).
[5] Gen. R. 10 (19 a).
[6] Onkelos, Exod. xxxix. 32.
[7] Targum Cant. vii. 14.

Exod. xx. 5;[1] 'to fulfil' a promise perfectly, in Targum Isa. xliv. 26. The passive participle of this would be *mushlam* or *mashlam*, which is close to the passive participle Pael *meshallam* of the Peshito. The latter adds at the beginning *hā*, 'behold', because the Peshito also considers the word by itself too short. The 'behold' would suggest that our Lord addressed the word to someone. But as it was not a word of diction but the last call of a Soul which had just now accomplished its life-work, the simple *mushlam* without any additions is more appropriate.

Moreover, it is assumed that our Lord did not merely mean to say that the Scripture which refers to Him (John xix. 28) was fulfilled, but that the programme sketched out for Him in Scripture has been brought to a successful close. It is the worker's cry of achievement when he puts away the finished article with the sense of satisfaction. Tarphon once said: 'It is not for thee to complete (Hebrew *ligmōr*) the work, but neither art thou free to desist from it (Hebrew *lebaṭṭēl*); but faithful is thy Employer to pay thee the reward of thy labour'.[2] The Rabbi here thought of the service rendered to the study of the Law to which, as to life itself, God alone can appoint the end. In the words of our Lord expectation of reward is not expressed. In any case, the life-work on which now He looks back is not the keeping of the 613 commandments and prohibitions of the Mosaic Law, but the work of which, according to John xvii. 4, He says to the Father: 'I have glorified thee on earth, because I have finished the work (Evang. Pal. Pesh. *shallēmt*) which thou hast given me to do'. In so far as it refers to the accomplishing of a Scriptural ordinance, as well as to that of a task laid directly by one person upon another, it means here a word of Scripture concerning the Son of God, who Himself is God's Word to the world. With its fulfilment Jesus was concerned until the last moment, and that, as His cry taken from Psalm xxii shows, in full consciousness. There are no entirely suitable parallels to this in Jewish literature. An important form of the glorification of God is in this connexion 'the sanctification of

[1] According to Cod. Soc., Part. Aph.: *mashlemīn*; edit. Sabbioneta, 1557 (in the original) has the Pael: *meshalemīn* (read *meshallemīn*).

[2] Ab. ii. 16.

the Name' (Hebrew *ḳiddūsh hash-shēm*), which, according to Lev. xxii. 32, is the task put upon every Israelite (but not on others), and which should be accomplished by doing more than the Law demands, and even at the cost of one's life, as soon as any different conduct would lead to a public desecration of God's honour.[1] 'Greater is the sanctification of the Name than the profanation of the Name',[2] meaning that the duty of honouring the Name of God is of greater value than that of protecting it from being profaned. Abraham sanctified (Hebrew *kiddēsh*) the name of God when he was thrown into the fiery furnace, but also when he built a hostel in Beer-sheba, where he gave hospitality to wayfarers, thus bringing men under the wings of the Shekina, and also proclaiming in the world the glory of God; as a reward for which he, like the angels, received a name consisting of the name of God.[3] He could claim before God: 'I am a "wall" (Cant. viii. 9) in order to deliver (Hebrew *mesar*) my soul for the sanctification of Thy name; and not only I, but all my descendants, Ḥananya, Mishael, and Azariah, and the generations of Rabbi Ḥananya ben Teradyon and his associates will give their souls for the sanctification of Thy name'.[4] In this tone Ḥiyya bar Abba said: 'Should I be commanded: "Give thy soul for the sanctification of the Name of God", I would do it, but I must be killed at once (without being tortured)—for, what the generation of the time of religious persecutions was able to go through, I could not bear'.[5] This manner of sanctifying God's name is, of course, also included in our Lord's scheme. He put the hallowing of God's name at the head of the Prayer which He taught the Disciples (Mt. vi. 9; Lk. xi. 2), and which He certainly did not consider merely as a doxology, after the example of the Jewish Kaddish.[6] Similar to the first petition in the Lord's Prayer is the prayer of Jannaį: 'May Thy name not be profaned on us, and make us not an object of chatter to all people'.[7] In both cases it means a Divine

[1] Siphra on Lev. xviii. 5 (86 b); cf. above, pp. 64, 80.
[2] p. Sanh. 23 d; Kid. 65 c. [3] Num. R. 2 (8 a).
[4] Tanchuma, lech lecha at the beginning.
[5] Cant. R. ii. 7 (29 b); Pesikta, 87 a.
[6] Cf. above, p. 19. The Kaddish begins: *yitgaddal weyitḳaddash shemēh rabbā*, 'exalted and hallowed may His great Name be', suggested by the corresponding expressions in Ezek. xxxviii. 23. [7] p. Ber. 7 d.

action which causes God's honour to be recognised in the world. Our Lord describes His own life-work as a self-sanctifying for the sake of the Disciples (John xvii. 19), wherein God is the One to whom He sanctifies Himself. In expression it is reminiscent of the Jewish saying: 'He who sanctifies himself a little, is sanctified much (by God); when it is done here, they (i.e. God) will sanctify him above; when in this world, then in the next'.[1] In content, however, the acting according to the legal standard, which is the *motif* of the Jewish conception of sanctification, belongs to a quite different sphere from that of the self-dedication of Jesus to His task of representing God in the world. Yet this also may include martyrdom. For, when Peter was to glorify God by means of his death (John xxi. 19), the Death of Jesus must certainly be considered to be an honouring of God, and hence a sanctification of His Name.

As well as the 'sanctification of ṯhe Name', 'the justification of the (Divine) judgment' (Hebrew *ṣiddūḳ had-dīn*) is an important religious concept in Judaism. This latter is achieved when the sinner not only bears his punishment willingly, but 'as if he had offered Him a Sacrifice' praises the God, who had condemned him, saying to Him: 'Thou hast judged rightly, Thou hast rightly acquitted, Thou hast rightly condemned, Thou art right in condemning the wicked to hell, and in sending the pious to Paradise'.[2] This justification of God was practised by Eleazar who, suspected of being a Christian, was called up by the Roman government to give an account of himself. He said: 'faithful is the Judge to me', even before he knew why God had brought him into that position.[3] Ḥanina advised the afflicted Joḥanan not to say, when in great pain: 'More is put upon me than I can bear', but simply exclaim: 'the faithful God'.[4] When the waves of the sea tore away from her hands, for the second time, the garments which she was washing, Miriam, the daughter of Boethos, exclaimed: 'Let the Tax-gatherer (God) receive what is due to Him!' and herewith justified the Divine judgment.[5]

[1] b. Yom. 39 a, Barayta.

[2] b. Erub. 19 a; cf. Targum Cant. vi. 5; the Psalter of Solomon ii. 16; iii. 3, 5; iv. 9; viii. 7, 13.

[3] b. Ab. z. 16 b.

[4] Cant. R. ii. 16 (35 b).

[5] Lam. R. i. 6 (35 b).

Even when the sin is unknown, can God's just punishment be thus accepted. Aaron's silence at the death of his sons (Lev. x. 3),[1] Abraham's humble speech before God (Gen. xviii. 27), Jacob's expression of his unworthiness (Gen. xxxii. 11), mean, as does also David's confession of sin (Psalm xxxviii. 6), a justification of the Divine judgment.[2] It became a submission to the Divine destiny (which is not a punishment for sin) when Ḥanina ben Teradyon and his wife and daughter were brave enough to acknowledge God's perfect truth under fearful martyrdom, taking certain Scriptural words as hints for their suffering. 'All three directed their hearts and justified (Hebrew *ṣiddeḳū*) the Divine judgment upon themselves.'[3] If a newborn child has died within a month, it is a good custom to praise God as 'true Judge' (Hebrew *daiyān emét*)[4] and in this way to justify His judgment.

That it is only the acknowledgment of God's righteousness that can lead to release from punishment, is emphasised in the above-mentioned description of the scene where God teaches the Law of the Messiah.

It will come to pass that the Holy One, blessed be He, will sit in Paradise and teach. And all the righteous will sit, and the whole family above (the angels) will stand upon their feet before Him. The sun and the planets will be at His right hand, the moon and the stars at His left, and He will proclaim a new Torah, which He will give through the Messiah. When He has finished, Zerubbabel the son of Sealtiel will stand up and say: 'May His great Name be magnified and sanctified!' And his voice will sound from one end of the world to the other; and all those who come into the world will answer: 'Amen!' The wicked among Israel and the righteous among the heathen who have remained in Hell will also answer: 'Amen!' until the world will be shaken by the sound, so that the voice of their crying shall be heard by the Holy One, blessed be He, and He shall ask: 'What is this tumult?' The angels shall answer: 'Lord of the world, this is the voice of the wicked in Israel and the righteous among the heathen, who have remained in Hell.' They also cry 'Amen' and *justify the judgment passed upon them.*

[1] Lev. x. 3; cf. Jer. I. Lev. x. 16; *tezakkon dina*, 'justify the judgment'.
[2] Siphra 45 a.
[3] Siphre Deut. 307 (133 a); cf. Sem. 8.
[4] *Siddur Kolbo* (Spanish rite), Wilna, 1877, 605 f.

Then will the Holy One, blessed be He, be greatly moved with pity and shall say: 'Why should I punish them more than this? It is evil imagination (sin personified) that has brought them to it'. In that hour the Holy One, blessed be He, will take the keys of Hell in His Hand and give them to Michael and Gabriel in the presence of all the righteous, and shall say unto them: 'Go, open the gates of Hell and take them out'. At once they will go, and with the keys will open the 8000 gates of Hell. Every hell is 300 parasangs long, 300 wide, 1000 thick, and 100 deep; and none of the wicked who have fallen in, is able to get out again. What will Michael and Gabriel do in that hour? They will take hold of the hand of each, and lift him out as though he were lifted out of a ditch by a cord. They will then wait upon them, and wash them, rub them with oil and heal them all from the boils of Hell. They will put before them beautiful garments and will bring them into the presence of the Holy One, blessed be He, and before all the righteous.[1]

When, in the above-mentioned examples, God is acknowledged as just, although in reality it means merely a bending before His inscrutable Will, God's justice is clearly apprehended, when the sufferer takes upon himself the punishment of others, as the Messiah does according to Pesikta Rabbati.[2] When He is being mocked in prison, 'He justifies (Hebrew *maṣdīḳ*)[3] His punishment for Israel'; which means that, notwithstanding the mockery, He carries His suffering willingly as a punishment justly deserved by His people. But He also perpetrates justification of the Divine judgment in another way, namely, when He says to His people: 'Ye are all my children. Are not ye all saved only by the mercy of God?' (i.e. by God's attribute of mercy using His suffering for their salvation).

Our Lord never said that He Himself needed God's mercy. His Death was necessary for the sake of others (John vi. 53; x. 15; xv. 13); He carries the sin of the world (John i. 29). But He also speaks of a justification of the Divine act for men's salvation, which the Spirit of God will accomplish (John xvi. 8 f.). Both absolving and condemning judgments will then be recognised. 'The people justified God' in undergoing the

[1] Yalk. Shim. II. 296 on Isa. xxvi. 2.

[2] Pes. Rab. 34; cf. Dalman, *Der leidende und der sterbende Messias*, 53; Levertoff, *Die religiöse Denkweise*, Append. vi.

[3] According to the reading of Codex De Rossi, 240, kindly supplied by Pierre Perreau in Parma.

baptism of repentance ordered by Him (Lk. vii. 29).[1] And when 'wisdom will be justified by all her children' (Lk. vii. 35; differently in Mt. xi. 19),[2] wisdom stands for God, whom those who follow Jesus' directions will justify. Moreover, our Lord exercised submission to the Divine will during His whole life, especially when He said at Gethsemane (Mt. xxvi. 40): 'Not as I will, but as Thou wilt'; and when He fulfilled God's will even unto death.

Thus, there are connexions in expression between the glorification of God which our Lord accomplished at the Cross, and Jewish thought concerning the glorifying of God by justification and sanctification. Yet, in reality, the difference is obvious. The acting and suffering of a law-observing Jew, and of Him who was to bring God to men, are essentially beyond comparison.

Hence, in the Fourth Gospel, there is a conception of 'glorifying' God, unusual in Jewish religious phraseology. Pal. Evang. and Peshito express it by the Aramaic *shabbaḥ*, 'to praise'. In Jewish Aramaic it is known from Targum Isa. lv. 5; lx. 9 as the rendering of the Hebrew *pē'ēr*, 'to beautify'; from Targum Judges v. 9 for 'to praise'; and in this meaning also from Dan. ii. 23; iv. 31, 34; v. 4, 23. From the Aramaic it has entered into the language of some of the later Psalms and the book of Ecclesiastes as well as into post-Biblical Hebrew.[3] In Hebrew it is once said (but only occasioned by the Scriptural expression *'alē zebaḥ*, Psalm l. 5) of those who 'uplift' (*'illū*) God and let themselves be slaughtered for His sake.[4]

According to Onk. Yer. I. Lev. xiii. 3, *yaḳḳar*, the usual Aramaic word for 'to honour', would also be appropriate for *δοξάζειν*. The popular language also used the Aphel *ōḳar* for it. 'His Creator honours him (*ōḳerēh*), and should I not honour him (*mōḳerēh*)?' it is said of a Jew.[5] 'He was honoured through

[1] Peshito has here *zaddīḳ(u)*; Pal. Evang. *shabbeḥū*.

[2] But compare Levertoff (*Commentary on St Matthew*) on this passage.

[3] E.g. Cant. R. i. 1 (5 b).

[4] Tos. Sanh. xiii. 11; p. Sanh. 29 c.

[5] Lev. R. 25 (67 a); Eccl. R. 2 (79 a); cf. also Esther R. ii. 4 (9 a); p. Mo. k. 81 c; Ber. 5 c; but Pael *meyaḳḳerin*, p. Makk. 32 c.

him' (Hebrew *hāyā mitkabbēd bō*).[1] Naturally, it is possible that in Aramaic a peculiar use of *ōḳar* and *shabbaḥ* was developed, similar to the δοξάζειν of the Fourth Gospel; but we do not find it in the Jewish religious sphere. Schlatter, alas, does not point out such differences in the Johannine vocabulary in his *Sprache und Heimat des vierten Evangelisten*. His parallels from Rabbinic literature always need to be examined, in order to judge how much they are founded on the connexion of ideas, or on merely a similarity in sound; and besides, his collection should be completed by showing which Johannine expressions are without parallels in Jewish thought.[2]

The question whether the word for 'it is finished' was first formed in Aramaic or in Greek, must remain unanswered. The unique life-work of our Lord had considerable influence on the languages which tell of Him. The last Word from the Cross expresses the fact that this life-work had been brought to a successful close; a superhuman task had been put upon Him, now, since it has been accomplished, He can go back to Him who had sent Him.

This means that it is not of much importance whether the Fourth Evangelist had the information that the Saviour's last Word was not as Luke records. The historic facts which lie before and behind the Death of Jesus testify that the 'It is finished', the greatest single word ever uttered, is, in truth, the superscription of His completed life and work.

After the concluding word 'Jesus bent His head and gave up the ghost' (John xix. 30). There are no Jewish parallels to the bending of the head at death. One 'bends one's head' (Hebrew *hirkīn rōshō*) in order to kiss someone,[3] and one 'nods the head' (Hebrew *hirkīn berōshō*) as a sign of agreement.[4] In Aramaic one says *itrekhīnat*, 'she bent' (respectfully);[5] *arkīnūn berēshēhōn*,

[1] Mech. 57 d.
[2] For other parallels and differences, cf. Levertoff, *Love and the Messianic Age*.
[3] Siphre on Num. 22 (7 b); Num. R. 10 (73 a); p. Ned. 36 d; cf. Tos. Naz. iv. 7; b. Naz. 4 b; Ned. 9 b, with different readings.
[4] Gitt. vii. 1; Tos. Gitt. vii. 1; Maas. Sh. v. 8; Sanh. xi. 2; xii. 7; p. Gitt. 48 c; Ter. 40 b.
[5] Gen. R. 60 (128 a).

'they nodded their heads'.[1] Of one who dies hanging, the bending of the head is the sign of departed life.[2] It may be meant as a proof of the actual arrival of death.

Mk. xv. 37 and Lk. xxiii. 46 designate the approaching Death by ἐξέπνευσεν, Mt. xxvii. 50, and John xix. 30 by ἀφῆκεν, or παρέδωκεν τὸ πνεῦμα. The last expression reminds Schlatter[3] of the Jewish phrase *māsar naphsō 'al* 'to deliver one's soul for something',[4] and the Pal. Evang. translates accordingly *mesar rūḥēh*. In that case it would not merely mean to 'die', like the phrase 'to give up the ghost', but would suggest a conscious and willing surrender of life. Then it would have had to be stated what it was given up for. On considering the last Word from the Cross according to St Luke, one might suggest *aphḳēd*, 'He entrusted', with which is akin the *ashlēm* of the Peshito. Then the person to whom the life is being entrusted would have to be mentioned. And so, as in John xix. 30, it is probably a Greek parallel to ἀφῆκεν τὸ πνεῦμα in Matthew and is meant to emphasise Jesus' own resolution to suffer death; according to His own word (John x. 17): 'I give my life in order that I may take it again'.

Neither is the expression in Matthew a Hebrew or Aramaic phrase. Pal. Evang. and Pesh. translate literally *shebaḳ rūḥēh*, 'He relinquished His ghost'; but they do not give any information concerning the expression which would have been used in an Aramaic original. For ἐξέπνευσεν in Matthew and Luke they did not venture to give a literal translation and were satisfied with *shelēm*, 'He ended', as they did not know of anything more appropriate. The fact is, that here also it is a genuine Greek phrase. Franz Delitzsch ought not to have used *waiyippaḥ naphshō* in his translation, since it is a reminder of the Jewish cursing formula: *tippaḥ rūḥēh dehāhū gabrā*, 'may thy ghost be exhaled'.[5] Among the Jewish terms for 'dying' the only one which could be used here, and which Delitzsch actually uses in John xix. 30, is the Hebrew *yāṣetā naphshō*[6] or *yāṣetā nishmātō*,[7] 'his soul went out (left him)'. In Aramaic it is said

[1] p. R. h. S. 58 d. [2] Tos. Gitt. vii. 1. [3] *Op. cit.* p. 140.
[4] Cf. above, p. 145. [5] p. Maas. Sh. 55 c; cf. *Gram.* 195.
[6] Ohal. i. 6; Sab. xxiii. 5; Sanh. vii. 3; b. Yeb. 120 b.
[7] b. Ber. 61 b; Ab. z. 18 a.

proverbially of a lean person: 'his soul goes out', *naphshēh naphḳat*,[1] and of camels who perish by being overburdened: 'is it not the spirit of life (*rūḥā*) which has flown from them (*naphḳat*)?' According to this the Aramaic phrase here would be: *wenaphḳat naphshēh*. The active *weāppēḳ naphshēh*, 'He let his soul go out', would be rather daring.

That Jesus really died as men die, is what all the records wish to testify. His Death is the necessary presupposition for their further account of His Burial and Resurrection. A state of death beyond the third day meant, from the popular Jewish point of view, an absolute dissolution of life. At this time the face cannot be recognised with certainty; the body bursts; and the soul, which until then had hovered over the body, parts from it.[2] The putrefaction of Lazarus' body also set in on the fourth day (John xi. 17, 39). For three days was Meyasha unconscious during an illness in childhood, and could then describe what takes place in the other world;[3] here death did not enter, but the soul visited the other world. To the Evangelists the Resurrection on the third day (Mt. xvii. 23; Lk. xxiv. 7), or after three days (Mk. ix. 31), presupposed real Death, but not necessarily decay.

A tear through the curtain at the entrance to the Temple,[4] and an earthquake which split rocks (Mt. xxvii. 51; Mk. xv. 38; Lk. xxiii. 45), testified to the fact that God wished this Death to be noticed. At the death of Rabbi Jassi, the castle of Tiberias fell; at the death of Ḥanina, the lake of Tiberias was divided, and seventy lintels of Galilaean houses were shaken.[5] The last miracle is reminiscent of what, according to St Jerome, was also recorded in the Gospel to the Hebrews; namely, that at the Death of our Lord it was the lintel of the Temple, not the curtain, that burst. This would have been a quite conceivable effect of an earthquake on a wooden lintel ten metres wide, notwithstanding its artificial construction.[6] Later, the scribes saw in the sudden opening of the eastern gate of the inner court of the Temple (perhaps according to Isa. xxiv. 12), a sign of

1 Lam. R. iii. 20 (52 b).
2 Eccl. R. 12 (129 b); Lev. R. 18 (45 b).
3 Ruth R. 3 (9 a).
4 *P.J.B.* 1909, 49; *W.J.* 56; *O.W.* 323.
5 p. Ab. z. 42 c; cf. b. Mo. k. 25 b.
6 Cf. *P.J.B.* 1909, 47.

the approaching entry of enemies.[1] One could similarly interpret the meaning of the torn curtains in the Gospels. But of far greater importance than the details of these signs is the Dying One Himself to whom they were meant to point, and the heaven-and-earth extent of the significance of His Death.

There is a touching narrative of the circumstances under which the great doctor of the Law, Rabbi Akiba, died, about a hundred years after the Crucifixion of our Lord.[2] When he was tormented to death with iron spears, the time arrived for the recitation of the *Shema*ʿ (confession to the One God). He began it smilingly. To one who asked him with astonishment the reason of his joyousness he answered: 'My life long was I troubled because of the word (Deut. vi. 5, which belongs to that confession of faith): "Thou shalt love the Lord thy God with all thy soul", which means, even when He taketh away thy soul. I said: "When shall I get the opportunity of fulfilling it?" And now when at last I have this opportunity, how can I be sad?' In the confession to the One God, uttered aloud, he drew out the sound of the word *eḥād* ('one') until his soul 'flew away' (*pāreḥā*).[3]

Thus died a Jewish Law-teacher for the Law, the practice of which the Roman government forbade. Jesus also died for a 'Law', namely, for the new Divine order which it was given to Him to establish, and which did not abrogate the old Law but confirmed it in a new fashion. Akiba's dying meant an intense devotion to the ordinance of the Law and the fulfilment of a ritual duty. It was limited, however, by the frame of a piety which expected a reward from God corresponding to the achievement, and which would benefit himself alone. Quite in harmony with this conception is the Rabbinic interpretation of Psalm ix. 13 ('for he that maketh inquisition for blood, remembereth them'): 'God writes the names of the martyrs on His purple robe. When He accuses the Gentile nations of having killed His saints, who, like Ḥanina ben Teradyon, died for the sanctification of His Name, and they deny it, He brings forth

[1] *Bell. Jud.* VI. 5. 2.
[2] p. Ber. 14 b; b. Ber. 61 b.
[3] p. Ber. 14 b. For the last expression cf. Gen. R. 93 (201 a).

His purple robe and gives them His verdict'.[1] In this way the death of martyrs receives the necessary propitiation. The Death of Jesus also means resignation to God's Will even unto death, but to a Will which signifies grace to men. In this resignation His own life is given up for the sake of others—self is delivered up to death. Therefore, here also God does something with His royal robe—He puts it upon the shoulders of Him who died in order to help others to live through all eternity.

[1] Midr. on Psalms, ix. 13.

APPENDIX

JEWISH PROVERBS AND MAXIMS

THE proverbs and maxims which our Lord incorporated in His teaching must be considered as a proof of the connexion between His words and ordinary Jewish life and manner of speech. Although He does not designate them as the common possession of His environment, He yet assumes that they would add to the strength of His arguments. Thus they must have either been quite familiar to His hearers, or, if He Himself coined them, His intention must have been that the form and the content should not only easily impress themselves, but, above all, be immediately grasped as necessarily true. A great portion of these proverbs has its counterpart in Jewish literature; of the rest it can be presumed that, in one form or another, they were also familiar to the people at the time of Jesus, although they had not been preserved. The sources in which they are found are, with the exception of the Book of Sirach, later than the Gospels; and also the men to whom they are ascribed are, almost without exception, of a later time. This led some scholars to the conclusion that our Lord was the originator of all these words, and it is believed by some that it would be a detraction from His creative power to assume that their origin is not due to Him. But here, as well as in the domain of the parables, the characteristic originality of Jesus does not consist in the outer form of His words, but must rather be sought in the ideas which the parables or the proverbs in His discourses illustrate. One and the same parable or proverb can be used for quite different purposes. And even when the nearest purpose of the application is the same in both cases, the deeper, to which the material used is put, can be a different one. He who pays attention to this will find that our Lord not only occasionally, but always deviates from the Rabbis, notwithstanding the similar application made of the same material in both cases. Hence a careful analysis of the so-called Rabbinic parallels to the Gospels is of greater importance than the mere grouping together of them, which misleads the superficial and has already caused a great deal of harm.

One example may suffice to show what is meant. Our Lord says (Mt. vii. 2): 'And with what measure ye mete, it shall be measured to you again'. The Mishna[1] gives the same warning: 'With the measure with which one measures it is measured (literally: they measure) unto him'. When this maxim is taken by itself, it is a

[1] Sota i. 7.

sentence which uses the idea of retribution as a warning. It means: one does well to arrange one's actions according to the expected reward or retribution. It would refer first of all to the reciprocity in human relationships. The Mishna raises the maxim into a higher sphere by assuming God to be the Retributor (the plural verb in the second part of the sentence must be taken, as often in such cases, as a veiled reference to God; compare: 'they give reward';[1] 'they remove from him';[2] 'they repute'; 'they demand';[3] where in all these passages 'they' refers to God). The sentence is applied to the conduct of the adulteress and its consequences in the divinely-prescribed procedure of her punishment. 'She made herself look beautiful to commit sin, therefore God made her look ugly. She has uncovered herself in order to sin, therefore God does the same to her. She started with the thigh, and then with the whole body, therefore the punishment begins with the thigh, and then with the belly, and lastly the whole body does not escape (the punishment).' In this way the Mishna itself interprets the sentence and herewith justifies the juridical procedure with the adulteress, when her ornaments are being taken away from her, her hair loosened, her breast uncovered, and, through the effect of the water, the thigh and the belly begin to swell.[4]

Our Lord also thinks of Divine retribution,[5] but He applies it to the judging and condemning of others, with which God's judgment over those who judge corresponds: if that was harsh, so will this be. It is essentially an inculcation of loving-kindness towards our fellow-men, by pointing to the fact that the lack of love towards our neighbour results in the loss of God's love toward us. The relationship to God is put, with the use of the idea of retribution, on a moral basis, and that at a point which is of essential significance as a principle of conduct. Moreover, God and man stand here as personally one against the other, as is man to man. The application of the maxim in the Mishna, on the other hand, lies in the circumference and puts in between God and man the legal paragraphs according to which He treats him.

Following the above considerations we present now Jewish proverbs and maxims in three groups: (*a*) such as are also found in the Gospels, which I give in an Aramaic translation; (*b*) such as are known to us only from the Gospels; and finally (*c*) such as are found in Jewish literature but which our Lord, as far as we know, did not apply in His teaching. The last group, in which only Palestinian

[1] Ab. ii. 15. [2] *Ibid.* iii. 5. [3] *Ibid.* iv. 4.

[4] Sota i. 5 f.; Num. v. 18 f.; cf. Levertoff, *Midrash Siphre on Numbers*, 23 f.

[5] For the Greek changing of the active 'to measure' into the passive, see *W.J.* 224 f.

material is given, should show how commonly human and naïvely popular sentiments were also represented among the Jewish people, as a proof against those who conceive of the Jews of that time only as 'scribes', and consequently find no Jewish environment to which Jesus and His disciples could have belonged. The proverbs are specially valuable for this end, since they help us to envisage, even more than parables (which are naturally formed for a special purpose), the world of the uneducated, *'amemē de'ar'ā*. Besides, they offer the possibility of considering the nature of the proverbs used by our Lord, in contrast to the great number of those of which He made no use. Completeness is not aimed at in this sphere.

A. GOSPEL PROVERBS AND MAXIMS WHICH ARE ALSO FOUND IN JEWISH LITERATURE[1]

'And with what measure ye mete, it shall be measured to you again'. Mt. vii. 2, Mk. iv. 24, Lk. vi. 38.

Aramaic: *bimekhīletā deattūn mekhīlīn bah yekhīlūn lekhōn.*

With the measure with which one measures, it will be measured unto him. (Hebrew.) Sot. i. 7; Tos. Sot. iii. 1, 2; Siphre, 28 b.

God only rewards measure for measure. (Hebrew.) Exod. R. i. (5 b).

Measure corresponds to measure. (Aramaic.) Tg. Yer. I. Gen. xxxviii. 26.

With the measure with which somebody measures (on earth) it will be measured to him in heaven, may it be a good or a bad measure. Tg. Yer. II. Gen. xxxviii. 26.

With the measure with which ye measured, I measure unto you. (Hebrew.) Siphre Deut. 308 (133 b).

As the weaver weaves on his spindle, so he receives it; with his (own) spindle he takes it. As the pan boils over, so it pours it (the contents) out down its sides. Every thing that one spits upwards into the air, falls back on one's own face. (Aramaic.) Judan. Eccl. R. vii. 9 (105 a).

[1] For the Aramaic texts of Jewish proverbs here quoted see Dalman, *Aramäische Dialektproben*, 2nd ed. (1927), 33 f.

'Therefore all things whatsoever ye would that men should do to you, do ye even so to them: for this is the Law and the prophets'. Mt. vii. 12; Lk. vi. 31.

Aramaic: *kōl mā deattūn bā'ayin de-ya'bedūn lekhōn benē nāshā hākhedēn uph attūn hawōn 'ābedīn lehōn, hādā hī ōrāyetā unebīaiyā.*

What is hateful to thee, do it not unto thy neighbour. (Aramaic.) This is the whole Law and the rest is the interpretation thereof. (Hebrew.) Go, learn! (Aramaic.) Hillel. b. Sab. 31 a.

What thou hatest for thyself, do it not to thy neighbour. (Aramaic.) Akiba. Ab. d. R. N. 26.

Do what is done unto thee; accompany [be present at funerals] in order that thou mayest be accompanied [that others may be present at thy funeral]. Lament, in order that thou mayest be lamented. Perform the duty of burial [literally, bury], in order that others may perform it on thee! (Aramaic.) Akiba. Tos. Ket. vii. 6; Meg. iv. 16; p. Ket. 31 b; Eccl. R. vii. 2 (102 a); cf. b. Ket. 72 a.

'Blessed are the merciful; for they shall obtain mercy'. Mt. v. 7.

Aramaic: *ṭūbēhōn derahmānaiyā deyihwōn meraḥḥemīn 'alēhōn.*

Whenever thou art merciful, God is merciful to thee. (Hebrew.) p. Bab. k. 6 c.

He who is merciful towards men (creatures), towards him 'one is merciful from heaven' (i.e. God is merciful towards him). (Hebrew.) Gamaliel. b. Sanh. 51 b; cf. Siphre Deut. 96 (93 b); Tos. Bab. K. ix. 30.

As we are merciful in heaven, ye must be merciful on earth. (Aramaic.) p. Meg. 75 c; Ber. 9 c; Tg. Yer. I. Lev. xxii. 28.

'Freely ye have received, freely give'. Mt. x. 8.

Aramaic: *'al maggān ḳabbēltūn, 'al maggān habūn.*

'As I for nothing, so ye for nothing', says God (in connexion with the teaching of the Law). (Hebrew.) p. Ned. 38 c; b. Ned. 37 a; Beḥ. 29 a.

'Blessed are the pure in heart; for they shall see God'. Mt. v. 8.

Aramaic: *ṭūbēhōn didekhē (dedakhyē) libbā.*

God loves him who is of a pure heart. (Hebrew.) Gen. R. 41 (84 b).

'For out of the abundance of the heart the mouth speaketh'. Mt. xii. 34; Lk. vi. 45.

Aramaic: *min mōterēh delibbā memallēl pummā.*

What is in the heart, is in the mouth. (Aramaic.) Midr. on Psalms, xxviii. 4; cf. Gen. R. 84 (179 b).

What the heart does not reveal to the mouth, to whom can the mouth reveal it? (Aramaic.) Eccl. R. xii. 9 (131 a).

'Wherefore if thy hand or thy foot offend thee, cut them off.... And if thine eye offend thee, pluck it out'. Mt. xviii. 8 f.; cf. v. 29 f.; Mk. ix. 43.

Aramaic: *in īdākh ō riglākh atkelākh keta'innūn, we'in 'ēnākh atkelākh 'akkerah.*

He who says: 'Blind my eye, for it harms me; cut off my hand, for it harms me', is guilty. (Hebrew.) p. Bab. k. 6 c; Tos. Bab. k. ix. 32; cf. Bab. K. viii. 7.

'Be ye therefore wise as serpents, and harmless as doves'. Mt. x. 16.

Aramaic: *hawōn 'arīmīn kegōn ḥiwwāwātā utemīmīn kegōn yōnaiyā.*

God says of Israel: Towards me they are without guile like the doves, but towards the nations of the world they are as wise as the serpents. (Hebrew.) Jehuda ben Simon. Cant. R. ii. 14 (32 b).

'For whosoever exalteth himself shall be abased; and he that humbleth himself shall be exalted'. Lk. xiv. 11.

Aramaic: *kōl man demerōmēm garmēh memakkekhīn yātēh uman dimemakkēkh garmēh merōmemīn yātēh.*

Who lowers himself, God will exalt. (Hebrew.) Ben Shammai. b. Erub. 13 b. But see also Ezek. xxi. 31.

When he exalts himself, God humiliates him, but when he repents, He exalts him. (Hebrew.) Joseph bar Ḥama. b. Ned. 55 a.

My humiliation is my exaltation, and my exaltation is my humiliation. (Hebrew.) Hillel. Lev. R. i. (2 b).

'Sit not down in the highest room; lest a more honourable man than thou be bidden of him; and he that bade thee and him come and say to thee, Give this man place....But when thou art bidden, go and sit down in the lowest room; that when he that bade thee cometh, he may say unto thee, Friend, go up higher'. Lk. xiv. 8 f.

Aramaic: *lā tirba' berēsh reba'tā begēn delā yihwē zemīn minnēh*

Go from thy seat two, even three, places down, and wait there, until thou art told: 'Go up higher!' And do not ascend in order that thou shouldst not be told: 'Go down'. It is better that it should be said unto thee: 'Go up higher, go up higher', than 'Go down, go down!' (Hebrew.) Shimon ben Azzai. Lev. R. i. (2 b).

meyaḳḳar minnākh weyētē wezamменēh weyēmar lākh hab atrā lehādēn, ēllā reba' be'atrā aḥrāyā wekhideyētē dezammenākh yēmar lākh reḥīmī sōḳ lākh.

'For many are called, but few are chosen'. Mt. xxii. 14.

Aramaic: *saggīīn de'innūn zemīnīn weṣībḥad de'innūn beḥīrīn.*

Not every one who is near, remains near; not every one who is afar off, remains afar off. There are elect, who are rejected, and again brought near; but there are also elect, who, once rejected, are never brought near again. (Hebrew.) Midr. on Sam. 8.

'So the last shall be first, and the first last'. Mt. xx. 16; cf. xix. 30; Lk. xiii. 30.

Aramaic: *yehōn aḥrāyē ḳadmāīn weḳadmāyē aḥrāīn.*

I saw (in the world beyond) those who were above (on earth) below, and those who were below —above. (Hebrew.) Abbahu. b. Bab. b. 10 b; Pes. 50 a.

I saw many men here—in honour: there—in dishonour. (Hebrew.) Ruth. R. iii. on i. 17 (9 a).

'For whosoever hath, to him shall be given, and he shall have more abundance; but whosoever hath not, from him shall be taken away even that he hath'. Mt. xiii. 12; xxv. 29; Mk. iv. 25; cf. Lk. viii. 18; xix. 26.

Aramaic: *man de' īt lēh yāhabīn lēh umittōsaph lēh uman delēt lēh uph nāsebīn minnēh mā de' īt lēh.*

He who does not increase, loses. (Aramaic.) Hillel. Ab. i. 13.

God gives wisdom only to him who *has* wisdom. (Hebrew.) Joḥanan. b. Ber. 55 a.

Among men it is an empty vessel which can be filled, but not a full one; it is not thus with God: a full vessel receives, an empty does not. (Hebrew.) b. Sukk. 46 b.

'He that findeth his life, shall lose it; and he that loseth his life for my sake, shall find it'. Mt. x. 39; cf. Lk. xvii. 33; John xii. 25.

Aramaic: *man demashkaḥ naphshēh mōbēd yātah uman demōbēd yātah beginnī mashkaḥ yātah.*

What should man do in order that he may live? Let him kill himself. What should a man do in order that he may die? Let him preserve his own life. (Aramaic and Hebrew.) b. Tam. 32 a.

'Ye are the salt of the earth'. Mt. v. 13; Mk. ix. 50.

Aramaic: *attūn milḥā dear'ā.*

The salt of money is parsimoniousness (*ḥéser*), but the salt of money is (also) benevolence (*ḥésed*). (Hebrew.) p. Dem. 21 d; b. Ket. 66 b; Sab. 153 a.

'But if the salt have lost his savour, wherewith shall it be salted?' Mt. v. 13; Mk. ix. 50; Lk. xiv. 34.

Aramaic: *in milḥā serī bemā mālehīn yātēh.*

Salt when it is beginning to stink wherewith can it be salted? (Aramaic.) Joshua ben Ḥananya answered: Can salt begin to stink? b. Beḥ. 8 b.

'Thou canst not make one hair white or black'. Mt. v. 36.

Aramaic: *lēt att yākhēl deta'bēd ḥadā sa'arā hiwwārā ō ikkūmā.*

Even when all should unite to make one wing of a raven white, they will not succeed. (Hebrew.) Alexandri. Lev. R. 19 (48 a); Cant. R. 5 (58 b).

'Thou hypocrite, first cast out the beam out of thine own eye; and then shalt thou see clearly to cast out the mote out of thy brother's eye'. Mt. vii. 5.

Aramaic: *appēḳ ḳadmay shārītā min 'ēnākh ubekhēn tiḥmē det appēḳ ḳēsāmā min 'ēn aḥūkh.*

Trim thyself and then trim others. (Hebrew.) Resh Lakish. b. Sanh. 18 a; 19 a; Bab. m. 107 b.

Let us pick off the straws from ourselves, before we do it to others. (Hebrew.) p. Taan. 65 a.

If one says to one: Take the mote from between thy eyes, he would answer: Take the beam from between thy eyes. (Hebrew.) b. Bab. b. 15 b; Arach. 16 b.

'Physician, heal thyself!' Lk. iv. 23; cf. Mt. xxvii. 42.

Aramaic: *āsyā assī garmākh.*

Physician, heal thy (own) lameness! (Aramaic.) Gen. R. 23 (49 b); cf. Sir. 18, 20.

'Do men gather grapes of thorns, or figs of thistles?' Mt. vii. 16 f.; cf. Lk. vi. 44 f.

Aramaic: *lā lāḳeṭīn 'inbīn min kubbaiyā welā tēnīn min dardāraiyā.*

A tree-stem (of the olive tree) which causes the olive tree to grow (read *saddānā* for *sarkhā*). In contrast to this it is also said: 'Out of the shrub of the thorn comes the rose'. (Aramaic.) Cant. R. i. 1 (2 a).

'The disciple is not above his master, nor the servant above his lord. It is enough for the disciple that he be as his master, and the servant as his lord'. Mt. x. 24; cf. Lk. vi. 40; John xiii. 16; xv. 20.

Aramaic: *lēt talmīdā le'ēl min rabbēh welēt 'abdā le'ēl min mārēh missat letalmīdā dīhē kerabbēh we'abdā kemārēh.*

It is sufficient for the servant to be like the master. (Hebrew.) Ulla. b. Ber. 58 b.

He considers the teacher like the disciple and the disciple like the teacher. (Hebrew.) Mech. 57 b.

'He that gathereth not with me, scattereth abroad'. Mt. xii. 30; cf. Mk. ix. 40.

Aramaic: *man delētēh mekhannēsh 'immihū mebaddar.*

At the time when one gathers—scatter; and at the time when one scatters—gather. (Aramaic.) Hillel. p. Ber. 14 d; b. Ber. 63 a; Tos. Ber. vii. 24. (Hebrew.)

'We have piped unto you, and ye have not danced'. Mt. xi. 17.

Aramaic: *zammarnān lekhon welā rakkēdtūn.*

Much as he may sing, it does not enter into the ear of the dancer. Much as he may sing, the son of the fool hears it not. (Aramaic.) Lam. R. Peth. (5 a).

'Ask, and it shall be given you; seek, and ye shall find; knock, and it shall be opened unto you'. Mt. vii. 7; Lk. xi. 9 f.

Aramaic: *sha'alūn weyāhabīn lehkōn pashpeshūn weattūn mashkeḥīn artekūn uphāteḥīn lekhōn.*

If someone says unto thee: 'I have endeavoured and yet I have not found', do not believe it! 'I have endeavoured to find and yet I have found', do not believe it! 'I have endeavoured to find and I have found', believe it! (Hebrew.) Jizchak. b. Meg. 6 b.

When he knocks, it is opened to him. (Hebrew.) Bannaa. Lev. R. 2 (55 a); cf. Pesikt. 176 a.

Answer (to prayer) is only near to the calling, and calling near to the answer. (Hebrew.) p. Taan. 67 a.

'It is easier for a camel to go through the eye of a needle than for a rich man to enter into the Kingdom of God'. Mt. xix. 24; Mk. x. 25; Lk. xviii. 25.

Aramaic: *ḳallīlā legamlā deyē'ōl benukbā dimeḥaṭṭā welā le'attīrā deyē'ōl lemalkhūtā de'elāhā.*

Know, that men are not shown (in a dream) either a golden palm, or an elephant passing through the eye of a needle (i.e. the impossible). (Aramaic.) b. Ber. 55 b; Bab. m. 38 b.

'Why seek ye the living among the dead?' Lk. xxiv. 5.

Aramaic: *mā attūn bā'ayin ḥaiyā 'im mītaiyā.*

Usually the dead are sought among the living; does one seek the living among the dead? (Hebrew.) Lev. R. 6 (18 b).

'Tell that fox' (Herod Antipas). Lk. xiii. 32.

Aramaic: *emarūn lehādēn ta'lā.*

Cast thyself down even before a fox, if it is his time. (Aramaic.) b. Meg. 16 b.

How? Thou hast lions before thee, and askest the foxes? (Aramaic.) p. Shebi. 39 a.

'And he would fain have filled his belly with the husks'. Lk. xv. 16.

Aramaic: *wehawā mitḥammad memallāyā me'ōhi beḥārūbīn.*

The Jew (Israel) needs the husks, before he repents. (Aramaic.) Acha. Cant. R. i. 4 (12 b); Lev. R. 13 (33 b); 35 (97 a); Pesikt. 117 a.

When the heathen enjoy themselves in the theatre, eating and drinking, they say mockingly: 'In order that we should not need the husks of the Jews'. (Aramaic.) Lam. R. Peth. (6 b).

'The sword (Hebrew *ḥéreb*) you should eat' (Isa. i. 20) means: ye should eat husks (Hebrew *ḥārūbīn*). (Hebrew.) Acha. Lev. R. 13 (33 b); Pesikt. 117 a.

Why dost thou eat husks? Because I have no figcake. (Hebrew.) Siphre Num. 89 (24 b).

It would be a vow of a lighter kind, but yet really a vow, when one had vowed not to eat husks. (Hebrew.) p. Kidd. 62 c.

'How many hired servants of my father's have bread enough and to spare, and I perish with hunger!' Lk. xv. 17.

Aramaic: *lekhamā agīrīn dile'abbā mōterā delaḥmā wa'anā nōbēd hākhā bekhaphnā.*

When the son goes about barefooted, he remembers the affluence of his father's house. (Aramaic.) Lam. R. i. 7 (30 b).

'She of her want did cast in all that she had, even all her living'. Mk. xii. 44; Lk. xxi. 4.

Aramaic: *hī min ḥusrānah remāt kōl mādelah kōl parnāsetah.*

A woman brought a handful of flour as an offering to the Temple. To the priest who thought lightly of her it was said in a dream: 'Do not despise her! It is as though she offered her own soul'. (Hebrew.) Lev. R. 3 (9 a).

'Blessed are the barren, and the wombs that never bare, and the paps which never gave suck'. Lk. xxiii. 29; cf. xi. 27.

Aramaic: *ṭūbēhōn dime'aiyā delā yelīdūn wedaddaiyā delā ōnīḳūn.*

Praised be the breasts that sucked such an one, and the wombs that brought him forth. Gen. R. 98 (214 b); Tg. Yer. I. Gen. xlix. 22; cf. Gen. R. 5 (10 b); p. Kil. 27 b.

B. PROVERBS AND MAXIMS USED BY OUR LORD, BUT NOT FOUND IN JEWISH LITERATURE

'No prophet is accepted in his own country', Lk. iv. 24. 'A prophet is not without honour, save in his own country, and in his own house', Mt. xiii. 57; cf. John iv. 44.

Aramaic: *lēt nebiiyā besīr ēllā beḳartēh ubebētēh*, or: *lēt nebiiyā meḳabbal beḳartēh.*

'For wheresoever the carcase is, there will the eagles be gathered together', Mt. xxiv. 28.

Aramaic: *hān de'īt pugrā mitkanshīn nishraiyā.*

'No man can serve two masters', Mt. vi. 24; cf. Lk. xvi. 13.
Aramaic: *lēt barnāsh yākhēl dīshammēsh litrēn mārīn.*

'Neither cast ye your pearls before swine', Mt. vii. 6.
Aramaic: *lā tiṭrephūn margeliiyātā dīlekhōn leḳummē ḥazīraiyā.*

'Let the dead bury their dead', Mt. viii. 22; Lk. ix. 60.
Aramaic: *arpē lemītaiyā deyiḳberūn mītēhōn.*

'The labourer is worthy of his hire', Lk. x. 7; 1 Tim. v. 18; cf. Mt. x. 10.
Aramaic: *agīrā shāwē (yizkē) agrēh.*

'For if they do these things in a green tree, what shall be done in the dry?' Lk. xxiii. 31.
Aramaic: *in 'āḇedīn hēkh beḳēsā raṭṭībā mā yit'abēd beyabbīshā.*

'For there is nothing covered, that shall not be revealed', Mt. x. 26; Mk. iv. 22; Lk. viii. 17; xii. 2.
Aramaic: *lēt ṭemīr delā yitgelē.*

C. PALESTINIAN PROVERBS AND MAXIMS IN JEWISH LITERATURE NOT USED BY OUR LORD

Preliminary note. The original of the following proverbs is Aramaic, and shows the popular Aramaic idiom: where 'Hebrew' is added, it signifies that it was transmitted in Hebrew.

1. PRACTICAL PRUDENCE

Do no good to one who is evil; then the evil will not come unto thee. Hast thou done good to him who is evil, thou hast done evil. Eccl. R. v. 10 (95 a); Ruth R. i. 1 (4 b); Lev. R. 22 (58 b); Num. R. 18 (146 b); Gen. R. 22 (47 b); cf. Sir. xii. 5.

While thou hast the sandals on thy feet, tread on the thorn bush! Gen. R. 44 (91 a); Pesikt. 94 b.

Approach the wicked one before he approaches thee. Gen. R. 75 (161 a); Midr. on Psalms xvii. 13; lvi. 1.

Eat according to thy income; dress thyself below thy income; let thy dwelling be above thy income. Gen. R. 20 (44 a).

Attach thyself to him who has been warmed, then thou also shalt get warm. (Hebrew.) Gen. R. 16 (33 b).

Mention first the ugliness (defects) which cling to thee! Gen. R. 60 (127 a).

Give thy blow, for it does good at the reception. p. Yeb. 4 a; Kidd. 64 d; Num. R. 19 (149 a); cf. Gen. R. 7 (13 a).

When the wheat of thy city is rye, then sow it! Gen. R. 59 (124 b).

A door which is not open to benevolence, will be open to the physician. Cant. R. vi. 11 (60 a); Num. R. 9.

Honour thy physician as long as thou hast need of him. p. Taan. 66 d; cf. Sir. xxxviii. 1.

One word—one denar; silence—two. Eccl. R. v. 5 (93 a); Lev. R. 16 (41 b).

Wherever this is, all things are there. Where this is not, what is there? He who acquires this, what lacks he? He who did not acquire this, what has he acquired? b. Ned. 41 a.

Hast thou gained knowledge, what lackest thou? Lackest thou knowledge, what hast thou gained? (Hebrew.) Lev. R. 1 (2 b).

The medicine for all things is silence. p. Ber. 12 d; cf. Eccl. R. v. 5 (93 a); b. Bab. b. 91 a.

Better one bird caught, than a hundred flying in the air. Eccl. iv. 6 (89 b).

The way has ears; ears has also the wall. (Hebrew.) Lev. R. 32 (87 a).

Should someone say unto thee: 'thou hast donkeys' ears', do not bother about it; when two say this, make thyself a halter! Gen. R. 45 (95 b).

Hast thou made a mess of things, take up the thread and sew. Gen. R. 19 (39).

Hast thou poured the water into the dough, add also flour to it Gen. R. 70 (151 a).

Thou wishest to take hold of the rope at both ends. Gen. R. 39 (78 b).

Hast thou fed (thy guest), given him to drink, accompanied him? (hast thou done thy full duty?). Gen. R. 48 (102 a).

Thou hast gone into the city, then follow its law! Gen. R. 48 (101 a).

Is thy sieve deaf, knock on it! Gen. R. 81 (173 b).

2. PRACTICAL JUDGMENT OF VALUES

Where the warrior hangs up his battle-axe, should the shepherd hang up his jug? Eccl. R. iii. 16 (86 b); cf. Lev. R. 4 (10 a); b. Sanh. 103 b; Bab. mez. 84 b; Pesikt. 94 b.

The most light-minded amongst the light-minded is the dancer. (Hebrew.) p. Sanh. 20 b; Sukk. 55 c; Num. R. 4 (25 b).

When the stronghold begins to shake, it is yet called a stronghold, and when the rubble becomes high, it yet remains the rubble. Pesikt. 117 a.

In the hour of need—the vow; in the hour of prosperity—frivolity. Gen. R. 81 (173 b).

From house to house—(the removal costs) a shirt; from place to place—the life. Gen. R. 39 (80 a).

According to the measure of the camel is his scab. Gen. R. 19 (38 a).

If one cord is separated (from the other), then two cords are separated. Lev. R. 14 (36 b).

At the end of a thing its beginning appears. Eccl. R. 2 (78 a).

The grave-bird ornates itself with what is its own and with what belongs to others. Esther R. 2 (8 a).

Here is the ware, and here is the seller. Pes. R. 21 (102 a).

He who spits returns to his spit; the fool to his folly. Lev. R. 16 (42 b); cf. 2 Peter ii. 22.

A joiner who has no tools is no joiner. (Hebrew.) b. Sab. 31 b; Exod. R. 40 (94 a).

She whores for apples and distributes them among the sick. Eccl. R. iv. 6 (89 b); Pesikt. 95 b.

He who lends money for usury, spoils his own property and that of others. Lev. R. 3 (7 b); Eccl. R. iv. 6 (89 b).

He who rents one garden eats birds; he who rents (several) gardens, him the birds eat. (He who is satisfied with one garden, will be able to eat the birds who sit in the trees, but he who has many gardens, loses all his income from them, because he cannot get at all the birds in the trees.) (Be satisfied with little.) Lev. R. 3 (7 b); Eccl. R. iv. 6 (89 b).

In the street of the blind the semi-blind is referred to as seeing. Gen. R. 30 (59 b).

Between the midwife and the woman in travail the son of the unfortunate dies. Gen. R. 60 (126 a).

One speaks of one's (former) poverty only when one is well-off. Eccl. R. i. 12 (72 b).

Can the fragments of a broken vessel be joined again? Gen. R. 14 (31 a).

Only the melody daily sung is a melody. p. Sanh. 99 a f.; cf. Tos. Ahil. xvi. 8; Par. iv. 7.

Reuben has joy, what does it matter to Shimeon? Gen. R. 53 (113 a); Pesikt. 46 a; cf. Pes. R. 42 (177 a).

Ground flour hast thou grinded; a dead lion hast thou killed; a burning house (town) hast thou burnt. Cant. R. iii. 5 (38 a); Lam. R. i. 13 (33 a f.); cf. b. Sanh. 96 b.

One says to a bee: 'neither thy honey, nor thy sting (do I desire)'. Num. R. 20 (157 b); Midr. on Psalms, i. 6 (22).

After the head comes the body. Tos. Taan. ii. 5.

The body carries the feet (not the reverse). Gen. R. 70 (151 a).

Throw the shoot of a tree in the air, it will manage to stand on its roots. Gen. 53 (114 b), 86 end; cf. Num. R. 20.

Behold, all faces are alike (one is like the other). Lam. R. Peth. (3 b); p. Sanh. 28 c.

Fennel (*shōmar*) means: 'her Lord waits' (*shāmar mārah*); who compares thee with the spices? (i.e. a fennel remains a fennel). (Galilaean.) p. Dem. 21 d.

Coriander (*kusberā*) is 'slaughter the daughter' (*kōs berattā*); who compares thee with the spices? (i.e. coriander remains coriander). (South Judaean.) p. Dem. 21 d.

He who eats fat-tail (of Arabian sheep), hides himself in the upper story; he who eats rotten food, sleeps on the dung-hill of the city. (MS. Mon.) b. Pes. 114 a.

He ate the half-ripe date and threw away the cress. b. Hag. 15 b.

Every one who is ill, will once be well again. Lam. R. i. 1 (26 b).

He who has been stung by a serpent, is frightened of a cord. Eccl. R. vii. 1 (101 a).

Before he goes to sleep, his substitute is at hand. b. Bab. b. 91 a.

Many colts died and their skins were spread as (saddle-blankets) on the backs of their mothers. (Hebrew.) Lev. R. 20 (56 a).

When the bull has fallen, his knives are sharpened (for slaughter). Lam. R. i. 7 (30 b); cf. b. Sab. 32 a.

The sow goes to the pasture with ten (piglets); the ewe not even with one. Gen. R. 44 (93 b).

Before the fat one gets lean, the lean one dies. Lam. R. iii. 20 (52 b).

What has passed has passed; from now the reckoning. Eccl. R. ix. 7 (114 a); Pesikt. 153 a.

One farthing (stater) makes a noise in a jug. b. Bab. mez. 85 b; Midr. on Psalms, i. 5 (21).

The uneducated (*hedyōṭ*) pushes himself to the front. (Fools rush where angels fear to tread.) (Hebrew.) b. Meg. 12 b; Esther R. i. 16 (14 b).

He who eats the palm-cob, will be punished by the palm-stock. Lev. R. 15 (39 b); 16 (42 a).

Wherever the king dwelleth, there is crown property. Cant. R. vi. 4 (63 b); Num. R. 12 (95 a).

Where the king is, there is peace. Pes. R. 21 (103 b).

A fat-tail, but a thorn in it. (Hebrew.) b. R. h. S. 17 a.

All agree with those who stand upright. With those who stand upright, one stands. Gen. R. 97 (207 b).

Rightly say the millers: Everyone has his reward (the wages for his work in the field) in his basket (with flour). p. Pea 15 c; Kidd. 61 c.

By three things one is recognised; by one's cup (*kōs*), by one's purse (*kīs*), and by one's anger (*ka'as*). (Hebrew.) b. Erub. 65 b; Tanch. Kor. end.

Wherever the robber commits violence, there he is hanged. (Hebrew.) Tanch. Tezawwe to Psalm lxxiii. 20.

He who takes part in the preliminary marriage-feast, participates also in the chief banquet. Lev. R. 11 (27 b); p. Shebi. 35 c.

Every one hates one of his own trade. Gen. R. 19 (39 a).

3. WIT AND RIDDLES

An Athenian demanded from a tailor in Jerusalem: 'Sew on for me this broken mortar!' The latter filled the mortar with sand, and replied: 'Twist together for me threads from it, then I will sew it for thee'. Lam. R. 1 (21 a).

An Athenian demanded from a boy in Jerusalem to buy for him something of which he could eat, be satisfied, leave a part, and take the rest on his journey. He brought him salt. The Athenian remonstrated that he did not send him for this. The answer was: 'By thy life! Thou canst eat from it, be satisfied, leave some over, and take some on thy journey'. Lam. R. 1 (21 a).

A Jerusalem schoolboy put the following riddle to an Athenian: 'Nine go out, eight come in, two mix, one drinks, twenty-four serve'. The solution which the Athenian could not find, runs: 'Nine months pregnancy, eight days till the circumcision, two sucking-breasts, one suckling, and twenty-four months the duty of nursing for the mother'. Lam. R. 1 (21 b).

INDEX OF NEW TESTAMENT PASSAGES IN ARAMAIC

From St Matthew.

v. 7, 8: ṭūbēhōn deraḥmānaiyā deyihwōn meraḥḥemīn ʻalēhōn. ṭūbēhōn didekhē (dedakhyē) libbā.

v. 13: attūn milḥā dearʻā. in milḥā serī bemā mālehịn.

v. 17 f.: lā tihwōn sebīrīn da-atēt limebaṭṭālā ōrāyetā (ō nebīaiyā), lā limebaṭṭālā atēt ēllā limeḳaiyāmā. āmēn āmarnā lekhōn ʻad delā yibṭelūn shemaiyā we-arʻā lā tihwē bāṭelā jōd ḥadā ō ḳōṣā ḥadā min ōrāyetā ʻad dejitḳaiyam kullāh.

v. 19: ūman dimebaṭṭēl ḥadā min hālēn miṣwātā zeʻēraiyā umeallēph kēn libnē nāshā (biryātā) hū ʻatīd lemitḳerāiyā zeʻērā bemalkhūtā dishemaiyā. ūman dimeḳaiyēm jāthēn umeallēph kēn hū ʻatīd lemitḳerāyā rabbā bemalkhūtā dishemaiyā.

v. 20: de-āmarnā lekhōn de-in lā tehē zākhūtekhōn meyatterā yattīr min desāpheraiyā wedipherīshaiyā lētekhōn ʻatīdīn lemētē lemalkhūtā dishemaiyā.

v. 21: shemaʻtūn de-it'amar leḳadmāyē lā tiḳṭōl uman deyiḳṭōl (yitmesar lebēt dīnā) hū yehē mitḥaiyab bēt dīnā.

v. 22: wa-anā āmar lekhōn dekhōl man dekhāʻēs ʻal aḥūh yeḥē mitḥaiyab bēt dīnā, uman de'āmar le'aḥūh rēḳā yehē mitḥaiyab sanhedrīn uman deāmar shāṭyā yehē mitḥaiyab nūr gēhinnām.

v. 29 f.: in īdākh ō riglākh atḳelākh ḳeṭaʻinnūn, we'in ʻēnākh atḳelākh ʻaḳḳerah.

v. 36: lēt att yākhēl detaʻbēd ḥadā saʻarā ḥiwwārā ō ikkūmā.

vi. 24: let barnāsh yākhēl dīshammēsh litrēn mārīn.

vii. 2: bimekhīletā deattūn mekhīlīn bah yekhīlūn lekhōn.

vii. 5: appēḳ ḳadmay shārītā min ʻēnākh ubekhēn tiḥmē detappēḳ ḳēsāmā min ʻēn aḥūkh.

vii. 6: lā tiṭrephūn margeliiyātā dīlekhōn leḳummē ḥazīraiyā.

vii. 7: sha'alūn weyāhabīn lekhōn pashpeshūn weattūn mashkeḥīn arteḳūn uphāteḥīn lekhōn.

vii. 12: kōl mā deattūn bāʻayin deyaʻbedūn lekhōn benē nāshā hākhedēn uph attūn hawōn ʻābedīn lehōn, hādā hī ōrāyetā unebīaiyā.

vii. 16 f.: lā lāḳeṭīn ʻinbīn min kubbaiyā welā tēnīn min dardāraiyā.

viii. 22: arpē lemītaiyā deyiḳberūn mītēhōn.

x. 8: ʻal maggān ḳabbēltūn, ʻal maggān habūn.

x. 10: agīrā shāwē (yizkē) agrēh.

x. 16: hawōn ʻarīmīn kegōn ḥiwwāwātā utemīmīn kegōn jōnaiyā.

x. 24: lēt talmīdā leʻēl min rabbēh welēt ʻabdā leʻēl min mārēh missat letalmīdā dīhē kerabbēh weʻ abdā kemārēh.

x. 26: lēt ṭemīr delā yitgelē.

x. 38: bar nāshā debāʻē mehallākhā bāteray, yehē khāphar begarmēh weyiṭʻan ṣelībēh weyētē bāteray.

x. 39: man demashkaḥ naphshēh mōbēd yātah uman demōbēd yātah beginnī mashkaḥ yātah.
xi. 17: zammarnān lekhon welā raḳḳēdtūn.
xii. 30: man delētēh mekhannēsh ʻimmi hū mebaddar.
xii. 34: min mōterēh delibbā memallēl pummā.
xiii. 12: man de'īt lēh yāhabīn lēh umittōsaph lēh uman delēt lēh uph nāsebīn minnēh mā de'īt lēh.
xiii. 57: lēt nebiiyā besīr ēllā beḳartēh ubebētēh; *or*, lēt nebiiyā meḳabbal beḳartēh.
xiv. 30: mārī shēzēbni.
xvi. 24: see Mt. x. 38.
xviii. 8 f.: in īdākh ō riglākh atḳelākh ḳeṭaʻinnūn, we'in ʻēnākh atḳelākh ʻaḳḳerah.
xix. 24: ḳallīlā dā legamlā deyēʻōl benuḳbā dimeḥaṭṭā.
xix. 30: yehōn aḥrāyē ḳadmāīn weḳadmāyē aḥrāīn.
xx. 16: see xix. 30.
xx. 26: bar nāshā lā atā deyishtammash ēlla dīshammēsh weyittēn naphshēh purḳān ḥulāph saggīīn.
xxii. 14: saggīīn de'innūn zemīnīn weṣībḥad de'innūn beḥīrīn.
xxiv. 28: hān de'īt pugrā mitkanshīn nishraiyā.
xxv. 29: see Mt. xiii. 12.
xxvi. 26: sábūn akhúlūn. dēn hū gūphī.
xxvi. 27: ishtōn minnah kullekhōn.
xxvi. 28: dēn (hādēn) hū idmī.
demishtephēkh ʻal saggī'īn.
xxvi. 29: āmēn āmar anā lekhōn delā nishtē min kaddūn (tūbān) min (hālēn) pēraiyā deguphnā ʻad yōmā denishtē minnehōn (ʻimmekhōn) we'innūn ḥadetīn bemalkhūtā de'abbā (de'elāhā).
xxvii. 40: way dephākhar hēkhlā ubānōhi bitelātā yōmīn.
xxvii. 42: āsyā assī garmākh.
xxvii. 46: ēlī ēlī lāmmā ʻazabtáni.
xxvii. 49: shubḳēh deniḥmē in yētē ēliiyā weyiphrōḳinnēh.
xxvii. 50: mesar rūḥēh.

From St Mark.

i. 11: att hū berī ḥabībā debākh itreʻīti.
ii. 5: berī ḥōbākh shebīḳīn lākh.
iv. 22: see Mt. x. 26.
iv. 24: see Mt. vii. 2.
iv. 25: see Mt. xiii. 12.
viii. 34: see Mt. xvi. 24.
ix. 7: dēn hū berī ḥabībā shimʻūn lēh.
ix. 40: see Mt. xii. 30.
ix. 43: see Mt. v. 29 f.
ix. 50: see Mt. v. 13.

x. 25: see Mt. xix. 24.
x. 43 f.: see Mt. xx. 26.
xii. 44: hī min ḥusrānāh kōl mādelāh kōl parnāsetah remāt.
xiv. 22: see Mt. xxvi. 26.
xiv. 23: unesab kāsā ubārēkh wīhab lehōn ushetōn minnah kullehōn.
xiv. 24: see Mt. xxvi. 28. dēn (hādēn) hū idmī deliḳeyāmā.
hādā kāsā hi ḳeyāmā ḥadattā be' idmī.
xiv. 25: see Mt. xxvi. 29.
xiv. 36: abba kullā yākhēl lāk, a'bar minnī hādā kāsā, beram lā mā deṣābēnā anā ēllā mā de'att sābē.
xv. 34: see Mt. xxvii. 46.
xv. 36: see Mt. xxvii. 49.
xv. 37: see Mt. xxvii. 50.

From St Luke.

ii. 49: lā hawētōn yāde'īn diṣerīkh anā lemihwē bide'abbā.
iv. 18 f.: rūaḥ nebūā min ḳodām adōnāy elōhīm 'alay, ḥalāph derabbī adōnāy yātī lebassārā 'inwetānaiyā, shalḥani letaḳḳāphā litebīrē libbā, lemiḳrē ledisheban ḥērū ūleda-asīrīn itgelū linehōr, lemiḳrē shenat ra'wā ḳodām adōnāy.
iv. 21: yōmā dēn itḳaiyam hādēn ḳerājā be-udnēkhōn.
iv. 22: lā hādēn hū berēh deyōsēph.
iv. 23 f.: min kōl atar tēmrūn lī matlā āsyā assī garmākh. kōl mā dishema'nān da'abadtinnēh bikhephar naḥūm hawē 'ābēd uph hākhā bimedīnetākh. āmēn āmarnā lekhōn, delēt nebiiyā meḳabbal bimedīnetēh. min ḳushtā āmarnā lekhōn dahawaiyān saggīān armelān beyisrāēl beyōmōhi de-ēliiyā kid-it'aḥedūn shemaiyā telāt shenīn weshittā yarḥīn wehawā kaphnā rabbā 'al kōl ar'ā welā ishtelaḥ ēliiyā leḥadā minhēn ēllā leṣārephat dileṣaydānāē le-ittetā armaltā.
iv. 23: see Mt. xxvii. 42.
iv. 24: see Mt. xiii. 57.
vi. 38: see Mt. vii. 2.
vi. 40: see Mt. x. 24.
vi. 44 f.: see Mt. vii. 16 f.
vi. 45: see Mt. xii. 34.
viii. 17: see Mt. x. 26.
viii. 18: see Mt. xiii. 12.
ix. 23: see Mt. x. 38.
ix. 60: see Mt. viii. 22.
x. 7: see Mt. x. 10.
xi. 1: māran allephan.
xi. 9 f.: see Mt. vii. 7.
xi. 27: ṭūbēhōn deme'aiyā delā yelīdūn wedaddaiyā delā ōnīḳūn.
xii. 2: see Mt. x. 26.

xiii. 30: see Mt. xix. 30.
xiii. 32: emarūn lehādēn ta'lā.
xiv. 8 f.: lā tirba' berēsh reba'tā begēn delā yihwē zemīn minnēh meyaḳḳar minnākh weyētē dezammenākh weyēmar lākh hab atrā lehādēn, ēllā reba' be'atrā aḥrāyā wekhideyētē dezammenākh yēmar lākh reḥīmī sōḳ lākh.
xiv. 11: kōl man demerōmēm garmēh memakkekhīn yātēh uman dimemakkēkh garmēh merōmemīn yātēh.
xiv. 34: see Mt. v. 13.
xv. 16: wehawā mitḥammad memallāyā me'ōhi beḥārūbīn.
xvi. 13: lēt barnāsh yākhēl dīshammēsh litrēn mārīn.
xvii. 33: see Mt. x. 39.
xviii. 25: see Mt. xix. 24.
xix. 26: see Mt. xiii. 12.
xxi. 4: see Mk. xii. 44.
xxii. 15: meḥammādā ḥammēdt denēkhōl hādēn pisḥā 'immekhōn 'ad delā nēḥōsh.
xxii. 16: deāmarnā lekhōn, delā nēkhōl tūb minnēh 'ad diyehē mitḳaiyam bemalkhūtā dishemaiyā.
xxii. 17: sabbūnah uphallegūnah bēnēkhōn.
xxii. 18: de'āmar anā lekhōn delā nishtē min kaddūn min pērōhi deguphnā 'ad detētē malkhūtā de'elāhā.
xxii. 19: dēn hū gūphī. hākhedēn 'abīdūn (hawōn 'ābedīn) ledukhrānī.
xxii. 26: bar nāshā lā atā deyishtammash ēlla dyshammēsh weyittēn naphshēh purḳān ḥulāph saggīīn.
xxiii. 28: benāt yerūshlēm, lā tihweyān bākhyān 'alay, ēllā bekhan 'al garmēkhēn we'al benēkhēn.
xxiii. 29: see xi. 27.
xxiii. 31: in 'ābedīn hēkh beḳēsā raṭṭībā mā yit'abēd beyabbīshā.
xxiii. 34: abbā shebōḳ lehōn lētēhōn ḥākhemīn mā 'ābedīn.
xxiii. 42: mārī anhar lī khidetētē bemalkhūtākh.
xxiii. 43: āmēn āmarnā lākh, yōmā dēn att 'immī beginnetā de'ēden.
xxiii. 46: abbā bīdākh aphḳēd rūḥī.
xxiv. 5: mā attūn bā'ayin ḥaiyā 'im mītaiyā.

From St John.

iv. 44: see Mt. xiii. 57.
xii. 25: see Mt. x. 39.
xiii. 16: see Mt. x. 24.
xv. 20: see Mt. x. 24.
xix. 26: ittā hā berīkh. hā immākh.
xix. 28: sāḥēnā.
xix. 30: mushlam.

From Acts.

xxii. 7 f.: anā yēshūa' nāṣerāyā deatt rā-dephinnēh.
xxvi. 14: schāūl schāūl mā att rādephinni.
man att māri.

From 1 *Corinthians.*

xi. 24: hādā hawō 'ābedīn ledukhrānā dīlī.
xi. 25: hādā kāsā hī ḳeyāmā ḥadattā be'idmī.
kol ēmat de'attūn shātayin.

A FURTHER LIST OF PASSAGES IN ARAMAIC FROM "ORTE UND WEGE JESU"

St Matthew.

viii. 22: ethā lākh bātheray, ushebōḳ mītaiyā ḳāberīn mītēhōn.

viii. 25 f.: mā attūn dāḥelīn, ze'ērē hēmānūtā!

xv. 11: mā de'ālēl lephummā lā mesāēb lebar nāshā, ēllā mā denāphēḳ mippummā hū mesāēb lebar nāshā.

xxii. 21: habūn dileḳēsar leḳēsar wedile-elāhā le-elāhā.

xxiii. 37: yerūshelēm yerūshelēm dimeḳaṭṭelā nebīaiyā werāgemā demishtalḥīn legabbah, kemā zimnīn be'ēt limekhannāshā libenayekhī hēkhmā de-mekhanneshā hādā tarnegōletā le-ephrōḥahā teḥōt agappahā weattūn lā be'ētōn.

xxiii. 38 f.: hā mishtebēḳ lekhōn bētekhōn weāmar anā lekhōn delā tiḥmōn yātī min kaddūn 'ad mā detēmerūn bārūkh ha-bā beshēm adōnay.

xxvi. 31: attūn kullekhōn titkashlūn bī.

xxvi. 39: abbā, in yākhēl, te'bar minni hādā kāsā, beram lā hēkh debā'ēnā anā, ēllā hēkh deatt bā'ē.

xxvi. 61: anā sātar hēkhelā hādēn ubitelātā yōmīn nibnē ḥōrānā.

xxvi. 64: tiḥmōn bar enāshā yātēb leyammīnā digebūretā weātē 'im 'anānēhōn dishemaiyā.

xxvii. 29: shelām lākh malkehōn dīhūdāyē.

St Mark.

ii. 9: mā hū ḳallīl denēmōr limerashshelā shebīḳīn lākh ḥōbākh, ō denēmōr ḳūm sab 'arsāk weṭaiyēl.

iv. 39: ishtattaḳ ḥashē.

INDEX OF NEW TESTAMENT PASSAGES

MATTHEW

MARK

LUKE

JOHN

ACTS

INDEX OF NAMES AND SUBJECTS